Issues in Mentoring

As the initial training of teachers becomes increasingly school-based, and as schools and colleges develop formal induction programmes for their newly qualified teachers, the role of the teacher mentor is fast becoming a pivotal one in teacher education. Individual sections look at mentoring as it relates to:

- Initial training
- Induction
- Assessment
- Whole institution staff development

Throughout, the emphasis is on the ways in which mentoring contributes at all points in the continuum of professional development. Anyone involved in mentoring in any setting – from the primary school to the adult education college – will find this book indispensable as a guide to reflection and a spur to action.

The Open University MA in Education

Issues in Mentoring

This Reader is part of a course, 'Mentoring', for the Open University MA in Education and is, therefore, related to other material available to students. Opinions expressed in it are not necessarily those of the course team or of the university. This disclaimer also applies to the use of sexist language within the articles.

If you would like to study this course, please write to The Central Enquiries Office, The Open University, Walton Hall, Milton Keynes MK7 6AA, for a prospectus and application form. For more specific information write to The Higher Degrees Office at the same address.

Issues in Mentoring

Edited by
Trevor Kerry and Ann Shelton Mayes
at The Open University

ROUTLEDGE

London and New York
in association with
The Open University

First published 1995
by Routledge
11 New Fetter Lane, London EC4P 4EE

Simultaneously published in the USA and Canada
by Routledge
29 West 35th Street, New York, NY 10001

Selection and editorial matter: © 1995 The Open University

Typeset in Garamond by
Mews Photosetting, Beckenham, Kent

Printed and bound in Great Britain by
Biddles Ltd, Guildford and King's Lynn

British Library Cataloguing in Publication Data
A catalogue record for this book is available from the British Library

Library of Congress Cataloging in Publication Data
A catalogue record for this book has been requested

ISBN 0-415-11681-3

Contents

Illustrations

Editors' biographies

Dr Trevor Kerry graduated from Durham University and taught in the London Borough of Havering. He became lecturer and then senior lecturer at Bishop Grosseteste College, Lincoln, before joining the Teacher Education Project in the Universities of Nottingham, Leicester and Exeter. After a brief spell as principal lecturer for educational research at Charlotte Mason College he became a project officer for the Schools' Council. Following some further teaching in a primary school he became Head of Department and Head of Site at Doncaster College, and then senior adviser for both In-service and Further Education in Norfolk. He is best known for a string of teaching skills books covering all phases of education from infant to further education. As staff tutor for the Open University he has been responsible for the implementation of the OU's distance-learning PGCE in the East Midlands.

Ann Shelton Mayes is currently Senior Lecturer and Deputy Director of the PGCE programme in the Open University School of Education. Her responsibilities include developing the mentor professional development programme for the PGCE and the associated MA in Education module in Mentoring. Before joining the OU Ann Shelton Mayes was Deputy Head, Curriculum, at a Northamptonshire school. Prior to this she was both Head of Science in a large Buckinghamshire Comprehensive, and a teacher-tutor for the University of Cambridge PGCE. Her INSET work has spanned classroom practice to whole-school management, as well as governor training. She has recently co-edited with Professor Bob Moon *Teaching and Learning in the Secondary School*, published by Routledge (1994).

Acknowledgements

PART A CONCEPTS OF MENTORING

1   Maynard, T. and Furlong, J. (1993) 'Learning to Teach and Models of Mentoring', in McIntyre, D., Hagger, H. and Wilkin, N. (eds) *Mentoring-Perspectives on School-based Teacher Education*, London: Kogan Page, pp. 69–85.
2   Anderson, E.M. and Lucasse Shannon, A. (1988) 'Toward a Conceptualisation of Mentoring', *Journal of Teacher Education*, 39(1), pp. 38–42. Copyright by the American Association of Colleges for Teacher Education.
3   Elliott, B. and Calderhead, J. (1993) 'Mentoring for Teacher Development: Possibilities and Caveats', in McIntyre, D., Hagger, H. and Wilkin, N. (eds) *Mentoring-Perspectives on School-based Teacher Education*, London: Kogan Page, pp. 166–189.

PART B MENTORING IN INITIAL TEACHER TRAINING

4   Bridges, D. (1993) 'School-based Teacher Education', in Bridges, D. and Kerry, T. (eds) *Developing Teachers Professionally*, London: Routledge, pp. 51–66.
5   Beardon, T., Booth, M., Hargreaves, D. and Reiss, M. (1992) *School-led Initial Teacher Training*, Cambridge: Department of Education, University of Cambridge.
6   Booth, M. (1993) 'The Effectiveness and Role of the Mentor in School: The Students' View', *Cambridge Journal of Education*, 23(2), pp. 185–197. Carfax Publishing Company, Abingdon, Oxon.
7   Rothera, M., Howkins, S. and Hendry, J. (1991) 'The Role of Subject Mentor in Further Education', *British Journal of In-Service Education*, 17(2), pp. 126–137.
8   Jacques, K. (1992) 'Mentoring in Initial Teacher Education', *Cambridge Journal of Education*, 22(3), pp. 337–350. Carfax Publishing Company, Abingdon, Oxon.

9   Watkins, C. and Whalley, C. (1993) 'Mentoring Beginner Teachers – Issues for Schools to Anticipate and Manage', *School Organisation*, 13(2), pp. 129–138. Carfax Publishing Company, Abingdon, Oxon.

10 Lucas, P. (1991), 'A Neglected Source for Reflection in the Supervison of Student Teachers', First published in *New Era in Education*, 72(1), pp. 2–6.

11 Reich, M. (1986) 'The Mentor Connection', *Personnel*, 63, pp. 50–56.

PART C MENTORING IN INDUCTION TRAINING

12 Turner, M. (1993) 'The Role of Mentors and Teacher Tutors in School-based Teacher Education and Induction', *British Journal of In-Service Education*, 19(1), pp. 36–45.

13 Waterhouse, A. (1993) 'Mirror, Mirror on the Wall, What is the Fairest Scheme of All? Reflections on the Induction Needs of Newly Qualified Teachers', *British Journal of In-service Education*, 19(1), pp. 16–22.

14 Kinder, K. and Earley, P. (1993) *Key Issues Emerging from an NFER Study of NQTs: Models of Induction Support*, London: National Foundation of Educational Research. Conference Paper for the Universities Council for the Education of Teachers: Annual Conference, Oxford, 12–14 November 1993. Reprinted by kind permission of the National Foundation for Educational Research.

15 Earley, P. (1993) 'Initiation Rights? Beginning Teachers' Professional Development and the Objectives of Induction Training', *British Journal of In-Service Education*, 19(1), pp. 5–11.

PART D MENTORING AND ASSESSMENT

16 Pring, R. (1992) 'Standards and Quality in Education', *British Journal of Educational Studies*, 40(1), pp. 4–22.

17 Whitty, G. (1992) 'Quality Control in Teacher Education', *British Journal of Educational Studies*, 40(1), pp. 38–50.

18 Whitty, G. and Willmott, E. (1991) 'Competence-based Teacher Education: Approaches and Issues', *Cambridge Journal of Education*, 21(3), pp. 309–318. Carfax Publishing Company, Abingdon, Oxon.

19 Hyland, T. (1992) 'Expertise and Competence in Further and Adult Education', *British Journal of In-Service Education*, 18(1), pp. 23–28.

20 Furlong, J. (1992) 'The Limits of Competence: A Cautionary Note on Circular 9/92', Conference Paper, UCET Conference, Oxford.

21 Moon, B. and Shelton Mayes, A. (1993) 'Integrating Values into the Assessment of Teachers in Initial Education and Training: A National Model Developed by Britain's Open University, paper for the Conference of the Association for Teacher Education in Europe, Lisbon, 5-10 September.
22 Gifford, S. (1992) 'Surrey New Teacher Competency Project', *British Journal of In-Service Education*, 18(3), pp. 159-165.

PART E MENTORING: PROFESSIONAL DEVELOPMENT AND INSTITUTIONAL ASPECTS

23 Kelly, M., Beck, T. and apThomas, J. (1992) 'Mentoring as a Staff Development Activity', in Wilkin, M. (ed.) *Mentoring in Schools*, London: Kogan Page, pp. 173-180.
24 Shaw, R. (1992) 'Mentoring', in Shaw, R. *Teacher Training in Secondary Schools*, London: Kogan Page, pp. 69-77.

Introduction

Mentoring has its professional origins in the world of business and over the past two decades it has evolved to become a prominent feature of many professions including teaching. First in the United States of America, where mentoring has played a key role across a range of teacher education programmes, in particular induction (see Klung and Salzman 1991); and more recently in Europe and the United Kingdom. In a review of the literature from 1972–1991 Mike Turner (1993) charts the development of the school-based mentor from the early 1970s, where a role for teachers in school-based induction of new teachers was raised, through to the 1990s and the establishment of mentoring in all phases of teacher education (pre-service, induction and continuing professional development).

Two changes in teacher education have served to place mentoring at the centre of institutionally based professional development in the UK. First, new regulations for initial teacher training in both the secondary and primary phases in England and Wales (DES 1992; DFE 1993) have introduced an extensive school-based component with a key role for teachers as mentors. Pilot studies to explore comparable school-based training were set up in Scotland in 1992; and a similar mode of training is proposed for Northern Ireland in 1995. Second, with the demise of the formal probationary year in England and Wales, there has been a growing awareness of the need to establish induction programmes for beginning teachers that build on initial training experiences. Since these induction programmes are most commonly based within a single institution, the role of the mentoring teacher has again been highlighted.

The rapidity of the rise of the teacher-mentor role in initial teacher education has been largely the result of a political agenda determined to wrest initial teacher education away from higher education institutions (HEI) and place it in schools. But teachers as mentors should be no less welcomed for that. As David Bridges (Part B) explains, the reality is that this new role forms a proper progression in the teacher's role, building on such developments as teachers as curriculum developers and researchers. It also offers a new professional role for those teachers who wish to remain primarily in the classroom and real job satisfaction as noted by Rowie Shaw (Part E); and opens up possibilities for genuine collaboration and partnership in teacher education between HEI and schools at each stage of the professional development continuum.

This notion of a continuum of professional development from pre-service through to induction and continuing service including appraisal, suggests that mentoring could evolve to serve a pivotal function in staff development. And given the widespread growth of mentoring there is a need to explore the issues and challenges that such a role offers for mentors, their institutions and the teacher education programmes they work within.

This book aims to explore some of these challenges and issues and provide access to this wider debate for those mentors actively engaged in critiquing their practice. It focuses mainly on mentoring within the context of initial teacher education and induction and the extracts have been drawn from research in a wide range of primary, secondary and FE contexts. But a central theme of this book is that mentoring is pivotal to institution-based professional development; and the extracts help us to speculate on the benefits that might accrue for pupils and staff in institutions which could be termed 'mentoring schools'.

The book examines a number of key questions. What is the mentor's role? What are the skills and strategies they need to learn? And most importantly, how does this relate to models of teacher learning and notions of the teacher's role – such as the development of the 'reflective teacher'?

It also pays particular attention to the mentor's assessment role now enshrined within the regulations for initial teacher training in England and Wales – which, in giving the school a major role in the assessment of student teachers, introduces a formal assessment role for the mentor. There are a number of questions that arise. How easily does this assessment role sit with other support functions of the mentor? And how is the mentor supported in making these professional judgements? Since mentors, in both initial and induction phases of teacher education, are now working with competency models of assessment, the debate about the use of competences in teacher education is an important feature of this book.

The volume falls into five parts. Each part is prefaced by a short introduction which identifies the main themes of the chapters.

Part A is concerned with *concepts of mentoring and the conceptual underpinning of the mentoring process*. Mentoring had its origins in the world of business, particularly in the United States of America. The degree to which concepts of mentoring construed in this context can be transferred into a UK educational scene are considered in this section.

Models of learning in teacher education are considered, leading in turn to some basic questions about appropriate mentor strategies to support particular stages in teacher learning. There is a first encounter in this part of the book with the 'reflective practitioner' model of teaching, and with the origins of mentoring in apprenticeship, role modelling and support. The chapters chosen here go on to take a first look at mentoring in practice, and at the attitudes of mentees themselves to the process of being mentored. The issues raised open up the debate about the nature of 'the mentoring school'; and how to provide a suitable learning environment for adult professionals.

Part B traces the *role of the mentor in initial teacher education*. The opening chapter in Part B deals with the political background of school-based teacher education. In it, Bridges traces recent moves by the government to put the responsibility for initial teacher education onto serving teachers. He makes an assessment of the relationships which can and should exist between teachers and tutors in higher education institutions. This part of the book looks at the ideals of mentoring: the ideal mentor, the ideal mentor behaviours and the ideal mentor relationships with mentees. By contrast, chapters taken from Booth, and from Rothera *et al.*, temper idealism with reality from the context of research projects in which initial trainees in schools and further education settings react to the realities of being mentored. How schools manage the process of mentoring is dealt with in some detail by Watkins and Whalley; and the conflict which arises for the mentor in playing the additional role of assessor is identified by Lucas, who offers an interesting suggestion about the involvement of pupils in the assessment of teachers. Finally, gender issues are addressed in an article by Reich which examines the specific issues which have been found to relate to women as mentors and mentees.

Part C moves on to examine the *role of the mentor in induction processes*. The first chapter, by Turner, opens up the 'reflective practitioner' debate in more detail. The theme is continued by Waterhouse using two case studies. Kinder and Earley examine the school and local education authority strategies in induction support programmes; and Earley's second extract examines the role that local education authorities may play in the future given their diminishing importance in political terms.

Part D tackles the difficult issues of *assessment in the context of mentoring*. In particular, it looks at the current concerns about the use of competency models in teacher education. In a series of chapters the political and philosophical issues in relation to quality and assessment are examined; competency models as curriculum, pedagogical and assessment tools are debated; and the importance of values as a dimension of assessment is explored. The professional development portfolio is used in many teacher education programmes as a means by which a trainee might most effectively reflect on practice, provide evidence of that reflection, and convince the assessor of development growth. Gifford's chapter in this section examines the portfolio approach at work for induction training in Surrey.

The final part speculates on how mentoring relates to staff development and institutional matters. Kelly *et al.* look at mentoring in the wider context of staff development: a clear link with the concept of the 'mentoring school'. While Shaw's final chapter draws together the themes of the book.

REFERENCES

DES (1992) Circular 9/92 *Initial Teacher Training (Secondary Phase)*.
DFE (1993) Circular 14/93 *The Initial Training of Primary School Teachers*.
Klung, B. and Salzman, S. (1991) 'Formal induction v. informal mentoring: comparative effects and outcomes', *Teaching and Teacher Education* (3).
Turner, M. (1993) 'The role of mentors and teacher tutors in school-based teacher education and induction', *British Journal of In-Service Education* 19(1).

BACKGROUND NOTE

This book has been prepared as part of a course, 'Mentoring', for the Open University MA in Education. The course has an accompanying resource of text and audio-visual material – including *Mentoring – A Professional Development Programme* which links to the Open University PGCE and explores mentoring skills and strategies. Together they provide the background for a study guide focusing on aspects of mentoring examined by the course.

Part A

Concepts of mentoring

Introduction

Part A focuses on the question 'What is mentoring'? The chapters included here reveal a range of definitions and descriptions indicating no current consensus as to the precise definition of mentoring or the functions associated with it. The uncertainty extends as to whether the term 'mentoring' actually relates to a single person carrying out a number of roles or a set of processes that can be carried out by many. The phrase 'mentoring school', for example, suggests a whole community that supports the professional development of teachers. Nevertheless common elements of mentoring do emerge: teaching and support, for example.

In exploring the concept of mentor the chapters here have sought to examine its theoretical underpinning. Anderson and Shannon start from a historical examination of the term and suggest that mentoring functions arise from an analysis of the essential qualities that reside in the relationship between mentor and mentee. They point to key characteristics of the mentor process: its intentional nature, nurturing the protégé, passing on wisdom in a protective context. Role modelling is seen to be an essential element. They quote Phillips-Jones's (1982) distinctions between six kinds of mentor:

- authority figures,
- supportive bosses,
- organization sponsors,
- career counsellors,
- patrons,
- invisible godparents.

Anderson and Shannon also describe a number of mentor functions, and point to the fact that mentoring can, in practice, be either a formal or an informal process. Daloz's (1983) definition of the mentor as a guide on a journey is also mentioned.

In the end, however, Anderson and Shannon conclude that none of these concepts is wholly adequate, and they present an alternative. For them, the five essential components of a definition are:

- nurturing,
- role modelling,
- functioning (as teacher, sponsor, encourager, counsellor and friend),
- focusing on the professional development of the mentee,
- sustaining a caring relationship over time.

It is interesting to note that an explicit assessment role does not appear in this list, in contrast to the major role in assessment given to schools in the ITT regulations for England and Wales (DES 1992; DFE 1993).

An alternative, and possibly more fruitful approach is suggested by Maynard and Furlong and by Elliott and Calderhead, who see an understanding of how teachers learn to teach as a fundamental pre-requisite for understanding what might constitute effective mentoring.

The chapter by Trisha Maynard and John Furlong begins by asking two pertinent questions. The first is why teachers should be part of the teacher training process, a process which until recently has been in the domain of higher education. The question is given preliminary attention here, but it is one developed further in Part B. The second question concerns how a trainee learns to teach. In answering this question Maynard and Furlong explore a number of models of mentoring: the apprenticeship model, the competency model and the reflective model.

What emerges from this discussion is a kind of 'successionist' view of mentoring: that just as, over time, the learning of trainee teachers needs to change as they move through progressive stages, so, over time, these changes must be matched by changes in the strategy of mentors: from mentors as models, to instructors and then co-enquirers.

The language used is particularly significant, for example:

> Helping trainees to look at their own practice is particularly important because the way in which they interpret school experi-ence is so often influenced and 'shaped' by their own set of attitudes, beliefs and values. . . . The trainee's own experience of schools and certainly the 'images' they hold of classrooms and pupils – will exert a powerful effect on their practice.

From this view of how trainees learn to teach at particular stages in their development emerges a view of mentoring which will be encountered elsewhere in this book – one that is strongly influenced by notions of 'reflective practice' and the 'reflective practitioner'. The mentor here plays a role in challenging the trainee to consider issues of belief and values in developing their practice. This notion of mentor as *agent provocateur* is returned to by Elliott and Calderhead.

In the third chapter in Part A, Bob Elliott and James Calderhead bring a research dimension to the problem of definition. Like Maynard and Furlong in the first chapter, they begin by exploring the nature of professional learning and growth. They adopt Daloz's (1986) view that growth requires both challenge and support. To explore the mentor role, they studied articled teachers in primary schools. The mentors were interviewed about their perceptions of the role, their approaches to it, the rationale for these approaches, and their views of how the articled teacher was learning to teach.

The research points up what these mentors did, and did not, understand about the role. Support is again noted as a fundamental element in any definition of mentoring. Generally, the mentors in this study did not adequately challenge the articled teachers and lacked an appropriate language in which to discuss professional development and the articled teachers' classroom understanding. In this context, mentors did not have an adequate grasp of teaching/learning in an adult milieu. Schools did not always behave as 'learning communities' – an important issue also described as 'the mentoring school', to which a return is made in Part C.

The message from these authors is that whatever the conception of mentoring mentors work within, they must have a clear understanding of that role and its associated functions; and have access to a range of strategies and a professional language for teaching and training if they are to support the mentee effectively.

REFERENCES

Daloz, L. (1983) 'Mentors: teachers who make a difference', *Change* 15 (6).
Daloz, L. (1986) *Effective Teaching and Mentoring*, San Francisco, CA: Jossey-Bass.
DES (1992) Circular 9/92 *Initial Teacher Training (Secondary Phase)*.
Phillips-Jones, L. (1982) *Mentors and Protégés*, New York: Arbor House.

Chapter 1

Learning to teach and models of mentoring

Trisha Maynard and John Furlong

INTRODUCTION

Learning to teach, as we all know but often fail to remember, is a complex, bewildering and sometimes painful task. It involves developing a practical knowledge base, changes in cognition, developing interpersonal skills and also incorporates an affective aspect. This chapter represents a preliminary examination of the ways in which teachers, acting as mentors, can most effectively help trainees in this difficult process.

Before starting to discuss the role of the mentor in facilitating the professional development of trainee teachers, it is necessary to ask a prior question – why, in principle, should school teachers themselves be part of the process? What is the rationale for the mentor's contribution? In these times of rapid change in teacher education it is more than ever necessary to have a clear and principled understanding of the rationale for each aspect of training and how it relates to other dimensions.

In order to try and answer that question we will briefly return to the research on school-based training undertaken by Furlong *et al.* (1988). In that analysis, Furlong *et al.* (p. 132) distinguished between four different levels or dimensions of training which, they argued, went on in all forms of teacher training course. These levels were as follows:

- *Level (a) direct practice*
  Practical training through direct experience in schools and classrooms.
- *Level (b) indirect practice*
  'Detached' training in practical matters usually conducted in classes or workshops within training institutions.
- *Level (c) practical principles*
  Critical study of the principles of study and their use.
- *Level (d) disciplinary theory*
  Critical study of practice and its principles in the light of fundamental theory and research.

Furlong *et al.*'s argument was that professional training demands that trainees in their courses must be exposed to all of these different dimensions of professional knowledge. Moreover, courses, they suggested, need to establish ways of working that help trainees *integrate* these different forms of professional knowledge. Trainees need to be systematically prepared in practical classroom knowledge – they need to be prepared at level (a) – it is a distinctive form of professional knowledge and training cannot be left to chance. But Furlong *et al.* suggested that it is only teachers who have access to that level of knowledge; it is only they who know about particular children working on a particular curriculum in a particular school. Lecturers can visit schools and give generalized advice but by definition that will always be generalized. Furlong *et al.* also argued that although individual teachers might be in a position to prepare trainees at levels (b), (c) and (d), the nature of their job meant that their greatest strength was at level (a). However, lecturers, because of their breadth of experience and because of their involvement in research, had access to other forms of professional knowledge. Training must therefore be a partnership between training institutions and schools.

Since publication, this analysis has been criticized for its notion of levels and certainly, given that the term does carry overtones of a hierarchy, then it would seem inappropriate – different *dimensions* of training might have been a more appropriate term. McIntyre (1990), in a lengthy critique, has also suggested that there is an implicit hierarchy in more than the language – he suggests that the model prioritizes academic knowledge at level (d) implying that it is the only route to professional rigour. McIntyre agrees that trainees need access to different forms of professional knowledge and that the practical knowledge of teachers must be a central part of that training process. However, he suggests that different forms of professional knowledge should all be used to interrogate each other. Practical classroom knowledge – the province of teachers – should be used to interrogate more theoretically based knowledge and vice versa.

The debate continues, but where many of those writing on initial teacher education would now agree is that trainees need systematic preparation in that practical classroom knowledge and by definition that aspect of training (and we would reassert that it is only one aspect of training) can only be provided by teachers working in their own classrooms and schools. As a consequence it is necessary to move from the notion of *supervision* in school, where teachers are supervising trainees in the application of training acquired elsewhere, to the notion of *mentoring*, which is an active process, where teachers themselves as practitioners have an active role in the training process.

Since the publication of that earlier study, the benefits of school-based training have become much more widely accepted.

STUDENT CONCERNS AND STAGES OF DEVELOPMENT

What do we know of the needs of trainee teachers? An examination of research literature on the process of learning to teach confirms the commonsense observation that trainees typically go through a number of distinct stages of development, each with its own focal concerns. These concerns can usefully be grouped under the following headings: early idealism; survival; recognizing difficulties; hitting the plateau; and moving on.

Early idealism

Research into the **pre**-teaching concerns of trainees has found that they are often idealistic in their feelings towards their students, identifying realistically with pupils but unsympathetic or even hostile to the class teacher (Fuller and Bown 1975). Moreover, they often seem to hold a clear image of the sort of teacher they want to be. They are terrified of ending up like that 'miserable old cynic in the corner of the staffroom'!

Survival

Once trainees embark on their teaching experience, however, their idealism often fades in the face of the realities of classroom life and they frequently become obsessed with their own survival. It is therefore not surprising that class control and management, 'fitting in' and establishing themselves as a 'teacher' often become major issues for them.

At this stage of training, trainees frequently refer to the problem of not being able to 'see'. Student-teachers in our own research have used phrases such as 'It's all a blur', 'I can't seem to focus' and 'feeling my way'. In the early stages of school experience, time is often given for trainees to observe classroom practice but as Calderhead (1988a) confirms, this is often wasted time – they cannot make sense of the noise and movement around them; they do not understand the significance of the teacher's actions – they simply do not know what it is they are supposed to be looking for. It is no wonder that at this stage trainees often express the need for 'quick fixes', and 'hints and tips' (Eisenhart *et al.* 1991).

Recognizing difficulties

At the next stage, trainees become sensitive to the varied demands made on them and are keen to give an impressive performance. With confidence shaken, the issue of assessment often starts to predominate. As college tutors are well aware, even at quite early stages, trainees constantly make the plaintive cry of, 'Am I doing well?', 'Will I pass?' This is despite the fact that an over-concern with assessment means that they have missed the main point of the experience. In this phase, trainees also begin to focus on the issue of teaching methods and materials, referring frequently to classroom constraints or lack of resources.

Hitting the plateau

After the first few weeks when basic management and control procedures have been established, trainees are liable to 'hit the plateau'; at last they have found a way of teaching that seems to work and they are going to stick to it! However, they frequently find great difficulty, as Feiman-Nemser and Buchmann (1987) explain, in shifting the focus from themselves to others, or from the subjects they are teaching to the issue of what the pupils need to learn. There often is, as Feiman-Nemser and Buchmann point out, a vast gulf that exists between 'going through the motions of teaching . . . and connecting these activities to what pupils should be learning over time' (p. 257).

Moving on

Trainees may eventually go on to experiment and/or show concern for pupils' learning but without positive intervention, Calderhead (1987) maintains that their level of reflection will be shallow and ineffective in promoting professional learning. A final phase of development has been identified as occurring after approximately seven years – that of 'teacher burn-out' (Calderhead 1984).

What are the reasons for these concerns at different stages of development? Are they warranted if, as many believe, learning to teach is just a matter of picking up practical hints and tips and gaining expertise through a process of trial and error? In the next section we examine what research tells us about a variety of processes in learning to teach: the nature of the practical knowledge trainees must acquire; the process of forming concepts; the interpersonal skills they must develop; and the affective issues they must confront. A more detailed understanding of these issues is, we argue, essential if we are to have a clearer vision of what the role of the mentor in school must be.

LEARNING TO TEACH

Developing a practical knowledge base

As we indicated above, there is now broad agreement that learning to teach demands that direct practical experience is placed at the heart of the training process. But what of the content of practical training? What exactly is it that mentors can help trainees learn through direct experience in schools and classrooms that cannot be gained elsewhere? Research into teachers' practical knowledge is, as Elbaz (1983) points out, patchy and fragmented, focusing on isolated characteristics and usually approached from a negative stance. This must be due, in part, to the fact that teachers are simply not seen as possessing a body of knowledge or expertise appropriate to their work. It is thought they possess knowledge in relation to, for example, subject matter, but not practical professional knowledge (Clandini, 1986; Elbaz 1983; Lortie, 1975; Wilson *et al.*, 1987). We would disagree and suggest that practical classroom knowledge can usefully be understood in terms of four broad areas – the four 'Ss'. They are knowledge of 'students' (or pupils), 'situation', 'subject matter' and 'strategies'.

At the most specific level, in terms of the *students* or pupils, the trainee needs to gain a knowledge of the actual students in the class: learn their names, discover their interests, attitudes, backgrounds, and find out what they are capable of achieving. But they also need to develop a detailed knowledge of the *situation* in which they must teach. This will involve developing a knowledge of the actual classroom, school and community in terms of its ethos, demands and constraints.

Subject matter, or content knowledge, has been called the 'missing paradigm' in research on teachers' thinking, particularly at secondary school level (Shulman 1986). Trainees may well know their subject from their own education but in becoming teachers they need to acquire a new type of subject knowledge: 'pedagogical content knowledge'. Pedagogical content knowledge involves ways of representing subjects that make them understandable to others (Wilson *et al.* 1987). While certain aspects of lesson 'content', for example evaluation of different types of subject matter and subject specific skills, may best be explored outside the classroom situation, trainees will be dependent on their observations of particular students in particular situations to evaluate just how effective their 'representations' of the subject matter have been.

Finally, and inextricably linked to pedagogical content knowledge, trainees need to develop a knowledge of which *strategies* may be used. Not simply a theoretical knowledge of different strategies that 'may' be used, but a practical knowledge of which techniques or tactics are most appropriate to facilitate learning in each case.

In practice these four domains (students, situation, subject matter and strategies) are never 'experienced' or 'used' in isolation. While they may differ in character, both 'students' and 'situation' are largely distinct but in a sense 'given' or 'fixed', whereas 'subject matter' and 'strategies' are inseparable but more mutable and open to choice. When planning, interacting or responding to problems, trainees need to weigh up and balance considerations of these four aspects. In reality, trainees' decisions and responses will also be influenced or modified by considerations of their own 'interests' and constrained by their particular stage of development.

Developing and exposing concepts

Learning to teach, however, does not merely involve acquiring a body of new practical knowledge, it actually involves changes in cognition, the perception and memory of less experienced teachers differing from that of 'experts' (Berliner 1987). Trainees need to form concepts, schemas and scripts in order to make sense of, interpret and come to 'control' aspects of classroom life (Carter and Doyle 1987). The fact that new trainees have not yet had the experience to form these concepts is associated with the problem of not being able to 'see'. Without such concepts, classrooms remain what Copeland (1981) describes as 'a bewildering kaleidoscope of people, behaviours, events and interactions only dimly understood' (p. 11).

Concepts can be held at the level of person theory, such as concepts of acceptable levels of movement and noise in the classroom or can be generalizations abstracted from the trainees' practical knowledge base – about typical students and situations or about subject matter and strategies that are likely to work. These concepts evolve only through experience; not life experience, not from observations of classrooms, but from actually doing the business of teaching (Berliner 1987). Since practical knowledge both at the level of the 'actual' and at the level of the 'typical' is formed through the trainee's classroom experience, this knowledge tends to be personal and largely tacit. Indeed, Sternberg and Caruso (1985) maintain that practical knowledge lends itself better to tacit or possibly mediated learning in that academic representation of this knowledge is 'poorly fit for practical purposes' (p. 149). Although this means that practical knowledge can not be 'passed on' in any traditional sense, it does not, however, negate the role of the mentor. Mentors are in a unique position to be able to support trainees as they begin to form concepts about their practical work. They are also uniquely placed to expose trainees' developing concepts and help them see the implications of various ways of working. This is what Schon (1991) refers to as 'guiding their seeing'.

Helping trainees to look at their own practice is particularly important because the way in which they interpret school experience is so often influenced and 'shaped' by their own set of attitudes, beliefs and values; their life values in general and their educational values in particular. The trainees' own experience of schools and certainly the 'images' they hold of classrooms and pupils and of the sort of teachers they want to be will exert a powerful effect on their practice (see Calderhead 1988b; Clandinin 1986; Nias 1989).

What we are advocating here is the importance of reflection on teaching: a notion that has assumed an important role in many teacher education programmes in recent years (Barrett et al. 1992). Trainees are today constantly urged to reflect, though it is not always made explicit what reflection means or what they should be reflecting on.

In our view, the aim of reflection must be to learn something wider and of more significance by 'making the tacit explicit' (Freeman 1991). Through helping the trainee to understand the underlying implications of working in particular and in different ways, mentors can be encouraging the formation of patterns of thinking. In terms of Furlong et al.'s (1988) model, reported above, trainees begin to work at level (c) looking at the 'practical principles' underlying their own practice and at level (d) examining the moral, political and theoretical bases of practice. It is these forms of thinking, these dimensions of professional knowledge, that are the 'link' to college-based aspects of training.

Making the tacit explicit also allows the trainee to make their developing concepts of practical knowledge and educational values known to themselves. This in turn gives them greater control over their own practice and therefore in a sense empowers them (Elbaz 1983; Freeman 1991). However, it may only be after basic competence and confidence in teaching is achieved, only with the help of a trusted mentor and possibly only after trainees have been 'prepared' in some way that their capacities to reflect can be developed (see Calderhead 1987, 1989, 1991; Feiman-Nemser and Buchmann 1987; Zeichner and Liston 1987).

The political and the personal

The practical business of learning to teach is therefore a complex and necessarily slow process. It is not possible to undertake all of the steps to effective professionalism at once. That process is often made more complex still by other pressures that impose on trainees – the pressure of conflicting expectations as well as demands on the self. Effective school-based training needs to recognize both of these.

Trainees have often reported that they feel under pressure to adopt a similar teaching style to their mentor. This is partly in an attempt to gain credibility in the pupils' eyes – Copeland (1981), for example, suggests that student teachers find that pupils respond better to known ways of working – but also in order to gain favour with the teacher.

Alongside the problem of sensing and adapting to conflicting expectations, the trainee also finds that teaching makes demands upon the 'self'. Teaching is a personal activity and as such exposes and makes calls upon the personality; it is an occupation that is felt as well as experienced (Nias 1989). Fuller and Bown (1975) describe teaching as a process of constant, unremitting self-confrontation.

Trainees desperately want to be liked by the pupils but are often accused of being 'over-friendly' and then react to this criticism by becoming over-controlling, stern and authoritarian; it is hard for them to find the right balance. They are, to an extent, reliant on pupils for feedback as to the effectiveness of their teaching and learn to detect, for example, signs of boredom and frustration as well as understanding and pleasure (Feiman-Nemser and Buchmann 1987). Trainees will also detect how pupils feel about them as people; they are 'on trial' as a person (Squirrell *et al.* 1990). Sometimes this information can be excruciatingly painful!

In summary, we would agree with Nias (1989) when she states that teachers, among other abilities, need to process densely packed information reaching them simultaneously on many channels and respond sensitively and with accuracy; not only orchestrating their skills but, as Schon (1991) explains, dealing with and making new sense of the uncertain, unique and value-conflicted situation that their existing practical knowledge will not fit.

MODELS OF MENTORING

If these then are some of the processes involved in learning to teach what can they tell us about the role of the mentor? What sorts of strategies and approaches should they be using in supporting trainees through these different stages? Unfortunately, if we examine the literature that already exists on the role of the mentor, most of it is extremely one-dimensional, reflecting the fact that much of the debate to date on the value of school-based training has been ideologically inspired (Furlong 1992). From looking at current literature it is possible to identify three rather distinct models of mentoring: the apprentice-ship model; the competency model; and the reflective practitioner model. As we will suggest, each of them is partial and inadequate,

perhaps only appropriate at a particular stage of a trainee's development. However, taken together, we suggest that they may contribute
to a view of mentoring that responds to the changing needs of trainees.

The apprenticeship model and 'learning to see'

The first model apparent in the literature is what might be called an
apprenticeship model. This is an approach to learning to teach that
is strongly advocated by O'Hear (1988) and the Hillgate Group (1989).
In one of their more coherent passages, the Hillgate Group argue that
there is a long tradition going back to Aristotle that some skills,
including many that are difficult, complex and of high moral and
cultural value, are best learned 'by the emulation of experienced practitioners and by supervised practice under guidance' (p. 9). In the case
of such skills, apprenticeship, they suggest, should take precedence
over instruction.

Of course the Hillgate Group argue that their apprenticeship model
is all that is necessary in learning to teach – all you need to do is to
work alongside an experienced practitioner. But before we fall into
the trap of dismissing their arguments out of hand, we need to
recognize the truth in their observation, for it would seem to us that
the work of a mentor does indeed contain elements of this apprenticeship model. Trainees need first-hand experience of real students,
teaching situations, classroom strategies and subject matter. In the early
stages of their training the purpose of that practical experience is to
allow them to start to form concepts, schemas or scripts of the process
of teaching. But in order to begin to 'see', trainees need an interpreter.
They need to work alongside a mentor who can explain the
significance of what is happening in the classroom. As we have argued
above, trainees also need to sense and fit into established routines.
They therefore also need to be able to model themselves on someone.
Such a model can also act as a guide, articulating and presenting
'recipes' that will work.

It is often advocated that in the first weeks of teaching experience
trainees should work with individuals or small groups of pupils. The
reason this is thought to be useful is that it is believed to reduce the
complexity of the teaching process. However, as trainees are mainly
concerned with 'survival' issues at this stage, small-group work of this
sort may only partially meet their needs. Small-group work can, for
example, help them focus on the issue of differentiation. It will not,
however, address their concerns with classroom management and
control. Moreover, if it detaches them from the main business of the
classroom, it reduces the opportunity for the mentor to act as a model
and interpreter. We would suggest that at this early stage, a more

appropriate strategy is for the trainee to work alongside a mentor, taking responsibility for a small part of the whole teaching process.

If we substitute the term 'collaborative teaching' for apprenticeship – a term used by Burn (1992) in describing part of her work as a mentor in the Oxford Internship Scheme – then we can perhaps start to see the power of this aspect of the mentor's role in the early stages of learning to teach. For example, Burn (p. 134) lists the following as some of the advantages of collaborative teaching:

- learning to plan lessons carefully through being involved in joint planning with an experienced teacher, finding out what the teacher takes account of and identifying with the planning and its consequences;
- learning certain skills of classroom teaching through having responsibility for a specified component of the lessons, while identifying with the whole lesson and recognizing the relationships of the part to the whole;
- gaining access to the teacher's craft knowledge through observation of the teacher's actions, informed by a thorough knowledge of the planning and probably through discussion of the lesson afterwards, with a heightened awareness of having joint responsibility for the lesson.

This is precisely the sort of training that students need in the early stages of school experience when they are 'learning to see'.

The competency model – systematic training

While the Hillgate Group and their friends are urging that learning to teach can best be understood as a form of apprenticeship, others are advocating a competency-based approach. For those in this camp, learning to teach involves practical training on a list of pre-defined competences. The mentor takes on the role of a *systematic trainer*, observing the trainee, perhaps with a pre-defined observation schedule and providing feedback. They are in effect coaching the trainee on a list of agreed behaviours that are, at least in part, specified by others.

Systematic training in this country has a long history, becoming particularly popular in the 1970s with the development of interaction analysis, micro-teaching and some interest in American competency-based teacher education. We have of late, of course, seen the approach re-emerge – initially somewhat tentatively in Circular 24/89 (DES 1989) and now much more forcefully in Circular 9/92 (DFE 1992).

What is right about the competency approach is that after an initial period of collaborative teaching, trainees will benefit from an explicit programme of training following a routine of observation and feedback. In this second stage of learning to teach, trainees must be given control of the teaching process. Learning at this stage necessitates trainees taking responsibility; they have to learn by actually doing the job of teaching. While still adopting some of the teachers' ready-made routines, they need to be helped progressively to form and implement some of their own while continually developing and modifying their own personal concepts and schemas. In order to help this process the mentor therefore needs, at this stage of the trainee's development, to take an active role, acting as a mirror or working as a coach.

There are very many models within the literature of how mentors can best approach systematic training (see Smyth 1991, for a critical review). Current British regulations are prioritizing one of these: the competency model. It may well be that this aspect of the mentor's work is facilitated if they utilize a pre-defined list of competences, though we would re-emphasize that it is not the only approach. However, we would suggest that if the phase of collaborative teaching has been gone through it is perfectly possible and educationally advantageous to involve the trainee in discussion of which competences they want their mentor to focus on.

One common problem that trainees face is that once they have taken control, once they have established routines that work for them, they can stop learning – they can hit a plateau. At this point the mentor therefore not only needs to 'remove the structure' of support but also encourage the trainee to observe and experiment with different teaching styles and strategies. Just because trainees are ready for more explicit training in relation to their own performance it does not mean that the benefits of modelling through observation and collaborative teaching are over. The foundations for an extended repertoire continue to be best laid by working alongside and observing experienced teachers. In other words, it is not appropriate to think of these phases of mentoring as discrete entities; rather, they are progressive.

The reflective model – from teaching to learning

The final approach to mentoring currently widely advocated is the reflective practitioner model. Some would argue that calling it a model is too generous – 'slogan' might be more appropriate for, as Calderhead (1989) has noted, there are great difficulties in defining what reflective teaching actually is and even more difficulty in suggesting what activities by mentors might promote its development. Indeed most courses, it would seem, try to promote the reflective practitioner by means other than involving mentors – by the way they structure the course with concurrent periods of school and college activity so that the lecturers can encourage trainees to reflect – or by particular assignments or activities such as keeping journals or undertaking IT-INSET assignments. All of these are valuable, but we would suggest that once trainees have, with systematic support from their mentor, achieved basic classroom competence, ways have to be found of introducing a critical element into the mentoring process itself. To put it more directly, if learning to teach is at the heart of training then reflection on teaching, however it is defined, must be part of that learning process.

In this final stage of practical preparation in teaching, trainees need to be encouraged to switch from a focus on their own teaching per-formance to a focus on the children's learning and how they can make it more effective. But to achieve this switch means more than the trainee simply extending his or her repertoire of routines. To focus on children's learning demands that trainees move beyond routines and rituals; they need to develop a deeper understanding of the learning process; thinking through different ways of teaching and developing their own justifications and practical principles from their work.

While it is common for mentors to withdraw and let the trainee get on alone once they have achieved basic competence, it would seem to us that if mentors are to facilitate this shift of focus they must continue to take an active role. However, we would argue that trainees are unlikely to be ready for this form of reflection on their own prac-tice until they have gained some mastery of their teaching skills; they need to be ready to shift their focus from their own teaching to the pupils' learning and that cannot come until they have gained some confidence in their own teaching.

Supporting trainees in this more reflective process necessarily demands a shift in the role of the mentor. To facilitate this process mentors need to be able to move from being a model and instructor to being a co-enquirer. Those other aspects of their role may continue but in promoting critical reflection a more equal and open relation-ship is essential. As we implied earlier, thinking critically about teaching and learning demands open-mindedness and involves confronting beliefs and values. This is difficult and challenging work but we believe it is an essential element in what a true mentor must be.

CONCLUSION

From this preliminary examination of trainees' learning needs at different stages of development, we are then able to propose a fuller and more complete view of the role of the mentor. In the early stages of school experience, when trainees are still 'learning to see', mentors need to act as collaborative teachers, working alongside trainees, acting as interpreters and models. Once trainees have moved beyond that initial stage and started to take increased responsibility for the teaching process itself, mentors need to extend their role. While continuing some periods of collaborative teaching, they also need to develop a more systematic approach to training, acting as instructors by establishing routines of observation and feedback on agreed competences. Finally, once trainees have achieved basic competence, the role of the mentor needs to develop further. While other aspects of the role may continue, mentors in this final stage of development need to establish themselves as co-enquirers with the aim of promoting critical reflection on teaching and learning by the trainee.

Effective mentoring is therefore a difficult and demanding task and teachers performing the role need the time and in-service support appropriate to the increased responsibilities being placed on them. But in our enthusiasm for analysing the role of the mentor we should not lose sight of the point made clearly at the beginning of this chapter. The work of mentors, however effectively undertaken, can, by definition, be only one aspect of professional preparation. Trainee teachers continue to need preparation in other dimensions of professionality. They need a broad understanding of different styles of practice; an understanding of the practical principles underlying practice; and an appreciation of the moral, political and theoretical issues underlying educational practice. All of these other dimensions of professional knowledge are still best provided by those in higher education. Effective mentoring is a way of complementing and extending forms of training traditionally made available through higher education institutions. It is not intended to be, nor can it be, a substitute for them.

ACKNOWLEDGEMENT

This paper is based upon research funded by the Paul Hamlyn Foundation. We gratefully acknowledge their support and the time given by teachers and trainees.

REFERENCES

Barrett, E., Whitty, G., Furlong, J., Galvin, C. and Barton, L. (1992) *Initial Teacher Education in England and Wales: A Topography*, Modes of Teacher Education Project, London: Goldsmiths College.
Berliner, D.C. (1987) 'Ways of thinking about students and classrooms by

more and less experienced teachers', in Calderhead, J. (ed.) *Exploring Teachers' Thinking*, London: Cassell.

Burn, C. (1992) 'Collaborative teaching', in Wilkin, M. (ed.) *Mentoring in Schools*, London: Kogan Page.

Calderhead, J. (1984) *Teachers' Classroom Decision Making*, London: Holt, Rinehart and Winston.

Calderhead, J. (1987) 'The quality of reflection in student teachers' professional learning', *European Journal of Teacher Education*, 10, 3.

Calderhead, J. (1998a) 'Learning from introductory schools experience', *Journal of Education for Teaching*, 4, 1.

Calderhead, J. (1988b) *Teachers' Professional Learning*, London: Falmer Press.

Calderhead, J. (1989) 'Reflective teaching and teacher education', *Teacher and Teacher Education*, 5, 1.

Calderhead, J. (1991) 'The nature and growth of knowledge in student teaching', *Teaching and Teacher Education*, 7, 5/6.

Carter, K. and Doyle, W. (1987) 'Teachers' knowledge structure and comprehension processes', in Calderhead, J. (ed.) *Exploring Teachers' Thinking*, London: Cassell.

Clandinin, D.J. (1986) *Classroom Practice: Teachers' Images in Action*, London: Falmer Press.

Copeland, W.D. (1981) 'Clinical experiences in the education of teachers', *Journal of Education for Teaching*, 7, 1.

DES (1989) *Initial Teacher Training: Approval of Courses (Circular 24/89)* London: HMSO.

DFE (1992) *Initial Teacher Training (Secondary Phase) (Circular 9/92)* London: DFE.

Eisenhart, M., Behm, L. and Riomagnano, L. (1991) 'Learning to teach: developing expertise or rite of passage?' *Journal of Education for Teaching*, 7, 1.

Elbaz, F. (1983) *Teacher Thinking: A Study of Practical Knowledge*, London: Croom Helm.

Feiman-Nemser, S. and Buchmann, M. (1987) 'When is student teaching teacher education?' *Teacher and Teacher Education*, 3, 255–73.

Freeman, D. (1991) 'To make the tacit explicit – teacher education, emerging discourse and conceptions of teaching', *Teacher and Teacher Education*, 7, 5/6.

Fuller, F. and Bown, O. (1975) 'Becoming a teacher', in Ryan, K. (ed.), *Teacher Education, 74th Year Book of the National Society for the Study of Education*, Chicago, IL: University of Chicago Press.

Furlong, V.J. (1992) 'Reconstructing professionalism: ideological struggle in initial teacher education', in Arnot, M. and Barton, L. (eds) *Voicing Concerns: Sociological Perspectives on Contemporary Educational Reforms*, London: Triangle.

Furlong, V.J., Hirst, P.H., Pocklington, K. and Miles, S. (1988) *Initial Teacher Training and the Role of the School*, Buckingham: Open University Press.

Hillgate Group (1989) *Learning to Teach*, London: The Claridge Press.

Lacey, C. (1977) *The Socialisation of Teachers*, London: Methuen.

Lortie, D. (1975) *Schoolteacher: A Sociological Study*, Chicago, IL: University of Chicago Press.

McIntyre, D. (1990) 'The Oxford Internship Scheme and the Cambridge analytical framework: models of partnership in initial teacher education', in Booth, M., Furlong, J. and Wilkin, M. (eds) *Partnership in Initial Teacher Training*, London: Cassell.

Nias, J. (1989) *Primary Teachers Talking*, London: Routledge.

O'Hear, A. (1988) *Who Teaches the Teachers?* London: Social Affairs Unit.

Schon, D. (1991) *Educating the Reflective Practitioner*, San Francisco, CA: Jossey Bass.

Shulman, L. (1986) 'Those who understand: knowledge growth in teaching', *Educational Researcher*, February.

Smyth, J. (1991) *Teachers as Collaborative Learners*, Milton Keynes: Open University Press.

Squirrell, G., Gilroy, P., Jones, D. and Ruddock, J. (1990) 'Acquiring knowledge in initial teacher training', *Library and Information Research Report*, 79, London: British Library Board.

Sternberg, R. and Caruso, D. (1985) 'Practical modes of knowing in learning and teaching the ways of knowing', in Eisner, E. (ed.) *84th Yearbook of the National Society for the Study of Education*, Chicago: University of Chicago Press.

Wilson, S., Shulman, L. and Richert, A. (1987) '150 different ways of knowing: representations of knowledge in teaching', in Calderhead, J. (ed.) *Exploring Teachers' Thinking*, London: Cassell.

Zeichner, K. and Liston, D. (1987) 'Teaching student teachers to reflect', *Harvard Educational Review*, 57, 1.

Chapter 2

Toward a conceptualization of mentoring

Eugene M. Anderson and Anne Lucasse Shannon

Articles about mentoring beginning teachers have pervaded educational journals during the past few years. Most have discussed responsibilities of a mentor (Nuefield 1987; Huffman and Leak 1986; Levinson, Darrow, Klein, Levinson, McKee and Braxton (1978), detailed the development of mentor programs within a school district (California mentor teacher program 1983), or provided a review of the current literature on mentoring (Galvez-Hjornevik 1985; Merriam 1983). Few, however, have provided the field of education with a clear conceptualization of the act of mentoring (Merriam 1983). This lack of clarity has created problems for school districts and collaborating schools of education that have wanted to develop teacher mentor programs around a sound conceptual framework.

This chapter establishes a conceptualization of the mentoring process that is rooted in historical reference and serves as a model for use by those who design and implement teacher mentor programs. In the discussion that follows, we (a) review the historical development of the term 'mentoring', (b) examine the problems inherent in current concepts of mentoring, (c) propose what we believe to be the essential characteristics of mentoring and (d) discuss implications of the proposed mentoring model for development of teacher mentor programs.

HISTORICAL PERSPECTIVES

The term 'mentor' has its roots in Homer's epic poem, *The Odyssey*. In this myth, Odysseus, a great royal warrior, has been away fighting the Trojan War and has entrusted his son, Telemachus, to his friend and advisor, Mentor. Mentor has been charged with advising and serving as guardian to the entire royal household.

The account of Mentor in *The Odyssey* leads us to make several conclusions about the activity which bears his name. First, mentoring is an *intentional process*. Mentor intentionally carried out his responsibilities for Telemachus. Second, mentoring is a *nurturing process* which fosters the growth and development of the protégé toward full maturity. It was Mentor's responsibility to draw forth the full potential in Telemachus. Third, mentoring is an *insightful process* in which the wisdom of the mentor is acquired and applied by the protégé. Clawson (1980) asserts that it was Mentor's task to help Telemachus grow in wisdom without rebellion. Fourth, mentoring is a *supportive, protective process*. Telemachus was to consider the advice of Mentor, and Mentor was to 'keep all safe'.

It is also reasonable to conclude from Athene's activities in *The Odyssey* that role modeling is a central quality of mentoring. Taking human form, Athene provided Telemachus with a standard and style of behavior which he could understand and follow. Athene helps us comprehend that mentors need to make themselves available to protégés as role models and to understand how their modeling can stimulate perspective, style, and a sense of empowerment within the protégé.

A New English Dictionary (Murray 1908), documents various uses of the term 'mentor' dating from around 1750. These uses confirm the historical meaning of mentoring and further imply that a mentor may be a person or a personified thing. It has not been until the last ten to fifteen years, however, that much about mentoring has appeared in the professional literature. Clawson (1980), for example, identifies the mid-1970s when mentoring for a professional career became a topic of research. Eng (1986) suggests that this emphasis on mentoring coincided with the Human Resources Development Movement in business. Since the mid-1970s, mentoring has increasingly been used to describe a variety of functions in a variety of vocational fields. Yet no commonly accepted meaning of the term has been developed (Speizer 1981).

CURRENT CONCEPTS OF MENTORING

There is a relatively small number of studies on mentoring, and most of these have centered on career development in the field of business (Alleman 1986; Murphy 1986; Zey 1984; Phillips-Jones 1982; Levinson *et al.* 1978). Within these studies various definitions of mentoring have been offered.

Phillips-Jones (1982) defines mentors as influential people who significantly help protégés reach their life goals: 'They have the power – through who or what they know – to promote . . . welfare, training, or career' (p. 21). She identifies six types of mentors: *traditional mentors* are usually older authority figures who, over a long period of time, protect, advocate for and nurture their protégés. They permit their protégés to move up the organizational ladder on their coat-tails. *Supportive bosses* are persons in a direct supervisory relationship with their protégés. Like traditional mentors, supportive bosses reach and guide, but they function more as coaches than as long-term protectors and advocates. *Organizational sponsors* are top-level managers who see that their protégés are promoted within the organization. Unlike traditional mentors and supportive bosses, they do not stay in day-to-day contact with their protégés. *Professional mentors* comprise a variety of career counselors and advisors. Protégés pay for services from these mentors. *Patrons* are persons who use their financial resources and status to help protégés prepare for and launch their careers. *Invisible godparents* help protégés reach career goals without their knowing it. They make 'behind the scenes' arrangements and recommendations (pp. 22–24, 79–89).

Alleman (1986) stipulates that a mentor is a person of greater rank or expertise who teaches, counsels, guides and develops a novice in an organization or profession. Expanding on her definition, she identifies nine mentor functions: (a) giving information, (b) providing political information, (c) challenging assignments, (d) counseling, (e) helping with career moves, (f) developing trust, (g) show-casing protégés' achievements, (h) protecting and (i) developing personal relationship/friendship (pp. 47–48).

Levinson *et al.* (1978) and Zey (1984) represent contrasting views of mentoring. Levinson *et al.* (1978:97) view mentoring as:

One of the most complex, and developmentally important, a man [sic] can have in early adulthood. The mentor is ordinarily several years older, a person of greater experience and seniority in the world the young man [sic] is entering. No word currently in use is adequate to convey the nature of the relationship we have in mind here. Words such as 'counselor' or 'guru' suggest the more subtle meanings, but they have other connotations that would be misleading. The term 'mentor' is generally used in a much narrower sense, to mean teacher, adviser, or sponsor. As we use the term, it means all these things, and more.

In contrast to this personal, relatively broad and informal view of mentoring, Zey (1984:7) defines a mentor as:

a person who oversees the career and development of another person usually a junior, through teaching, counseling, providing psychological support, protecting, and at times promoting and sponsoring. The mentor may perform any or all of the above functions during the mentor relationship.

In this definition, mentoring is viewed as a formal process within an organization that promotes the career development of the protégé to the benefit of the organization and the individual.

Those within the field of education have also provided us with definitions of mentoring. Fagan and Walter (1983) very simply define a mentor as 'an experienced adult who befriends and guides a less-experienced adult' (p. 51).

Similarly, Klopf and Harrison (1981), conceptualizing mentoring as an enabling process, state that mentors are 'competent people who serve as teachers, advisors, counselors, and sponsors for an associate, who may be younger and of the same or different sex' (p. 42). Klopf and Harrison go on to say that the mentor and associate mutually gain 'insight, knowledge, and satisfaction from the relationship' (p. 42). They stipulate that all of the processes or functions found within this definition must be enacted for mentoring to occur.

Daloz (1983) draws upon a travel metaphor when he characterizes a mentor as a guide on a journey. During the trip the mentor carries out three functions: (a) pointing the way, (b) offering support and (c) challenging.

While additional definitions from business and educational literature could be cited, we believe that these definitions serve as a representative sample from which we can express several concerns.

First, some definitions of mentoring, by their generality, are too vague or ambiguous to be helpful to teachers assuming a mentor role. An example of vagueness is found in Fagan and Walter's conception of a mentor as 'an experienced adult who befriends and guides a less-experienced adult' (p. 51). Such definitions do not give mentors enough specific direction for what they are to do or how they are to do it. Further, it is difficult from studying the definitions as a group to know whether mentoring involves a set of functions that are conjunctively or disjunctively joined. This ambiguity is found in the contrasting definitions of Zey (1984) and Klopf and Harrison (1983). While Zey indicates that mentoring may be expressed within *any or all* of a number of mentoring functions (i.e. teaching, counseling, supporting, protecting, promoting and sponsoring), Klopf and Harrison (1983) emphasize that all processes or functions of mentoring (i.e. teaching, advising, counseling, sponsoring and modeling) must be present or the role being enacted is not mentoring. The question is, must the mentor exhibit, or have the disposition to exhibit, all of the designated mentoring functions within a particular mentoring context, or can the mentor specialize in only one or another of the designated mentoring functions to the exclusion of the others? We will return to this point.

Second, while we recognize the complexity of the mentoring process, we are concerned by the lack of conceptual frameworks for organizing the various mentoring functions and behaviors found within the definitions of mentoring. For example, Alleman (1986) cites four mentoring roles and nine mentoring functions without establishing a clear relationship between the two sets. Lack of a rationale for and relationship among these thirteen variables constrains what contribution they might make.

Third, while most of the definitions of mentoring indicate that a mentor should promote the professional and/or personal development of the protégé through a set of mentoring functions, they do not highlight as much as we think they should that (a) mentoring is fundamentally a nurturing process, (b) that the mentor must serve as a role model to the protégé, and (c) that the mentor must exhibit certain dispositions that help define the process. In summary, most definitions do not provide what we believe to be the essence of mentoring in light of its etymological and historical derivation.

A PROPOSED CONCEPT OF MENTORING

In light of the problems expressed above, what constitutes a fruitful concept of mentoring for those who wish to develop and implement mentor programs for new teachers? We will respond to this question by offering a basic definition of mentoring, discussing five mentoring functions and related behaviors, delineating some basic mentoring activities and specifying some necessary dispositions of mentors.

First, we believe that mentoring can best be defined as:

a nurturing process in which a more skilled or more experienced person, serving as a role model, teaches, sponsors, encourages, counsels, and befriends a less skilled or less experienced person for the purpose of promoting the latter's professional and/or personal development. Mentoring functions are carried out within the context of an ongoing, caring relationship between the mentor and protégé.

(Anderson 1987)

The essential attributes of this definition are: (a) the process of nurturing, (b) the act of serving as a role model, (c) the five mentoring functions (teaching, sponsoring, encouraging, counseling and befriending), (d) the focus on professional and/or personal development and (e) the ongoing caring relationship. A brief discussion of each of these attributes will provide a better context for their inclusion.

Nurturing implies a developmental process in which a nurturer is able to recognize the ability, experience and psychological maturity of the person being nurtured and can provide appropriate growth-producing activities. The concept of nurturing also implies several notions embedded in the 'gardening' metaphor. The nurturer helps provide an environment for growth, considers the total personality of the person being nurtured in deciding how best to be helpful, and operates with a belief that the person being nurtured has the capacity to develop into fuller maturity.

Closely related to the nurturing process is the act of serving as a role model. Mentors provide the protégés with a sense of what they are becoming. Protégés can see a part of their adult selves in other adults (Levinson *et al.* 1978). By their example, mentors stimulate growth and development in their protégés.

We view the five basic mentoring functions as *conjunctive* (i.e. a mentor must stand ready to exhibit any or *all* of the functions as the need arises). We take this position for two reasons. First, the five functions as a group historically have been associated with a person called a mentor. Second, requiring a mentor to engage in all five functions carries with it the potential for better discriminating who is and is not mentoring and assigning more potency to the role.

Mentoring can focus on professional and/or personal development. We allow this option because we believe, as does Clawson, that mentoring can vary in terms of its scope of influence (Clawson 1980). While their scope of influence can and does vary within mentoring relationships, the spirit of mentoring, as we understand it, suggests that true mentors are inclined to be concerned about the comprehensive welfare of their protégés.

Lastly, in our definition of mentoring, we stipulate that mentoring must involve an ongoing, caring relationship. Levinson *et al.* (1978) assert that the essence of mentoring may be found more within the kind of relationship that exists between the mentor and protégé than in the various roles and functions denoted by the term, 'mentoring'. We believe the caring relationship is at least of equal importance. The kind of relationship we advocate in mentoring is similar to that of a good substitute parent to an adult child.

With the above definition as our base, we now expand briefly on the five functions of mentoring: teaching, sponsoring, encouraging, counseling and befriending. First, by teaching we mean basic behaviors associated with teaching, including: modeling, informing, confirming/disconfirming, prescribing and questioning. In the context of mentoring, these behaviors are guided by principles of adult education.

Sponsoring involves being a kind of guarantor. Sponsoring within the context of mentoring involves three essential behaviors: protecting, supporting and promoting. Teacher mentors can protect their protégés from something in the environment (e.g. helping to get a very troublesome student removed from their class), or by helping protect protégés from themselves (e.g. encouraging them not to stay up late every night preparing lessons until their health is impaired). Teacher mentors can support their protégés when they participate in an activity assigned to them (e.g. preparing lesson plans together). As sponsors, teacher mentors can promote their protégés within both the instructional and social systems of the school program. They can, for example, not only introduce them to other teachers and help them feel included but also recommend that their protégés serve on a school committee.

Encouraging is a process that includes the behaviors of affirming, inspiring and challenging. Teacher mentors can affirm their protégés for who they are and what they can do; they can inspire them by their example and words; and they can offer challenge by inviting them to become involved in a variety of growth-producing experiences.

Counseling is a problem-solving process that includes behaviors such as listening, probing, clarifying and advising. To the degree that protégés are willing and able, teacher mentors can help them solve their own problems.

Lastly, mentoring demands befriending. While it is difficult to delineate all of the behaviors associated with befriending, two critical ones stand out: accepting and relating. As a friend, teacher mentors will in continuing ways convey to their protégés that they understand and support them; and that they have time for them.

Again, we have selected teaching, sponsoring, counseling, encouraging and befriending as basic functions within our conception of mentoring for two reasons. First, they logically flow from the historical meaning of the term mentoring. Second, they have the capacity to organize a number of more specific functions of mentoring cited in the literature.

To clarify the concept of mentoring, we need to illustrate how mentoring functions are carried out within the teaching context. Examples of basic mentoring activities in the area of education include: demonstrating teaching techiques to a protégé, observing the protégé's classroom teaching and providing feedback, and holding support meetings with the protégé. The point is this: as we think about the concept of mentoring we need to identify various activities in which mentoring functions can be expressed. To be of even further assistance, we might eventually identify times in which these activities can best take place.

To take the concept of mentoring one final step further, we need to identify dispositions that mentors should have as they carry out their mentoring functions and activities. Drawing on the definition of dispositions offered by Katz and Raths (1985), we define a mentoring disposition as an attributed characteristic of a mentor, one that summarizes the trend of the mentor's actions in particular contexts.

Dispositions are broader constructs than skills and denote recurring patterns of behavior.

Mentoring dispositions may arise from the concept of mentoring and also from the values held by those who develop mentor programs. We offer three dispositions that we believe are essential to the concept of mentoring. First, mentors should have the dispositions of opening themselves to their protégés by, for example, allowing their protégés opportunities to observe them in action and conveying to them reasons and purposes behind their decisions and performance. Second, mentors should have the disposition to lead their protégés incrementally over time. Third, mentors should have the disposition to express care and concern about the personal and professional welfare of their protégés.

Figure 2.1 summarizes the essence of mentoring and its basic components. It indicates that basic to mentoring is a relationship in which the protégé views the mentor as a role model and the mentor nurtures and cares for the protégé. Entailed in the mentoring relationship are five mentoring functions and related behaviors that

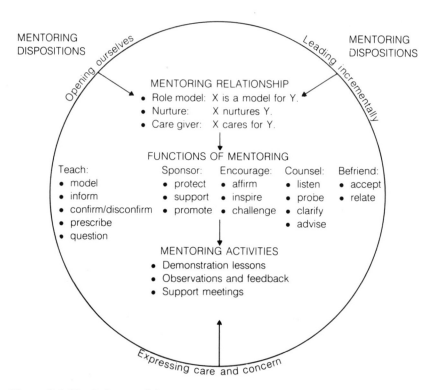

Figure 2.1 Mentoring model

are carried out within various mentoring activities. The entire mentoring process is styled by a set of dispositions displayed by the mentor.

IMPLICATIONS

In developing teacher mentor programs it is all too easy to focus prematurely on such tasks as designing job descriptions for mentors, selecting mentors and protégés, providing some initial orientation sessions and then getting a program underway. To do so, without first thinking carefully about the concept of mentoring, is to run the risk of developing programs that are incomplete, lack integrity, and duplicate programs that in some form have already been tried.

We believe that those who develop mentor programs for beginning teachers should embed them in a definition of mentoring that captures the essence of the mentoring relationship. Further, developers must decide what they believe are the essential functions of mentoring; they must identify possible mentoring activities in which these functions can be expressed; and they must develop the dispositions that mentors are to exhibit as they carry out the functions and activities.

Only when a strong and clear conceptual foundation of mentoring is established can effective mentor programs for beginning teachers be constructed.

REFERENCES

Alleman, E. (1986) 'Measuring mentoring – frequency quality impact', in W.A. Gray and M.M. Gray (eds), *Mentoring: Aid to excellence in career development, business and the professions*. British Columbia: The Xerox Reproduction Centre.

Anderson, E. (1987) *Definitions of mentoring*. Unpublished manuscript.

California mentor teacher program, program advisory (1983, November) Sacramento: California State Department of Education.

Clawson, J.G. (1980) 'Mentoring in managerial careers', in C.B. Derr (ed.), *Work, family and the career*. New York: Praeger.

Daloz, L. (1983) 'Mentors: Teachers who make a difference', *Change* 15 (6), 24–7.

Eng, S.P. (1986) 'Mentoring in principalship education', in W.A. Gray and M.M. Gray (eds), *Mentoring: Aid to excellence in education, the family and the community*. British Columbia: Xerox Reproduction Centre.

Fagan, M.M. and Walter, G. (1982) 'Mentoring among teachers', *Journal of Educational Research* 76 (2), 113–17.

Galvez-Hjornevik, C. (1985, April) *Mentoring: A review of the literature with a focus on teaching*. Austin: The University of Texas at Austin. Education Annex 3.203, Communication Services, Research and Development Centre for Teacher Education. (ERIC Document Reproduction Service No. ED 262 032)

Huffman, G. and Leak, S. (1986) 'Beginning teachers' perceptions of mentors', *Journal of Teacher Education* 37 (1), 22-5.

Katz, L.G. and Raths, J.D. (1985) 'Dispositions as goals for teacher education', *Teaching and Teacher Education* 1 (4), 301-7.

Klopf, G. and Harrison, J. (1981, September) 'Moving up the career ladder: a case for mentors', *Principal*, 41-3.

Levinson, D., Darrow, C., Klein, E., Levinson, M. and McKee, B. (1978) *Seasons of a man's life*. New York: Knopf.

Merriam, S. (1983) 'Mentors and protégés', *Adult Education Quarterly* 33 (3), 161-74.

Murphy, S. (1986, July) *Mentoring and adult development*. Paper presented at First International Conference on Mentoring, Vancouver, BC.

Murray, A.H. (ed.) (1908) *A New English Dictionary*, Oxford: Clarendon Press.

Nuefield, B. (1987, April) *Making a match: the structural and personal sides of mentoring beginning teachers*. Paper presented at the annual meeting of the American Educational Research Association, Washington, DC.

Phillips-Jones, L. (1982) *Mentors and Protégés*, New York: Arbor House.

Speizer, J.J. (1981) 'Role models, mentors, and sponsors: the elusive concepts', *Signs* 6 (4), 692-712.

Zey, M.C. (1984) *The mentor connection*, Homewood, IL: Dow Jones-Irving.

Chapter 3

Mentoring for teacher development
Possibilities and caveats

Bob Elliott and James Calderhead

INTRODUCTION

This chapter is concerned with how growth in teaching can be fostered in student teachers through mentoring. It begins with an analysis of the growth process by drawing upon recent research on student teachers' learning. It then compares and contrasts this with the conceptions of mentoring and student teachers' learning held by a sample of mentors involved in an articled teacher training scheme. This comparison of the two is used to raise issues concerning the roles and responsibilities of mentors, their potential contribution to student teachers' professional development and obstacles that may have to be overcome to reach this potential.

THE NATURE OF PROFESSIONAL GROWTH

Attempts to understand teacher development have recently drawn upon research on teachers' beliefs and mental processes (e.g. Richardson 1990). Such research suggests that the professional growth in neophyte professionals is influenced by a range of factors with particular emphasis on the following:

- the expectations for professional development that the neophytes bring with them to their training (Calderhead 1988; Elliott and Lange 1991);
- the structure, style and content of the formal curriculum of teacher education (Blum and Labasco 1984; Doyle 1986; Eraut 1985; Teich 1986);
- the learning strategies employed by trainees (Brown 1978; Calderhead 1988, 1990; Kober 1980);
- the nature of the work environment into which graduates will move (Mitchell and Marland 1989; Zeichner and Gore 1990).

While it might be argued that research on beginning teachers should provide the basis for the design of initial teacher education programmes (Floden and Klinzing 1990), policy directions tend to be shaped more by political forces than research initiatives. For example, in Britain there are clear moves from central government that 'schools should play a much larger part in initial teacher training' and that 'higher education institutions . . . focus on the competencies of teaching' (DES 1992:1). At the same time, research findings point towards the difficulties of cultivating the professional knowledge and thinking of the teacher and the complexities of teachers' work that take it beyond conceptualization in terms of a list of competences (e.g. McGaghie 1991).

While there is acceptance by politicians, researchers and teachers that development programmes for student teachers should be more 'school-based', there appears to be little agreement about what that entails or even why it is desirable.

Within such a climate, institutions concerned with teacher education need to take considerable care in how they conceptualize teacher development and how they structure training programmes to foster this. Simply placing students in schools may not always result in students learning how to teach (Edwards and Mercer 1987) and school-based programmes, depending on how they are structured and developed, may produce at best teachers who have demonstrated behaviours listed in sets of pre-defined competences. At worst they may produce para-professionals who are able to reproduce little more than what they have observed in other teachers.

This is not to deny the real possibilities and potential that exist in such programmes but they need to be well thought through and founded on appropriate principles of professional learning.

PROFESSIONAL GROWTH

The following analysis describes the nature of professional growth in teachers in terms of a series of significant dimensions.

Growth is multidimensional

Research highlighting the differences between experienced and novice teachers (Berliner 1987) and the changes reported by students during their training (Calderhead and Robson 1991) implies that teachers undergo a growth process which is complex and multidimensional in nature. For example, learning to teach involves changes in knowledge and beliefs and not simply changes in skill suggested by much of the earlier process–product research (Brophy and Good 1986).

In a review of contemporary research on teacher learning, Kagan (1992) concludes that growth occurs within a number of domains:

- there is an increase in the knowledge that novices have about pupils, how they learn and the importance of their backgrounds;
- the focus of the beginners' concerns moves away from themselves as actors in the classroom to those learners to whom their teaching is directed;
- routines for teaching become automated and the need to think through each minute step is diminished;
- novices become more aware of their own thinking about what they are doing and its impact on pupils – there is an increase in metacognition;
- there is an increase in instructional problem-solving on behalf of the beginning teacher which is 'more differentiated, multidimensional, and context-specific'.

It follows that not only is growth complex but, given that knowledge associated with teaching assumes a range of forms (Shulman 1986a), development programmes for teachers may need to incorporate a range of experiences, learning tasks and environments to develop these different forms of knowledge.

Growth is based on prior learning

Research also indicates the importance of students' previously acquired images of teaching. Experience during their own school days appears to shape how novices see themselves as beginning teachers (Leinhardt 1988). Images of teaching formed during this period appear to be not only stable across time (Calderhead and Robson 1991) but 'powerful influences' on how novices develop (Calderhead 1988:54).

Research illuminating the imagery in teacher knowledge is useful in highlighting a number of aspects of professional growth in teaching. Growth in knowledge about teaching begins prior to formal teacher preparation courses. The difficulty here, however, is that knowledge formed during these very early times creates images of teaching from the perspective of the pupil. Such images are often not helpful to the novice teacher because they are based on what teachers can be seen to be doing rather than what they are thinking in order to achieve these states.

Such conclusions contrast with what we know about the nature of more experienced teachers' thinking and action. For example, Shulman's research (1987) with teachers in the early stages of their careers has led him to conclude that teachers engage in progressing cycles of thought involving comprehension, transforming, instructing, evaluating, reflecting and forming new comprehensions of teaching. This conclusion suggests a constructivist perspective on teachers' work which intimately relates thought and action.

This theorizing points out the contrast between the images of growth and teaching that underpin the work of more experienced teachers and the images of teaching that novices bring with them to their initial training. Professional growth requires novices to confront previously constructed images of teaching, acknowledge them and their sources and subsequently adapt them.

Growth in teaching involves different forms of learning

One of the difficulties of language is that we often use the same word for different referents. When we refer to the outcome of an educational experience, irrespective of the nature of that experience, we claim that learning has occurred. We then conclude that, irrespective of the experience, learning has an invariant quality about it and, for example, that learning to ride a bicycle, learning to count and learning to teach are similar phenomena.

Much learning in schools is often linguistically oriented involving 'book knowledge' (Calderhead 1991). The assumption here is that if we are able to talk about a phenomenon or practice then we have learned it and consequently are able to engage in associated practices. Teacher preparation courses have sometimes been developed on such a premise. Such courses assume that learning to teach and learning about teaching are either one and the same or that the latter is a prerequisite for the former. Such assumptions are questionable.

Students come from school with not only images of teaching but, perhaps more importantly, images of development and learning (Elliott, 1992) which influence how they think about their own development. Professional growth probably requires novices to recognize the existence of such images and accommodate them in their learning to teach. In this sense growth in teaching involves an increase in metacognition.

Shulman's (1986) analysis of forms of knowledge has encouraged debate about the importance of case knowledge in fostering professional development. Since that time there has been increasing interest in the possible use of case knowledge in teacher development in the same manner that it is employed in the professional development of doctors and lawyers. However, it may be argued that the powerful cases that student teachers bring to the profession are those which they have developed across their extended apprenticeship period (Lortie 1975) and such cases have emotional and personal components attached to them, making them quite different from those employed in legal or medical education.

The individually created case knowledge *of teaching* is different from the case knowledge *about teaching* that is often created by researchers. It is the latter which is often the basis of the claim that learning to teach could use case knowledge in the same manner as medical and legal education. Cases about teaching may be useful in assisting the growth process of student teachers in that they may assist the novices to develop generalizable analytical skills. On a broader frame they may also assist in establishing the situated knowledge of the teacher as a central component of teacher education. However, notwithstanding these points, it seems to be the novices' personally developed cases that are powerful influences on their learning. Learning to teach appears to be quite distinctive and does not find ready parallels with other professions.

Growth implies cognitive and affective changes

One of the difficulties concerning checklists of competencies, such as those published by accrediting authorities, is that they list only the behaviours expected of teachers. There are, however, obvious cognitive and affective elements of teaching. The assumption is often made that if novices have particular knowledge about teaching they will be able to exhibit these behaviours. What the lists do not recognize is that growth in teaching requires interrelated changes in cognition, beliefs, attitudes and behaviours. To focus on one in the absence of others is unlikely to bring about significant changes in the beginning teachers. Affective components of learning to teach, including attitudes towards children, parents and other teachers, as well as attitudes about subject matter, are often developed during periods of stressful academic study in teacher preparation courses.

Growth occurs in a range of contexts

Student teachers claim that there is a range of contexts in which they develop their ideas about teaching. These range from formally structured learning environments, through semi-structured environments that the students organize amongst themselves, to being alone (Elliott 1992). Being alone is important for students, so that they can work through the complexities of their task, but the need to learn in a school context is also important. In such contexts it is probably more than the individual teachers that are important in assisting the novice to develop appropriately. Just as a supportive environment is an important pre-requisite for reflection amongst teachers (Calderhead and Gates, 1994) so also an appropriately supportive school environment may be necessary to foster cognitive and affective orientations to teaching amongst novices. A total school environment, including leadership from the head, an acceptance of professional debate and challenge as well as encouragement amongst the staff, may be essential characteristics of a school if a student is to develop those essential orientations to practice.

Growth requires both support and challenge

Daloz (1986:214) has argued that a two-dimensional model such as that indicated in Figure 3.1 is a useful device for discussing different approaches to fostering professional growth.

In the quadrant where challenge and support are both low the *status quo* is likely to be maintained but when challenge is increased without comparative changes in support there is likely to be no growth. In this case the student is likely to withdraw physically from the

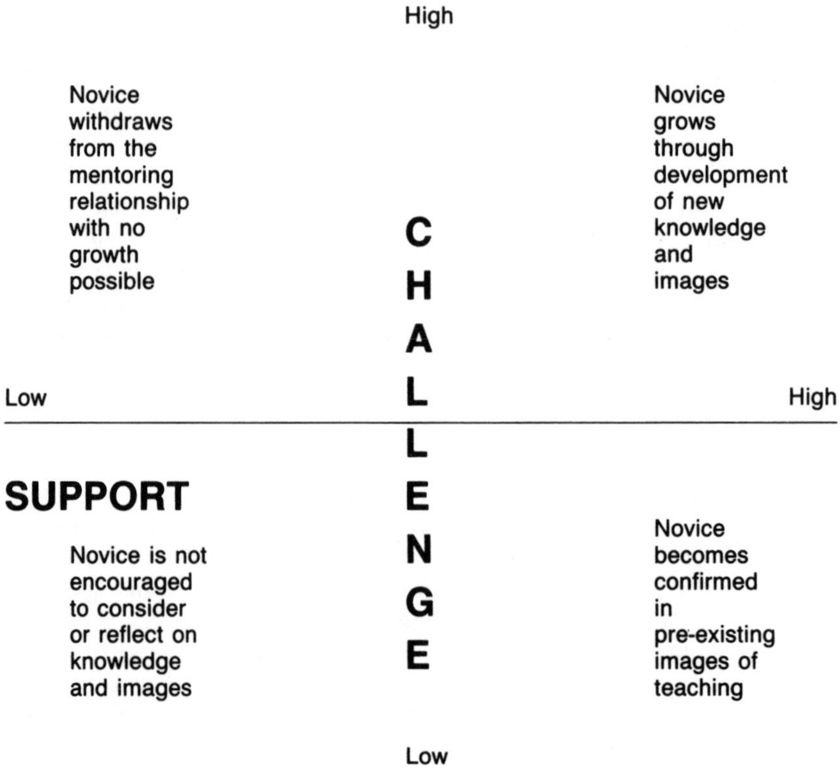

High

| | C | Novice grows through development of new knowledge and images |

Novice withdraws from the mentoring relationship with no growth possible

C
H
A

Low   L   High

L
SUPPORT   E
N
G
E

Novice is not encouraged to consider or reflect on knowledge and images

Novice becomes confirmed in pre-existing images of teaching

Low

Figure 3.1 Two-dimensional model of mentoring relationships (adapted from Daloz 1986)

development programme or, at best, resort to using previously formed ideas. In other words, there will be little increase in problem-solving characteristics and the student will sternly defend practice in terms of images from the past.

There is evidence to suggest that challenge is a necessary component for professional growth to occur. For example, Hollingsworth (1988, 1989) has argued that where there is a mismatch between the beliefs of student teachers and their supervisors in schools, the student is more likely to reflect on their own belief systems. In discussing findings such as these, which suggest that student teachers may be more satisfied with supervisors who are warm, Kagan (1992) concludes that although students experience cognitive dissonance when challenge is high, this is often uncomfortable.

Conclusions

A number of factors emerge from the above analysis. First, growth in teaching is a process that occurs across a considerable period of time and needs to be fostered in ways that are unique to the profession. Such fostering needs to attend to both the affective and cognitive aspects of teaching. It means, for instance, that 'throwing students in at the deep end' will probably, at best, produce teachers whose prime aim is the development of survival skills.

Second, because growth is complex and multidimensional in nature, learning to teach will probably occur at different rates for different students. The stage models of growth proposed by Fuller (1969), and more recently by Berliner (1987), suggest an invariant developmental pattern. Given the different profiles that students bring with them, it is likely that some will be quite advanced in some dimensions and novices in others. Such differentiation probably continues throughout their career where teachers move to expertise in different areas at different rates. Thus, it is unlikely that there would be a uniform linear progression in all domains of development as suggested by the stage models. Rather, what is more likely is development across a range of dimensions at different times for different students. Learning to teach, in this sense, is idiosyncratic and personal.

Third, growth can be fostered or hindered by the knowledge, values and ideas that the beginning teacher brings to teaching as well as the context in which such growth is developed. Further, given the unique combinations of support and challenge required to address these prior orientations, growth needs to be fostered in a range of contexts.

Fourth, those who foster growth in novices require a distinctive and comprehensive language to assist them in the process. Such language would not only enable a diversity of classroom experiences to be incorporated into the novice's image of teaching but it would enable developers to adequately reflect on their complex task.

Finally, there is need for considerable individual support, in both emotional and cognitive spheres, for beginning teachers if they are to develop and grow as teachers. While current demands for a reflective profession suggest that student teachers study and develop in traditional university academic environments, such environments may not provide the necessary support for the students to grapple with previously constructed and reinforced images of pupils and teachers which are at the heart of their learning to teach.

Such conclusions beg the question of how such growth can be fostered within teacher education courses through processes of mentoring. For example Shulman (1986b) has argued that the most substantial contribution that a mentor can make is to help other teachers extend their thinking about their educational practices but what it means to 'extend their thinking' and how such initiatives are conceived by practitioners are not clear.

The above review of the research also points to some implications for mentoring. In order to facilitate growth, mentors need to have well formulated ideas about how teachers develop professionally. Also, they need to be able to recognize the images of teaching that novices bring with them to their training, the diversity of possible teaching styles and how the latter can be constructed from the former. They require not only skills for counselling but also a language of practice which incorporates the complexities of training and teaching.

As a way of moving forward to identify how mentoring can best facilitate professional growth, as identified in the research literature, these issues are examined here in the light of how a sample of mentors perceive their role and the contexts in which they undertake the task.

MENTORING: A RESEARCH PROJECT

The research discussed here is related to an articled teacher training scheme for primary teaching in which student teachers spend four days per week in schools under the guidance of a mentor. In the scheme, a tutor from the higher education institution organizing the programme was attached to the mentor–articled teacher pair and nine such mentor–articled teacher pairs were studied. The mentors spanned a full range of teaching experience and tended to be teaching in lower primary or infants grades.

The findings relate to interviews conducted towards the end of the first year of the two-year course. Each mentor was interviewed for about an hour with questions focusing on:

- perceptions of mentoring roles;
- specific approaches the mentor was adopting;
- the rationale for these approaches;
- the mentors' perceptions of how the articled teacher was learning to teach.

Each interview was transcribed and analysed by examining similarities and differences across the range of mentors' responses to the four questions noted above.

Perceptions of mentoring roles

Each of the mentors in this study recounted the variety of mentoring roles in different ways. For example, some mentors discussed their role in terms of being a 'guide' or a 'leader'. These mentors appeared to believe that the role required them to open up the context of the school for the articled teacher so that she could encounter what was to be learned and be ready to assist if the articled teacher strayed into difficult territory.

Such perceptions may imply that these mentors felt that they had a good grasp of the terrain to be traversed by the student and a view of where the journey should end. It may also imply that the mentors believed that there was only one way to teach and that they were guiding or leading the novice to that viewpoint.

The mentors often discussed their roles in terms of being a 'good listener', 'being a friend or 'enabling'. On occasions, some of the mentors implied that there was a dependency relationship between themselves and the novice which shaped the way they viewed the role.

It was quite common for the mentors to refer to the role in terms of being an organizer of experiences for the novice throughout the school. Such experiences enabled the novice to complete a range of tasks set by the higher education institution.

Most of the mentors referred to the organizational aspect of their role where they organized activities for the articled teacher to enable her to complete various tasks for her campus learning. Also, many mentioned a collaborative aspect of the role such as planning of the timetable, 'narrowing it down with the week and the daily programme'.

In some cases, although only rarely, there was reference to the articulation of craft knowledge to the articled teacher. Such articulation was either in response to questions from the novices or as a result of watching the novices teach and comparing it with their own teaching. These mentors often interrelated their own development with that of their students. They linked the articulation of their personal knowledge with reflection on their teaching.

On only a very limited number of occasions were there references to the role of *agent provocateur* with the novice. In fact, only one mentor specifically focused on the importance of such a role. In terms of the earlier review of research she alone appeared to understand the multidimensional aspect of learning to teach.

On balance, the mentors appeared to perceive the mentoring role more in terms of nurturing or supporting the novices so that they can learn 'by whatever works' in their school or their classroom. In this sense there appears to be a conforming rather than critical orientation to the role.

Specific approaches to mentoring

Given the different views that mentors had of their roles, it is not surprising that they reported a wide range of mentoring strategies. For example, some reported approaches which built on the nature of the personal relationship that had developed between them and the student. Generally, these mentors arranged for the novices to be located in their classrooms for almost all of the time, although some did indicate that they had arranged for the novice to visit other teachers' classrooms. Their views appeared to stem from the fact that, in teaching, the 'relationship is central'.

One of the most frequently reported approaches that mentors claimed to be using was that of 'active listening'. Using such an approach, articled teachers reported on their experiences in the school and classroom context and, subsequently, mentors became sounding-boards for the novices' ideas. Many argued that such an approach not only encouraged students to think of creative solutions to problems but encouraged a level of independence in problem-solving. It could be argued that such an approach not only encourages such problem-solving but also empowers novices by placing the learning and development agenda directly in the hands of the articled teacher.

While most of the mentors were able to discuss particular strategies, such as active listening, a small number were unable to discuss their approaches in any detail.

A significant point of note with regard to the approaches adopted by the mentors, is that very few of them appeared to adopt an approach whereby they openly challenged their novices' ideas and images of teaching, particularly those which they brought with them to their training. In nearly all cases, when asked directly whether they challenged the students' ideas and beliefs, most replied that either there was no need to do so or that such an approach was inappropriate for novice teachers.

Some mentors, however, did indicate that during discussion sessions they encouraged the novices to 'discuss' their views about teaching.

With regard to the issue of when the novice should be encouraged to reflect on practice and beliefs, most of the mentors indicated that it was 'when things go wrong' that they encouraged the novice to think about an incident. It was as if a breakdown in class management or other teaching routines were needed in order to generate reflection. Mentors did not appear to adopt approaches in which they deliberately provoked students to reflect on their previously developed images of teaching by setting puzzles for the students to resolve, by deliberately adopting contrary positions to the student or asking the student to justify particular teaching events in terms of what the student believes or knows.

A final point concerns views about the scope of experiences and the breadth of the environment in which the novice should learn about teaching. Some mentors felt that it was appropriate, during the first year of development to keep the student primarily in the single classroom. Others felt it more appropriate to begin with a wider scope. These latter mentors saw the school and other local institutions as the environment in which development should occur.

In conclusion, while a diversity of approaches was reported by the mentors in this study, the particular approaches that were adopted by any particular mentor appeared to be compatible with the way the mentor perceived her role. Those who perceived 'the relationship' as central to the role advocated a series of interpersonal counselling encounters as most effective in developing understandings about teaching. Others, for example, who perceived the role more in terms of revealing personal knowledge of teaching, highlighted the importance of personal reflection and discussion of the outcomes of this process.

Rationale for mentoring approaches

Most of the mentors were able to provide rationales for their approaches to mentoring. In many cases mentors indicated that they began to think about mentoring in the same terms as they thought about their own teaching. In fact, the first image of mentoring that they formed was often based on their images of teaching. Others indicated how they formed subsequent images based on relationships with other teachers on the staff, relationships with family members and, in some cases, based on other career roles. For example, one mentor referred to her role as a counsellor and another to her role as a trainer in the retail business.

Some mentors indicated that their rationale for mentoring was based on how *they* would have liked to have been trained. In other words they were reflecting back to their own student days in order to assist them with ideas about mentoring. It appears that, just as novice teachers begin with images of teaching and development based on their own career as a student in a classroom, novice mentors may begin with images of mentoring based on experiences in other contexts which may or may not be appropriate.

In some cases, the mentors indicated that they adopted particular strategies because of the way they thought about their teaching. For example, some mentors appeared to believe that teaching is a set of behavioural routines and so knowledge of teaching was simply information about when to enact these routines.

Other mentors believed that differences amongst teachers are accountable for in terms of individual personalities. In such cases it seemed to be the resourcefulness of the articled teacher which often determined the learning agenda. She was expected to 'find things out', although the mentor would provide the 'shoulder to cry on, someone to talk to and with, and to set her on her guidelines'.

Another point of interest here is how a small number of the mentors sought to interrelate the learning which the novice experiences in the school context with that which occurs in the higher education institution. In order to achieve this interrelationship, one mentor indicated that 'we analyse the theory in terms of what the reality is'. In indicating how this interrelationship actually influenced the direction of the novice's development, the mentor said that she was 'adjusting the goalposts every week'.

The conclusion from this section is that mentors' assumptions about the mentoring task are often embedded in a network of other assumptions and values. For example, it appears that assumptions about the very nature of teaching and how learning occurs provide part of the rationale for the mentors' approaches. These are supplemented by the values that are attached to learning which the articled teachers undertake outside the mentors' control and direction.

Perceptions of how novices learn to teach

Often, amongst the mentors, there was a view that learning to teach required students to experience a range of teaching environments from which they could select specific teaching events and 'absorb' them. From the mentor herself, other teachers or the whole school environment, the articled teacher would obtain 'anecdotes . . . experience and knowledge'. Such information sometimes concerned 'mistakes' that the mentor said she had made in her own teaching and 'passed to the articled teacher so that she would not have to make the same mistakes'. On other occasions it concerned specific children to be taught. These mentors believed that absorption of information should preferably take place after discussion of the information or personal trialing of suggested strategies. It was a common view amongst the mentors that such experiences would assist the novice to learn the 'nitty-gritty' of teaching.

In some cases the mentors seemed to imply that the growth which occurs in the mentoring relationship is a mirror of the growth process in learning to teach. Confidence in teaching follows confidence in the mentor. In order to encourage novices' growth, these mentors indicated that they needed to be extremely supportive and positive so that mistakes can be made and learning occur. In this sense learning was seen to progress through three stages: gaining confidence in the relationship, gradually doing things with less support and, finally, being independent of the support.

Other mentors referred to different stage models of growth. For example, it was common for mentors to claim that because the novice had progressed from teaching a small group to teaching the whole class or progressed from teaching a half-hour to teaching a half-day that growth in teaching had occurred. These mentors seemed to have a unidimensional model of growth where teaching behaviours are extended to a greater number of children or for longer periods of time.

In most instances there appeared to be only lukewarm support from the mentor for growth attributable to learning in the higher education institution, although most pleaded ignorance of what was undertaken at the institution. At the other extreme, one mentor recounted how she spent a considerable amount of her spare time reading the papers associated with the novice's courses in order to 'marry the two together – the theory and the practice'.

Finally, it is also interesting to note the different ways that mentors thought about the outcomes of their mentoring. Some mentors indicated that the focus of their novices' learning had been on specific teaching techniques embedded in experience. Growth in teaching, in these terms, is identified with being able to take the class for larger periods of time. It is as if these mentors held a definition of growth expressed in quantifiable terms, equating competence with sustainability in teaching. For example, one mentor noted that growth involved 'experience and absorbing different things from courses', while another indicated that the novice was 'taking over lessons and preparing them for herself . . . so she's developed that far . . . from just observing to taking small groups and then taking whole classes'. In contrast, there were scant references to any changes in novices' beliefs about teaching, their perspectives on children or how they thought about subject knowledge.

One conclusion from this analysis is that mentors had views about learning to teach which were more simplistic than those implied in the research literature. Such a conclusion is perhaps not surprising given the limited opportunities that the mentors had to reflect on their new role and develop a language to discuss and reflect on a process which is both distinctive and complex.

CONCEPTIONS OF MENTORING: A DISCUSSION

A number of themes run through the above analysis and interrelate how mentors perceive their role and tasks, how they justify their ideas and actions and how they believe teachers learn to teach. These highlight a number of issues for school-based teacher training and the development of beginning teachers.

A question of responsibility

All the mentors stressed the high levels of responsibility that they felt for the articled teacher. In traditional preparation courses, where students are located in schools for practice teaching experiences, the students are only passing visitors and school supervisors generally regard the higher education institution as being responsible for the students' development. In the case of mentoring in articled teacher schemes, the role of school personnel is entirely different. One mentor explained the responsibility associated with this change in these terms:

> It's more of an intimate responsibility rather than general because you are reponsible for a particular person for two whole years, which is really quite a commitment. You are, I suppose, in overall charge of her. The college do their bit but ultimately it is us who are responsible for their development.

Inherent in this description is the realization of what it means to care for an articled teacher and to facilitate her growth for the greater part of her training, often with little outside support.

The importance of interpersonal relationships

Many of the mentors talked about the importance of the personal relationship between themselves and their students. In many cases mentoring was seen as a direct function of an extremely intense personal relationship which the mentor developed with the articled teacher. Such a relationship often spanned the boundaries between personal and professional issues where, according to the mentors, no problems of either nature are 'hidden'. Often such mentors discussed the nature of this relationship between themselves and the student as an extension of other relationships in the school. For example, one of the mentors indicated that the school in which she worked was a place where 'we work on a very friendly basis. We've all got a relationship with everyone . . .'.

In thinking about their role as mentors in these terms, they often referred to the similarity between the mentor–articled teacher relationship and their own family relationships. Where the age and gender factors were appropriate, the relationship was referred to as 'mother–daughter' by some mentors and a 'sister' relationship by another. Friendship, with honesty and mutual respect, were key words used by the mentors in describing these relationships.

In contrast, a couple of mentors saw their role more in terms of simply being available when needed. For these mentors, the focus seems to be simply on ' being there' for discussions and guidance. Such a conception of the mentor role is rather informal and less intense than that previously outlined.

In one case, the mentor noted that her role was 'quite an informal sort of job I would think. I have the responsibility (for the novice) but I don't think it's a formal role as such.' This case illustrates the complexity of issues involved in mentors' role conceptions. On the one hand she indicated that 'it was better that she [the student] spent time away from me to start with and it's worked very well that way – we're not under each other's feet', and her task was to 'arrange timetables [for the novice] . . . and to be there if she needs me'. On the other hand, while she 'made an effort as far as possible to make sure she's [the articled teacher] ok each day', this mentor also outlined how 'the relationship has deepened quite a lot . . . and over the past few months we've got to know each other more intimately'. These points highlight the complexity, and sometimes possible inconsistency, in how the mentors conceive their roles. It could be that the mentor believed that distance between herself and the novice was one way of sustaining the relationship between them. Alternatively, it could be that she maintained the distance because she had a different notion of 'the relationship' from other mentors.

Finally, the question of why the mentors in this study placed such importance on the relationships with their students needs to be considered. The initial training which the mentors received obviously provided a way for the mentors to think about their role. However, the analysis also suggests that mentors' extrapolations of ideas from school communities and classroom teaching models also play a part in their trying to identify their role in promoting professional growth.

The nature of interrelated development

While many of the mentors discussed their role in terms of the development of their articled teacher, there was another side to the role which a number of them recounted. This focused more on how the mentor herself gained from the experience and how this personal growth related to the growth of the novice. Some indicated how valuable the experience of having an articled teacher in the classroom had been. Some recounted the difficulties of professional isolation, commonly reported by teachers, and how the presence of another professional in the classroom had provided opportunities to share their work.

Some of these mentors reported complex relationships between the role of encouraging growth in the novice teacher and their own professional development. For example, some indicated that having an articled teacher present with them prompts them to think about, and subsequently articulate, the knowledge which is associated with their teaching. This process appears to be prompted either by the mentor simply observing the novice or by contrasting her own teaching behaviours with what she observes through watching the beginner.

It appears that the mentors had different orientations to professional learning and this, in turn, influenced how they viewed the role of mentoring. Given the earlier analysis, indicating the dimensions of professional growth required in novices, it would seem that mentors who have broad views of their own learning would be more likely to encourage growth, in all its dimensions, in their novices.

The interface of school and campus learning

If mentors were to value learning from contexts other than their own, it may be possible for them to draw upon similarities and differences between this knowledge and knowledge in the school situation to provoke incidents of cognitive dissonance for the novice, and hence promote growth.

While the data analysis indicates that very few mentors adopted such strategies, some mentors indicated that they encouraged the articled teacher to 'discuss' what they had learned during their visits to the higher education institution and to build this into their teaching. This was also seen by such mentors as a valuable way of incorporating newer approaches into their own teaching repertoire. Others indicated that they felt that they knew little about what was occurring in campus courses and that this had little to do with the 'nitty-gritty of teaching'.

The importance of challenge in professional growth

The earlier review of research indicated that challenge is essential for professional growth to occur. It is not clear why the mentors in this study generally did not adopt approaches involving open challenge of novices' images of teaching, but a number of reasons may be postulated. It may be that the intensity, or nature, of the relationship established between the mentor and articled teacher may impede such strategies. Neither the mentor nor the articled teacher may wish to place the relationship at risk – the mentor because of the high level of responsibility she feels for the novice and the novice for the level of dependency on the mentor which she may feel. Alternatively, it may be that these mentors felt that the first year of development was too early for such challenge or that coming to grips with the task was itself sufficiently challenging.

From a learning theory perspective, it is possible that the only model for learning and development to which the mentors have access is one which is grounded in classroom teaching. The only adult relationships in the school to which the mentor can relate (such as those among other teachers and helpers in the classroom) are based on friendships and not related to learning. As such, they are inappropriate models for fostering growth in beginning teachers.

From another perspective, since these mentors did not have extensive experience in professional development they had not formulated an appropriate language to talk about alternative ways of viewing classroom contexts. Not only might they have been unaware of the importance of cognitive, affective and behavioural orientations in learning to teach but they may be hampered in bringing about changes in these orientations because of the lack of an appropriate framework in which to do so.

While it seems that these issues require further clarification through longitudinal studies, they also point to possible implications for reconceptualizing teachers' work and school environments as places of learning if the move to school-based teacher education is to continue. While many would claim that costs are the inhibiting factors for school-based teacher development, the professional implications outlined here suggest other less tangible inhibitions.

Coherence in teachers' conceptions

Most of the mentors in this study appeared to have a view of mentoring which they expressed in terms of metaphors and images. These metaphors and images, often drawn from classroom experience, appear to be a focus for them to think about roles, strategies and conceptions of learning to teach. For example, one mentor referred to mentoring as 'enabling', comparing it to an approach to teaching writing: 'with our writing with the children we support them as long as they need our support . . . and gradually the children take over these things, so we are enabling them'. She then explained that being a mentor was 'someone to whom . . . she [the novice] can talk and put anxieties and joys to', and 'gradually allowing her to do more in the classroom'. The novice was 'usually very aware of why it's gone wrong', and 'it's very much like the children, absorbing a new idea and trying it out'.

There were also some inconsistencies in the way the mentors described their role and the study did not examine the possible inconsistencies between what the mentors said they did and their actual practices. Notwithstanding these possible inconsistencies, the study suggests an overall coherence in the way each mentor conceives the role. This coherence may be important in examining training implications for the future. These coherences may need to be the building blocks for developing mentors' skills and changing their orientations.

Relating teachers' and researchers' conceptions

This study suggests that mentors understand the importance of supporting novices during their formative period. It also indicates that they have a limited language with which to discuss practice and professional growth. While there is variation in understandings amongst the mentors, the data suggest some gaps between the expectations as implied by research and mentors' conceptualizations. The conclusions suggest that mentors need to adopt more of a challenging orientation to their role, drawing on the diversity of approaches to teaching, and that they require a more expansive language with which to discuss professional development and classroom understandings in general.

CONCLUSIONS: POSSIBILITIES AND CAVEATS

It is clear that the use of mentors as part of school-based training of teachers has real potential and this chapter has highlighted a number of implications for school-based training. Because the conclusions are based on one study in primary schools, they should be regarded as tentative.

First, there are caveats concerning changes required to the concept of teachers' work and school climates if the notions of mentoring are to be maximized. The move to school-based training implies that teachers need to change their traditional orientation to their role. For some centuries, teaching, particularly in primary schools, has been identified with teaching young children. Teachers' notions of learning are built on the fact that they teach young pupils. The mentors in this study indicated that they often thought of their mentoring tasks in terms of their teaching but realized the inadequacy of such a model.

The notion of the school as a 'learning community' in which learning occurs at various levels will need to become widely accepted. In such a community open debate amongst all professionals would have to characterize the school environment. Teachers will need to interact with each other, challenging each other and supporting each other in order to sustain that challenge. Many mentors often refer to their happy and friendly school and what is required is the transformation of this climate to sustain professional development for all.

Second, there are implications for re-examining the nature of 'partnerships' between schools and higher education institutions. Staff in both organizations are very busy and it is difficult for each to find time to work together. Of greater importance is the history and feelings each brings with them to their meetings. The irony is that greater professional growth for novice teachers is a real possibility if the differences in orientations of these two groups can be used as the basis of professional challenge and debate. This requires the schools to be less defensive about their practices and look for the reasons why practice and theory often sit uneasily beside each other. In parallel, it requires higher education institutions to value the craft knowledge of teachers and seek ways that it can be legitimated and brought within the mainstream of teacher preparation. In this sense, the initiatives reported by McAlpine *et al.* (1988) to teach novices specific strategies to elicit that craft knowledge while in the higher education institution require further exploration. If the difficulties which these authors report can be addressed, then mentoring has real potential for both the mentor and novice.

Third, there are implications for training programmes for mentors. As noted above, the relationships between a mentor and a novice teacher do not presently find a parallel in schools. Training for mentors to recognize this fact is necessary. However, considerable care needs to be taken in formulating such programmes. The notions of support and challenge and the delicate relationship between these need to be carefully considered. Further, while skill development in areas such as counselling may be necessary, the conceptions that mentors hold and the values and beliefs that they bring to a mentoring context appear to be important factors in determining whether or not these skills are actually exercised. In this sense, the research on teachers' learning, illustrating the powerful images that students bring with them to their training, is perhaps generalizable to all professional development. Development programmes should seek to establish conceptions of mentoring in such a way that the unique combinations of challenge and support necessary to foster growth are realized in mentoring contexts.

REFERENCES

Berliner, D. (1987) 'Ways of thinking about students and classrooms by more and less experienced teachers', in Calderhead, J. (ed.) *Exploring Teachers' Thinking*, London: Cassell.

Blum, B. and Labasco, G. (1984) 'The case against the case system', *California Lawyer*, 4, 30–4.

Brophy, J. and Good, T. (1986) 'Teacher behaviour and student achievement', in Wittrock, M. (ed.) *Handbook of Research on Teaching*, 3rd edn, New York: Macmillan.

Brown, A. (1978) 'Knowing when, where and how to remember: a problem of metacognition', in Glaser, R. (ed.) *Advances in Instructional Psychology*, Hillsdale, NJ: Erlbaum.

Calderhead, J. (1988) 'The development of knowledge structures in learning to teach', in Calderhead, J. (ed.) *Teachers' Professional Learning*, London: Falmer Press.

Calderhead, J. (1990) 'Conceptualising and evaluating teachers' professional learning', *European Journal of Teacher Education*, 13, 3, 153–60.

Calderhead, J. (1991) 'The nature and growth of knowledge in student teaching', *Teaching and Teacher Education*, 7, 5/6, 531–5.

Calderhead, J. and Gates, P. (eds) (1994) *Conceptualising Reflections in Teacher Development*, London: Falmer Press.

Calderhead, J. and Robson, M. (1991) 'Images of teaching: student teachers' early conceptions of classroom practice', *Teaching and Teacher Education*, 7, 1, 1–8.

Daloz, L. (1986) *Effective Teaching and Mentoring*, San Francisco, CA: Jossey-Bass.

Department of Education and Science (1992) *Reform of Initial Teacher Training: A consultation document*, London: DES.

Dyle, W. (1986) 'Content representation in teachers' definitions of academic work', *Journal of Curriculum Studies*, 18, 4, 365–79.

Edwards, D. and Mercer, N. (1987) *Common Knowledge: The development of understanding in the classroom*, London: Methuen.

Elliott, R. (1992) 'Moving toward teaching: a model of teacher development', paper presented at European Conference on Educational Research, University of Twente, Enschede, The Netherlands, June.

Elliott, R. and Lange, J. (1991) 'Becoming the reflective professional: evolving models for understanding', paper presented at Australian Teacher Education Association meeting, Melbourne, July.

Eraut, M. (1985) 'Knowledge creation and knowledge use in professional contexts', *Studies in Higher Education*, 10, 117–33.

Floden, R. and Klinzing, H. (1990) 'What can research on teacher thinking contribute to teacher preparation? A second opinion', *Educational Researcher*, 19, 5, 15–20.

Fuller, F. (1969) 'Concerns of teachers: a developmental conceptualisation', *American Educational Research Journal*, 6, 207–26.

Hollingsworth, S. (1988) 'Making field-based programs work: a three-level approach to reading education', *Journal of Teacher Education*, 39, 4, 224–50.

Hollingsworth, S. (1989) 'Prior beliefs and cognitive change in learning to teach', *American Educational Research Journal*, 26, 160–89.

Kagan, D. 'Professional growth among preservice beginning teachers', *Review of Educational Research*, 62, 2.

Kober, P. (1980) 'The Socratic method on trial: are law schools a failure?, *Case and comment*, 26, 26–35.

Leinhardt, G. (1988) 'Situated knowledge and expertise in teaching', in Calderhead, J. (ed.) *Teachers' Professional Learning*, London: Falmer Press.

Lortie, D. (1975) *Schoolteacher: A sociological study*, Chicago, IL: University of Chicago Press.

McAlpine, A., Brown, S., McIntyre, D. and Hagger, H. (1988) *Student-teachers Learning from Experienced Teachers*, Edinburgh: The Scottish Council for Research in Education.

McGaghie, W. (1991) 'Professional competence evaluation', *Educational Rsearcher*, 1, 3–9.

Mitchell, J. and Marland, P. (1989) 'Research on teacher thinking: the next phase', *Teaching and Teacher Education*, 5, 2, 115–28.

Richardson, V. (1990) 'Significant and worthwhile change in teaching practice', *Educational Researcher*, 197, 7, 10–18.

Shulman, L. (1986a) 'Those who understand: knowledge growth in education', *Educational Researcher*, 15, 2, 4–14.

Shulman, L. (1986b) 'Opportunities of a mentorship: the implications of the California mentor teacher programme', paper presented at American Education Research Association, San-Francisco.

Shulman, L. (1987) 'Knowledge and teaching. Foundations of the new reform', *Harvard Educational Review*, 57, 1, 1–22.

Teich, P. (1986) 'Research on American law teaching: is there a case against the case system?' *Journal of Legal Education*, 36, 167–88.

Zeichner, K. and Gore, J. (1990) 'Teacher socialisation', in Houston, W (ed.) *Handbook of Research on Teacher Education*, New York: Macmillan.

Part B

Mentoring in initial teacher training

Introduction

Part A examined conceptions of mentoring. In Part B the focus is on mentoring in the context of initial teacher training.

This subject cannot be approached without visiting some political issues. The growth of mentoring is related (as seen already in passing in Part A) to the move towards school-based initial teacher training. But the decision to place greater emphasis on school-based training, as opposed to training located substantially in higher education institutions, has been one which in England and Wales has emanated from the government as a result of political rather than educational decisions.

In the first article of Part B, David Bridges looks at the political background of initial teacher training. He traces the origins of the notion of the school as the unit of educational responsibility, and applauds it. Indeed, he sees the notion as grounded in a maturing relationship - a partnership - between schools and initial training institutions: a notion which did not need a political intervention, least of all one which has distorted its focus.

This distortion Bridges sums up in his contrast between a corporate model of initial teacher training and what he labels the collaborative/professional model (see Table 4.1 on p. 70). If the corporate model is adopted then an individual school (as opposed to teachers/schools/the profession) becomes the locus for selection of students, for providing most, or all training opportunities, for assessment and for ultimate employment. Though it needs to be acknowledged that 'partnership' arrangements between Higher Education Institutions (HEIs) and schools for initial teacher training lie on a continuum between these two models.

Bridges argues that it is difficult to resist the implication that teachers whose roles have expanded to include that of curriculum developers and researchers, should play a prominent and effective role in initial teacher training (ITT). But he makes no secret of his reservations about the role of teachers in ITT; drawing attention to the *different* skills required in training adults and explicating practice (a point referred to by Elliott and Calderhead in Part A). There are also reservations related to the idea of 'protected professionalism' (see p. 72) and to the 'distraction' (p. 73) from their main concerns of teaching children.

Bridges also comments on the issue of how initial trainees learn. He seeks a more rigorous definition of experiential learning, on which much school-based training is allegedly grounded, and argues for 'the collecting together and passing on of the fruits of other people's experience' (p. 77) to quicken that process of learning – a role HEIs have previously fulfilled.

Though Bridges does not deal explicitly with the definitions and skills of mentoring he does offer a backdrop against which mentors are expected to act out their roles. These are dealt with more overtly in the next chapter by Beardon *et al.*

In the Beardon *et al.* chapter the scene is apppropriately set in the context of the political debate about standards in schools. But their summary of the issues cuts through the political motives of the main protagonists to set out a professional agenda (p. 83). This is followed by a predictive look at teacher training in the year 2000, which focuses on the key role which will be played by mentors. The full text of this chapter forms a pamphlet which makes proposals for reorganizing initial teacher training under a General Teaching Council and around training schools. The authors go on to identify the nature of training schools, the qualities required of staff, and the ways of achieving a transition from the present system of initial teacher training to their proposed one.

Here, however, you will find extracted those sections of the chapter which bear most closely on the mentor's role. In reading the chapters about mentoring from these four authors you will notice that some aspects of their proposals are not really very radical. For example, the contents of training (the basic skills listed on pp. 85–6) are likely to be replicated in every extant course. The qualifications and skills required of mentors themselves are, of course, highly desirable, if marginally idealistic. That mentors should be trained, and be awarded time for their work, are fair proposals that certainly are not currently fulfilled. But proposals, by their very nature, tend towards identifying the best possible scenario. What is open to debate is the degree to which the proposals can be achieved in practice.

From the ideal, Martin Booth moves us on to the real. Booth studied forty-five English, History and Geography students' views of the mentoring they received during a block teaching practice in secondary schools. The mentors and the mentoring process are given a generally positive, but not uncritical, reception by the initial trainees. A crucial mentor skill is identified as the ability to draw out professional learning in discussion, both formal (e.g. a weekly mentoring meeting) and informal. Mentors were especially helpful in aiding subject-specific performance but gave limited support in other areas (e.g. in handling special needs or information technology). These findings have implications for the selection and training of mentors. The student teachers emphasized the mentor as counsellor (p. 95), and certainly as a conveyor of professional attitudes: two qualities requiring care in the selection of mentors. But, it could be argued that mentoring should, more appropriately, involve a number of teachers with different areas of expertise.

It is interesting to compare and contrast Booth's school-based study with a similar piece of research among In-service FE teachers following programmes of initial training. An appointee to an FE institution (in contrast to a school) does not need to be already in possession of a PGCE or equivalent, but initial training courses are provided. In this case, Maurice Rothera, Stephanie Howkins and James Hendry studied two cohorts of initial trainees to explore the role of their subject mentors. While many of the trainees found that they preferred their mentors to be located in the same institution (60 per cent), drawn from the same subject area (83 per cent) and of a more senior status (41 per cent), these figures show that other models were also perceived to work well. What mattered most was the quality of trainee–mentor interaction in guiding course work (83 per cent rated this highly), and the detailed, constructive and practical advice given in teaching practice reports (93 per cent). But the study raised an ambiguity in the mentor role to which it will be necessary to refer again: that of mentor as support and formal assessor. Two-thirds of those questioned accepted the duality of the role mainly on the grounds that the mentor had the most detailed and accurate knowledge of them – while one-third emphasized the guidance-without-judgement role as paramount.

This research by Booth in schools and Rothera *et al.* in FE gives a generally positive response to mentoring from the mentee's perspective. The chapter from Kate Jaques is taken from the mentor's perspective and highlights the stresses and tension the role can create. These problems revolve around several key issues:

- understanding the nature of the mentor role;
- coping with a close interpersonal relationship with the mentee;
- feeling adequately trained and briefed;
- being realistic about the attitudes of staff not selected to be mentors;
- accepting responsibility for making judgements and assesssments, and for communicating these to the trainee;
- coming to terms with the demanding nature of the role, knowledge and emotional commitment.

So where does this leave us in understanding the mentor role? Clearly it is not a simple issue: for *both* mentor and mentee have roles to play, and these are complementary and require reciprocal behaviours. Mentors interact not just with mentees but with other professional colleagues; and expectations are imposed on them by government, by headteachers and by other staff. Mentees may be slow to learn, or may lack insight, fail to take advice or fall short of professional standards. There is a genuine emotional difficulty in failing another adult with whom the mentor has developed a close working relationship. This emerges as a major stumbling block in carrying out the role of formal assessor. An important issue, therefore, emerges for assuring the quality of these judgements. How do school-based training schemes build in checks and support for assessment? The suggestion offered by Jaques is the role of the HEI tutor. An alternative model would look for other staff within the school to carry out this verification role. Such a model fits within the partnership framework and gives each partner a role in quality assurance.

In Part B, there has been a transition from the ideal systems by Beardon *et al.* to the realities of mentoring explored by Jacques. And the caveats are continued to a degree in the next chapter, taken from an article by Chris Watkins and Caroline Whalley.

Watkins and Whalley leave behind concerns about the mentor role itself in order to tackle issues for schools to manage. It is important to return here to the concept of the 'mentoring school'. Much of the debate so far in this part of the book has been the tacit assumption that there is a tripartite relationship in initial teacher education: between an HE tutor, a school-based mentor and a mentee. In *practice*, that is often the case. But it is also argued that the most effective mentoring can happen only when a school as a whole takes on the full implications for being a conducive learning environment for initial teacher training: where all staff have a reflective approach to their work; where professional knowledge and standards are shared; and where team work is the norm. Such a school is a 'mentoring school'. Watkins and Whalley also (p. 126) identify that the 'gains' of mentoring benefit not just the mentee but the school when the process is conceived in these terms. This is indeed an important principle and one to which, for example, the Open University's PGCE scheme of mentoring is inextricably wedded.

Next in Part B we revisit an issue raised earlier: the assessment of the initial trainee. The tension in combining the functions of assessment and support within the mentor role have been noted. In this extract Peter Lucas proposes a model involving pupils themselves as a source of evaluative data. This reinforces the argument that teacher education must stress pupil learning. In fact what

what is proposed is a triangulation of view between trainee teacher, pupils and supervisor. Whether that supervisor is also a mentor is an open question worthy of more rigorous consideration.

Finally, in this part of the book there is a return to the mentor process in the American literature of business management. This is to raise an issue which is not well documented in the UK educational literature: the role of women in mentoring. Murray Reich's study sounds cautionary notes in attempting to identify mentors and match them with mentees and asks whether women accrue different benefits from being mentored. This is an issue relevant for mentoring with ITE and induction.

Chapter 4

School-based teacher education

David Bridges

INTRODUCTION

The 1980s saw a substantial shift of attention and resources in in-service education from higher education-based courses to school-based in-service programmes and from LEA held and managed in-service budgets to budgets under the control of schools. The most visible manifestation of this was the introduction of five professional development days when staff were required to attend school, when pupils were not present, for staff development. The 1990s have seen the extension of this shift in responsibility to the initial training of teachers, with the introduction of the articled and licensed teachers schemes and in 1992 of the requirement for substantial proportions of initial training courses for secondary schools (24 weeks of the 36-week postgraduate course) to take place in schools (DFE 1992).

These developments in the in-service and in the initial training of teachers are separable in recent history and have tended to be treated separately in the literature, but they appear to express several common principles concerning, for example, the school as a unit of educational responsibility, the extended professionalism of teachers and the nature and sources of teachers' professional knowledge; and they raise many common questions. For these reasons and because I count it as desirable in any case to view the initial and in-service training of teachers as part of a continuous process, I propose to discuss school-based initial and in-service training together.

Some rather different arguments and programmes for change underlie the development of school-based teacher training. Three which have been especially significant and which I want to discuss more fully in this chapter are:

- the political and to some extent professional programme to strengthen the school as the unit of educational responsibility;
- the professional concern to enhance or to acknowledge the enhancement of teachers' professionalism;

- the political promotion of and professional sympathy for what one might loosely label as experiential learning.

Certain features of these arguments or programmes for change are worth noting straight away. The first is the intertwining of educational arguments about learning, of programmes of change related to professional aspirations of teachers (and indeed the aspirations of people not directly involved in teaching for the professional advancement of teachers) and of explicitly political programmes. In this field, as in most others today, political arguments dominate more strictly educational discourse.

This is partly why many of those in and around education feel ambivalent about the changes. For teacher educators based in higher education this ambivalence is particularly acute since the enthusiasm they may share for the enhanced professionalism of teachers and their interest in experiential learning require them to associate themselves with developments publicly presented as designed to 'slit the throats' (in the delicate expression of one government spokesperson) of their own institutions.

Sober consideration of the rationale for school-based teacher training requires us, therefore, to separate some of the underlying arguments and consider them in their own terms.

THE SCHOOL AS THE UNIT OF EDUCATIONAL RESPONSIBILITY

Partly as a reaction against the disappointments of earlier attempts at centralized curriculum change generated by the Schools Council, the late 1970s saw the repeated affirmation of the centrality of teachers and of the school in the processes of educational development. This was reflected in the language and practice of 'school-based curriculum development'; 'school self-evaluation' and 'the self-acccounting school' (see Elliott *et al.* 1981).

Comfortably associated with all these was the notion of school-based in-service education. As early as 1972 the James Report had recommended:

In-service training should begin in schools. It is here that learning and teaching take place, curricula and techniques are developed and needs and deficiencies revealed. Every school should regard the continued training of its teachers as an essential part of its task, for which all members of staff share responsibility.

(DES 1972:11)

In the 1980s political commitment to the devolution of extended managerial responsibility to schools strengthened. This was informed by a management philosophy which supported the devolution of financial responsibility and empowerment to units closest to practical working realities. It was primarily this philosophy which inspired, for example, the early piloting of local financial management (LFM) and local management of schools (LMS) in Cambridgeshire and elsewhere. The shift was also explicitly motivated as far as central government was concerned by its desire to 'free' schools from what is presented as the burdensome bureaucracy and political tutelage of the local education authorities. This desire was reinforced by the government's undeclared determination to destroy what were in practice all the significant and informed sources of independent criticism or 'subversion' of its educational programme – the LEAs, colleges and departments of education and HMI.

With LMS came the requirement for schools to produce school development plans, and these were expected to incorporate staff development plans. At the same time the provision for five 'non-contact days' gave schools a resource in terms of teachers' time roughly equivalent in value to the whole of the previous national INSET budget though happily at no extra cost to the Exchequer. With delegated in-service budgets, staff development plans, non-contact days and, in most larger schools at least, a senior teacher holding direct responsibility for staff development, school-based in-service training had apparently come of age. However, the coincidence of these developments with training required to support the government's introduction of the National Curriculum, which was provided on the whole by local authority trainers, meant that schools did not get quite the sense of ownership of in-service training that they might otherwise have done.

The twenty-year span covered by this brief historical review also saw significant shifts in the location of the financial resources available to support INSET, with first an expansion of in-service provision within colleges and departments of education (filling the vacuum left by the reduction in the number of students on initial training programmes); then a shift in funding from the higher education institutions to the local education authorities, which could then choose whether or not to buy in training from higher education; and then most recently a shift in funding and responsibility from LEAs to schools which, similarly, might or might not choose to purchase the services of LEA advisers.

One principle associated with and underpinning the development of school-based in-service training is, therefore, a commitment to the increased responsibility or even empowerment of schools at the expense of LEAs (directly) and higher education (indirectly).

Associated with this has been the increasing corporatism of schools and attempts to strengthen the professional identity of teachers with their place of employment rather than a wider professional group. An early evaluation of school-based INSET illustrated the contrasting emphasis evident in some secondary schools between the desire of some teachers (and in particular of senior management) to give priority to whole staff INSET on whole-school issues and the preference of other teachers (notably subject heads of departments) for INSET through professional networks of teachers working within the same subject area (Bridges 1981).

Recent government measures (for example, the publication of examination results, the freeing of constraints upon admissions, parental choice of schooling and the award of grant maintained status) have deliberately encouraged competitiveness between schools, have provided a disincentive to collaborative work and have identified the individual school, rather than the group of schools operating in a district or the LEA, as the unit for the delivery of educational service. Of course, the sense that this represents an impoverished vision of educational service leads many teachers and others to oppose such developments. Nevertheless, while these remain firmly on the political agenda it is clearly the case that they reinforce the notion of the school as the unit of professional identity, the school as the focus for the identification of staff development needs and the school as the base for the delivery of the staff development which flows from that identification.

Initial training has been slow to follow in-service training either in being sucked into what have been, with the rather important exception of curriculum determination, the expanding responsibilities of schools or in reflecting their developing corporatism. In 1984, and again in revised form in 1989, the Secretary of State published criteria which all teacher training courses had to satisfy (DES 1984, 1989). These established a minimum requirement for the amount of school-based work and set clear expectations for the involvement of teachers in, for example, the selection of students, the supervision of their practical work and the assessment of their classroom competency. But these expectations required little change in most initial training institutions (the criteria relating to the substance of academic pro-grammes in the B.Ed. created more problems) and did little in themselves to transform the roles of schools in initial training.

In a significant sense the impetus towards a closer partnership with schools in initial training was growing out of a maturing relationship between schools and initial training institutions and was a consequence not of new regulations but of collaboration in school development programmes, advanced courses, classroom action research and school-based INSET. These relationships provided the foundation for what in some cases were adventurous collaborations between individual tutors in higher education institutions and individual heads or teachers in schools, and in other cases some of the early pilots in systematic versions of school-based training.

By 1991 HMI were able to report on a variety of developments in 'school-based initial training' (DES 1991) including the recently established articled teachers and licensed teachers schemes. The report makes explicit the shift in control ('influence' and 'determination' to be precise) bound up in the concept of school-based training.

> The extent to which a course is school-based cannot be determined adequately just by counting the hours students spend in school; the more influential role for teachers implied by the criteria needs to be evident, too. It would be hard, for example, to think of a course as being school-based if teachers had only a marginal voice in determining its content, or were not significantly involved in its delivery and in deciding whether, at the end, students were fit to join the profession or not.
>
> (DES 1991:6–7)

This same association between the location of training in schools and the control of training by schools was evident in the Secretary of State's consultative document and in his successor's revised criteria (Circular 9/92; DFE 1992) – though there remained some ambivalence between the rhetoric of 'partnership', the assertion that schools should be in the lead role and the proposal that higher education institutions should be the validating bodies.

Circular 9/92 makes it clear that the new partnership is between higher education institutions and schools as institutions, not just with teachers as individuals or as a wider professional group (see especially paras 12–14). It is schools that should approach their local teacher training institution; the contribution of schools that will be described; schools that will carry the responsibility and schools that will receive their share of the financial resources. On the face of it, therefore, this development will, like those already described, strengthen the corporatism of schools.

But the reality is not as simple as this. Some universities have already developed plans to work with clusters of schools. Both headteachers and university staff recognize that within schools some departments are much more suitable than others in terms of their ability to provide acceptable training. Different schemes place different kinds of emphasis on the range and variety of schools which students will encounter during their initial training. In fact one of the interesting features of the variety of responses to the new requirements can be expressed in terms of the strength or weakness of school corporatism in the training model. The following headteacher, for example, is clearly concerned that her school's role in initial teacher education should support rather than undermine her corporatist strategy for school improvement. Considering a Leeds approach to school-based training which concentrates five students in one department with time allowed to an individual member of staff, she observes:

> This apparently works well . . . for those schools involved. The view at Fearnhill [her own school] is that the whole staff are working together to improve their delivery of education, and this arrangement would place an emphasis and recognition on one department at the expense of another; it would be difficult to justify the involvement of such a large number of students within a limited area to parents and staff.
>
> (Monck 1992:21)

A strongly corporate model of school-based training (stronger certainly than Monck was advocating) would be one which treats the individual school as the central unit for the delivery of training, provides for the tightest association between the trainee teacher and that school and allows that school the greatest opportunity to promote its own professional culture through the training process. In rather the same way some of the old teacher training colleges left their own distinctive mark – and major corporations such as ICI or Sony would reckon to provide management or sales training programmes which bear their own distinctive corporate style. Such a strongly corporate model of school-based training contrasts with what one might call a more collaborative professional training in the ways indicated in Table 4.1.

In practice the licensed teacher scheme, in particular, and the articled teacher scheme, to a lesser degree, have reflected the features of the more strongly corporate model and in this way have echoed some of the characteristics of school-based INSET. However, other forms of school-based initial training, which retain strong associations with higher education institutions, seem likely to reflect the broader collaborative professional model. This is not only because the institutions themselves have traditionally had a commitment to a broader or more liberal conception of the professional socialization of teachers but also because, in spite of the several pressures towards a more isolated and competitive corporateness already described, many teachers in many schools continue to affirm their identity with a larger educational service and to recognize the regenerative benefits of communication and collaboration across a wider professional community. A letter from forty-five staff to the governors of a Cambridgeshire school which was contemplating the move to grant maintained status asserted these principles succinctly:

Table 4.1 Corporatism in school-based initial training

	Strongly corporate model	Collaborative professional model
Selection of students	By the school in which they will do their main practice or, more strongly, by the school in which they will be employed.	By trainers and teacher/ mentors, for the course but not necessarily for training in their own school.
Contract	between HE institution and an individual 'training school'.	Between HE institution and a cluster or consortium of schools.
Placement	(a) School has major role in determining which student(s) it has; (b) Students placed in a *school* with a variety of departments involved in training.	(a) Schools accept students allocated by HE; (b) Students placed with a selected *department* in one school or with the cluster.
Training	Largely focused on one school; strong socialization into the ways of that school.	Provides wide basis of experience and comparison across schools; weak socialization into the ways of any one school.
Assessment	Students assessed by training school on its own criteria of success.	Students assessed collaboratively by those participating in training on common criteria of success.
Employment	Within school in which trained.	Anywhere.

As teachers we believe we share collective responsibility for the education of pupils in this LEA, and that the school is part of a community of schools. ... We would be unhappy to isolate ourselves from other schools in the area. The LEA enables us to communicate, share ideas, and collaborate with other schools.

(Snapper and Charles 1992)

There remains an important choice of identity for teachers (though it is not obvious that the choice lies any longer with teachers) and an important decision concerning the focus of the professional socialization of new teachers: are they to be socialized into a department; a school; a school district; or a wider educational profession? The narrower the focus of this socialization perhaps the more powerful ('effective'?) it can be. But it would be sad, in a decade in which even international obstacles to the mobility of professional competence are being pulled down, if school-based teacher training were used to legitimate professional parochialism.

THE ENHANCED PROFESSIONALISM OF TEACHERS

The attribution to teachers of responsibility for their own professional development is presented and perceived both as a recognition of their extended professionalism (see Hoyle 1974) and as a contribution to that extension. It fits comfortably with two decades of development which have provided a fertile range of possibilities for the expansion of teachers' roles as:

- curriculum developers;
- researchers – notably within the framework of classroom action research;
- self-evaluators – within the context of school reviews and personal appraisal;
- self-developers – within the context of school-based staff development;
- advisers – either formally as advisory teachers or less formally as 'consultants' available to support development and training across schools.

It is difficult to resist the implication that if teachers have come to be able to handle these complex responsibilities for professional and educational development, then they ought also to be able to play a prominent and effective part in the initial training of teachers. As Hargreaves was able to observe, in arguing for school-based initial training, 'a striking change of recent years is the growing confidence and skill of heads and teachers in all aspects of training and professional development' (Hargreaves 1989).

The argument presented is a combination of the view that teachers' extended professionalism now equips them to provide initial as well as in-service teacher training with the view that they should be providers of initial as well as in-service teacher training because this will enhance their professionalism.

Recent debates have tended to qualify rather than to contradict this comfortable conjunction, but the qualifications offer important cautions for the way in which school-based initial and in-service training develops. The main qualifications are as follows.

The first reservation is to acknowledge that whatever one's admiration for the professionalism of teachers, the training of adults as teachers requires some different skills from those involved in successful classroom teaching. These arise partly out of the different requirements of teaching adults, some of whom may well be older than the classroom teacher and have all sorts of child rearing and work experience outside schools. They arise too out of the different subject content. The classroom teacher may (a) teach mathematics and do it extremely well, but does s/he also (b) communicate to someone else how s/he does it and does s/he (c) help them to develop an approach to the same task which will work for them? Plainly, a high level of competence in (a) is not sufficient for (b) nor (b) for (c). Indeed it is questionable whether (a) is even necessary to (c) though no doubt this sort of personal competence in the classroom adds credibility and authority to the trainer.

This argument amounts only to a caution, however, since it is generally acknowledged that practising school teachers do need support and training if they are to function effectively either as in-service trainers or as trainers or mentors of students in initial training. Norfolk LEA has worked actively to provide training for those with responsibilities for staff development in schools (see, for example, the resource pack for INSET co-ordinators distributed to all schools, Norfolk LEA 1991), and all school-based initial training schemes are required to make provision for mentor training. There is considerable evidence (e.g. Furlong *et al*. 1988) which suggests, however, that the task which practising teachers have in communicating and explicating their own craft knowledge to students is a complex one which defeats many teachers and leads others to avoid even trying.

A second reservation to teachers' assumption of the role of teacher trainer is linked to one of the more negative sides of extended professionalism. At its worst the strengthening of the professionalism of the delivery of a service to any community is a reinforcement of the exclusivity of that service. In the case of teachers' roles, the greater the span of activity which is deemed to fall within the province of teachers' professionalism, the narrower the range of agencies or voices involved in the delivery of that service. In medicine, in law and in the church the protected professionalisation of the sphere of activity has served to disqualify or invalidate a whole range of 'lay' contributions to its discourse and practice. In any context in which the professionalism of one group is extended, it is important to ask – at whose expense? In many ways the parental role in the education of their children has been diminished by the widening professionalisation of child rearing and education (or perhaps it is the other way round). Recent administrations in England and Wales have hardly been marked by their enthusiasm for the enhanced professional status of teachers, so why are they so supportivve in this instance? The reason is not difficult to find. Whatever the government's distrust of classroom teachers, it is even more suspicious of the perceived ideological predilections of what successive ministers continue – ignorantly or bloody-mindedly – to refer to as 'the teacher training colleges'. Teachers may or, more likely, may not be flattered by the idea that government finds their opinions safer than those of colleagues in higher education, but either way it would be a betrayal of some profoundly important educational and indeed democratic principles if the extended professionalism of teachers in the area of initial as well as in-service training were acquired at the cost of excluding educational voices perceived fairly or unfairly to be dissonant with those of the government in power.

Fortunately the notion of partnership described in DFE Circular 9/92 does give scope for students to have contact both with teachers and with staff from higher education. There remain, however, influential right-wing ideologues who insist that government has not yet gone far enough in taking initial teacher education right out of the hands of the universities. It will in time diminish teachers' professionalism and constitute a quite unwarranted restriction on student teachers' access to alternative ideas if this is allowed to happen.

A third reservation to the extension of teachers' professional roles into initial teacher training is of a quite different kind. It stems from concern about the distraction of teachers – and especially successful teachers – from their central and overriding commitment to the teaching of their children in the classroom. There is considerable evidence, which in this case supports what common sense would surely suggest, that children learn best when (a) they themselves spend the maximum time on task and (b) when their teachers spend the maximum time on task. If successful teachers are to give significant attention to the training of student teachers, then this must surely be at the cost of their classroom pupils. If they give whole-hearted attention to their pupils then this must surely be at some cost to the students? Not surprisingly, therefore, a significant portion of the resistance to the extension of school-based training has come from parents and teachers alarmed about its potential impact on children's learning. 'It will be impossible for a school to take the leading role in the training of teachers', wrote Lynne Monck, head of Fearnhill School, Letchworth, 'because schools must be first and foremost concerned with education of pupils in their care. The student teachers will always take second place to this' (Monck 1992).

The equation in terms of costs and benefits to schools of involvement in initial teacher training is by no means as simple as is described here. Schools recognize that student teachers can contribute positively to the life of a school and to pupils' learning. For a considerable part of their training they may be working alongside the experienced teacher rather than taking his or her place. The presence of small groups of students can provide individual attention for pupils quite beyond the scope of a single teacher. And experienced teachers commonly acknowledge the boost to their own enthusiasm, the fresh ideas brought in by student teachers or the benefits of collaboration with staff from higher education (see, for example, Benton 1990 on the Oxford Internship Scheme).

These kinds of arguments have application too in the context of in-service teacher education, except that here the provision of school-based training is seen as less disruptive of pupils' learning than the away-based course which requires the regular teacher's absence and the deployment of a supply teacher.

I have indicated three sets of considerations which qualify our enthusiasm for extending the professional role of teachers to include the initial and in-service training of their fellow professionals. But these suggest conditions for the implementation of programmes of school-based training rather than overwhelming objections to that implementation. With proper safeguards, training and support, and developed in a context of partnership with higher education, such programmes should be able to enhance the professionalism of teachers and to contribute to quality of learning in the classroom.

SCHOOL-BASED TRAINING AND EXPERIENTIAL LEARNING

I have so far couched the arguments relating to school-based training rather narrowly in terms of the location of control and the professional interests of teachers. A spectator to recent government and allied pronouncements could be forgiven for imagining that this is what the debate is all about. However, intertwined with these arguments are other considerations regarding how teachers acquire or develop their professional knowledge. Plainly what school-based training (and in particular initial training) most readily provides is the opportunity for learning through practice and through observation of practice, in other words (though we should not lose the distinction between practice and observation) experiential learning. If we regard experiential learning as a particularly potent form of learning, or even an essential condition for the development of practical competence, then we must clearly welcome developments which maximize the opportunity to found professional learning in professional practice (see Jamieson 1992 for a discussion of 'Experiential learning in the context of teacher education').

There is, of course, no context to the argument that the initial, let alone the continuing, training and development of teachers should include a significant and central ingredient of practice of teaching.

Nor does anyone seriously maintain that practice is by itself sufficient for the professional development of teachers. The real issues are located inside this framework of assumptions. There are four which have particular relevance to the context of teacher education and which I will comment on briefly.

The first issue concerns the conditions under which people best learn from experience or indeed the conditions under which they properly experience something at all, since it is evident that two people, who are equally well equipped with healthy sensory organs, can be present in the same place at the same time, attending to the same events, and have totally different experiences and that the time spent can constitute for one of the two a rich experience while for the other it barely constitutes an experience at all. Experience awaits the experiencing mind, that is, one motivated by interest, curiosity or purpose; one equipped with sufficient conceptual apparatus to allow it to discern, to discriminate, to analyse and to interpret; also one receptive to having ideas and assumptions challenged or expanded by what is beheld.

These conditions of experience-based learning were well appreciated in the classical works of the Chicago pragmatists, which are the progenitors of much contemporary thinking (see Bridges 1991). In pragmatic theory, practical experience provides the challenge or testing ground to the assumptions or hypotheses which inform our attempts to do things. Our attempts are frustrated when, from time to time, those assumptions or hypotheses are not adequate to the world in which we attempt to act. Experience challenges our beliefs and we have, through our imagination and intelligence, to refine or adjust those beliefs to experience so that we are once more able to go about our business.

This is a crude summary of a complex set of theories which were developed in different ways by Dewey, Pierce, James and others (see Rucker 1969; Scheffler 1974) and revived in recent times in the popular but philosophically less sophisticated form of Kolb's 'experiential learning cycle' (Kolb 1984), but it will serve to illustrate the active and informed intelligence which is brought to experience, which wrestles to interpret the significance of experience and which constantly refines belief structures so as to allow the individual to function effectively in the experienced world.

In the context of in-service teacher education already, and in initial training increasingly, there is plainly no shortage of participation in school and classroom events. However, if 'participation' is to contribute to teachers' professional development, it must be rendered as richly as possible as 'experience', as articulated here; that is, as something which engages our interest and curiosity, as something to which we bring a sophisticated and appropriate conceptual armoury and as something to which we are sufficiently receptive that we allow it to modify our assumptions. Notions of 'the reflective practitioner' (Schön 1983) and of 'teacher as researcher' (Elliott 1991) provide important foundations for this kind of dynamic and conceptually laden notion of experience-based learning, though perhaps neither notion has yet been represented in a form which adequately captures the interplay between the understanding which a teacher brings to classroom practice and the understanding which he or she takes from engagement in or observation of that practice.

These last considerations bring me to my second reservation about school-based learning, in so far as this takes the form of experiential learning. This echoes similar criticism of pragmatic theory of knowledge from which, I have suggested, it is derived. Pragmatism – and theories of experiential learning – work reasonably well when they are applied to the domain of technology in which the test of whether 'it works' or not is the singular significant consideration and in which the determination of whether 'it works' or not is firmly grounded in experiment and experience. But, as we have become increasingly aware, we run into all sorts of trouble if we take technological decisions on technological grounds without reference to, among other things, moral and social principles. This is especially the case in the context of the education of children, which is an activity governed at every turn by moral and social considerations. But neither pragmatism nor any experiential theory of learning provides an adequate account of, and still less an adequate justification for, the moral framework which has to be applied to our experience of teaching and has to be interpreted within the context of that experience but cannot plausibly be derived from it.

The problem extends wider than this. Many teachers today observing a classroom in which boys were engaging in 'hands on' work with the computers while girls stood back to offer occasional supportive advice would identify this as an instance of sexism. Similarly a student spending a term in a school in which Christian festivals were marked with intensive activity while those of other faiths were unselfconsciously ignored would recognize this as one of the ways in which the cultures of minority ethnic groups in Britain were structurally devalued and discriminated against. In so far as this awareness is abroad, however, it is only because the wider significance of features of school and classroom work, to which practising teachers had managed to remain oblivious for many years, was repeatedly brought to their attention by critical theorists, most of whom stood at some distance from the classroom but had a wider perspective on social structures. Critical theory developed in this way and communicated to teachers mainly through university departments has come to provide a significant part of the conceptual apparatus which now informs their observation and the way in which they experience classrooms. It is theory which has in some sense to stand the test of experience, but it is not theory which (in any simple sense at least) is going to be derived from experience. Thus, the professional education and development of teachers must continue to include engagement with challenging conceptual structures, not as an antidote to experiential learning but as a condition of experiential learning properly understood.

A third set of reservations about experiential learning are of a more elementary but no less important nature. They are neatly summarized by the nineteenth-century historian Froude (1877): 'Experience teaches slowly, and at the cost of mistakes.' In a sense the fundamental rationale of education and training is to quicken a process of learning which, if it were left to experience alone, would be interminably slow. So we quite sensibly expect teachers to be familiar with, to collect together and to communicate to others the lessons of experience of previous and contemporary workers in the field under consideration. Learning derived at second or third hand like this may not have the immediacy of one's own experience and may be less powerful in modifying one's actions, but access to it is nevertheless a condition of any serious kind of social progress. More especially in areas like education, where the mistakes of teachers can have damaging consequences for children, we have plainly a particular obligation to provide education and training in advance of the practice of teaching, which will at least limit the damage resulting from the otherwise stumbling and inadequately informed efforts of new practitioners. The principle applies both to pre-service training of classroom teachers and to that of headteachers, though only relatively recently has its application to the second case been taken seriously.

This discussion of experiential learning sets out not to challenge the importance of experiential learning in teacher education but to describe (a) the conditions under which learning from experience becomes even intelligible, (b) some of the limits to what can be derived from experience in the ordinary sense of the term (i.e. setting aside the consideration that all learning is derived from experience of something even if it is only the monotonous drone of someone dictating the declension of a verb) and (c) some of the limitations on what we sensibly rely on experience to teach.

In the context of teacher education all of this argues for:

- the collecting together and passing on of the fruits of other people's experience to new entrants to the profession and to people taking on new responsibilities in their professional careers;

- the development (by pre-service and in-service teachers) through discussion, reading and reflection of the thinking, the ideas, the conceptual structures which inform, shape and direct their observation and experiencing;
- Specific attention in pre-service and in-service programmes to the development of moral schemata and wider socio-political frameworks of thinking without which teachers will fall prey to the lowest forms of unquestioning pragmatism and lose that personal integrity without which they are scarcely entitled to invite the trust and confidence of their students.

None of this is incompatible with pre-service or in-service training which is substantially school-based (in the sense of being physically located within schools) but it does suggest, first, that practice alone cannot substitute for teaching and learning of the kinds described here and, second, that schools as they function institutionally at the moment and with the legitimate priorities they have in relation to their pupils' education may have some difficulty in providing the kind of adult learning environment described here.

But, of course, we do not have to assume that schools will stay as they are, as they take increasing responsibility for the initial as well as continuing professional development of teachers. The Oxford Internship Scheme has illustrated both some of the difficulties faced in turning the school into a proper learning environment for new teachers and some effective strategies developed through the partnership between schools and higher education; these strategies include giving articulation to teachers' craft knowledge; developing 'reflectivity' in both established and new teachers; investigating and examining the taken-for-granted aspects of schooling and teaching (see Benton 1990 and especially Judith Warren Little's overview).

CONCLUSION

This indeed is part of the exciting potential of the best forms of school-based teacher training run in partnership with higher education: the contribution which it can make to the invigoration of the professional and intellectual context of teachers' working lives. In the United States the location of teacher training in so-called 'professional practice schools', in which university staff work in collaboration with school staff and in which part of the initial socialization of new teachers is into the process of educational change, has provided a dynamism which is reported as a successful if not trouble-free approach to educational reconstruction (Anderson *et al.* 1992; Grossman 1992; Whitford 1992; Miller and Silvernail 1992).

But, as Miller and Silvernail argue, with reference to their study of Wells Junior High, any success has clearly not been the result of rational linear planning. It rests on an approach which requires 'a map rather than itinerary, being long-range, being adaptive, and being value-based' (Miller and Silvernail 1992:31). And these are the conditions which the development of school-based teacher education requires in England and Wales: the opportunity for universities and schools to establish new kinds of partnerships; the opportunity to experiment and to test approaches in practice; the opportunity to research and reflect upon experience; and freedom from incessant political interference so that the next stages in the development of teacher training can be based on the evidence of research and on reflection rather than contorted to satisfy the shrill but ignorant invective of politically unaccountable ideologues.

REFERENCES

Anderson, E.M., Stilwell, J.L. and Trevorrow, L.B. (1992) 'Educational reform: issues and answers in the Patrick Henry/University of Minnesota Professional Practice School', Paper presented to the Annual Meeting of the American Educational Research Association, San Francisco.

Benton, P. (1990) *The Oxford Internship Scheme*, London: Calouste Gulbenkian Foundation.

Bridges, D. (1981) *The Secondary School Curriculum: Theory into practice: An evaluation of an extended school-based in-service programme at City of Ely College, Cambridge*, Mimeo, Cambridge: Homerton College.

Bridges, D. (1991) 'From teaching to learning', *Curriculum Journal* 2(2): 137–51.

Department for Education (1992) *Initial Teacher Training (Secondary Phase)*, Circular 9/92, London: HMSO.

Department of Education and Science (1972) *Teacher Education and Training* (the James Report), London: HMSO.

Department of Education and Science (1984) *Initial Teacher Training: Approval of Courses*, Circular 3/84, London: HMSO.

Department of Education and Science (1989) *Initial Teacher Training: Approval of Courses*, Circular 24/89, London: HMSO.

Department of Education and Science (1991) *School-based Initial Teacher Training in England and Wales*, a report by HM Inspectorate, London: HMSO.

Elliott, J. (1991) *Action Research for Educational Change*, Milton Keynes: Open University Press.

Elliott, J., Bridges, D., Ebbutt, D., Gibson, R. and Nias, J. (1981) *School Accountability*, London: Grant MacIntyre.

Froude, J.A. (1877) *Short Studies on Great Subjects: Party Politics*, London: Longman Green.

Furlong, V.J., Hirst, P.H., Pocklington, K. and Miles, S. (1988) *Initial Teacher Training and the Role of the School*, Milton Keynes: Open University Press.

Grossman, P.L. (1992) 'In pursuit of a dual agenda: creating a middle level professional development school', paper presented to the Annual Meeting of the American Educational Research Association, San Francisco and to be published in L. Darling-Hammond (ed.) (1994) *Professional Development Schools: Schools for Developing a Profession*, New York: Teachers' College Press.

Hargreaves, D. (1989) 'Judge radicals by results', in *Times Educational Supplement*, 6 October.

Hoyle, E. (1974) 'Professionality, professionalism and control in teaching', *London Educational Review* 3 (2): 21–37.

Jamieson, I. (1992) 'Experiential learning in the context of teacher education', in G. Harvard and P. Hodkinson (eds) *Action and Reflection in Teacher Education*, Norwood, NJ: Ablex.

Kolb, D.A. (1984) *Experiential Learning: Experience as the Source of Learning and Development*, Englewood Cliffs, NJ: Prentice Hall.

Miller, L. and Silvernail, D.L. (1992) 'Wells Junior High School: evolution of a professional development school', Paper presented to the Annual Meeting of the American Educational Research Association, San Francisco.

Monck, L. (1992) 'A problematic partnership', in *Times Educational Supplement*, 21 February, 21.

Norfolk LEA (1991) *Making the Most of Curriculum Development Days*, Norwich: Norfolk, LEA.

Rucker, D. (1969) *The Chicago Pragmatists*, Minneapolis, MN: University of Minnesota Press.

Scheffler, I. (1974) *Four Pragmatists*, London: Routledge & Kegan Paul.

Sehön, D.A. (1983) *The Reflective Practitioner*, New York: Basic Books and London: Temple Smith.

Snapper, B. and Charles, A. (1992) *Letter to Governors*, Cambridge: Netherhall School.

Whitford, B.L. (1992) 'Permission, persistence and resistance: the context of high school restructuring', Paper presented to the Annual Meeting of the American Educational Research Association, San Francisco and to be published in L. Darling-Hammond (ed.) (1994) *Professional Development Schools: Schools for Developing a Profession*, New York: Teachers' College Press.

Chapter 5

School-led initial teacher training

*Toni Beardon, Martin Booth, David Hargreaves
and Michael Reiss*

THE BATTLEGROUND

The location and content of training

The debate about the reform of ITT has frequently focused on two
particular issues: first, the amount of time student teachers should
spend in school rather than in the training institution, and second,
the relationship between theory and practice. Both issues have been
a matter for concern among teacher trainers as well as to their critics.

Over the last few years almost all training courses have increased
the amount of time the trainers spend in school. Nobody doubts that
such on-the-job training is of the utmost importance or that trainees
themselves frequently regard this as the most significant aspect of
training. Both the Conservative government and the Labour Party seek
what for most courses would be an increase in the numbers of days
trainee teachers spend in schools.

A few of the critics would make training *entirely* school-based. They
adopt this position because they see the college-based elements as being
the theoretical component and the school-based as the practical
component. This is, of course, an inaccurate representation. The
training institutions teach both theory and practice; indeed, their major
concern has been how theory and practice can be better integrated.
The schools also teach both theory and practice, for almost everything
that a trainee or the supervising teacher does in the classroom is deeply
embedded in some kind of theory – theories about how classrooms
are best managed and organized, about the best ways of teaching and
learning, about the selection and pacing of the content of the
curriculum. The difference between the training institution and the
school is that in the former the theories are more likely to be very
explicit and to be underpinned by some academic or research-based
rationale, whereas in the latter the theories tend to be more implicit or
taken for granted as good practice derived from the long experience of

the supervising teacher. All practice is grounded in some kind of theory: it is impossible to get rid of theory simply by emphasizing practice or a particular location for that practice.

The critics, then, are in reality not attacking theory as such, but the particular theories and values that are purportedly held by the teacher trainers and which they believe are transmitted to the trainees. One possible line of objection is that the training institutions teach too much of the academic foundations for educational studies – the psychology, sociology and philosophy of education. It is true that these used to be taught fairly extensively on the PGCE courses, but today they have virtually disappeared. If they exist at all, it is in the form of a short optional course. A second line might be that training institutions convey to trainees a rather different kind of theory – the value of mixed ability teaching, or multi-cultural or anti-racist education or creative writing and so on. If this is the objection, then the question is whether the total abolition of the training institutions and the location of training entirely in schools would eradicate these emphases. In fact, many of these features are common in schools, so a system of 100 per cent school-based training would not achieve the objectives of the critics.

This is why we believe much of the recent debate has been so fruitless. The muddle about the nature of theory and its relationship with practice has become entangled with the issue of the location of the training: the resulting confusion has served as a distraction from what we regard as more basic and central questions.

Without doubt there is a need to raise standards of the education provided in our schools. The important matter is not so much whether they have fallen, as some allege, or whether they have risen, as others claim. Whatever the present standards are, they need to be higher, if only because the kinds of knowledge, skills and attitudes required in the world of work in a fiercely competitive international market so demand. If students in schools are to learn more and to learn it more effectively – and that is what the creation of the National Curriculum and new modes of assessment and testing have been about – then the quality of teachers and teaching must also rise. The education of teachers, and their initial training in particular, are bound to come under scrutiny at this point.

The issues of the theoretical elements in ITT and the location of training are of secondary significance. The primary question is how to raise the quality of teachers to achieve their fundamental purpose, that of enabling pupils to learn more effectively than before.

On the basis of our experience of teacher training and our investigations of how other professions respond to the task of professional training, we offer a new set of assumptions about what is needed for a course of ITT that would be successful, rigorous and satisfying. We believe that such training must:

- be school-led in the sense that practising teachers in schools take the main responsibility for trainees;
- treat trainee teachers not as students but as members of the profession from the very beginning of training;
- be based on a model of team-work between trainees and those who supervise them;
- be under the overall control of a General Teaching Council;
- after completion of ITT, allow for continued professional development throughout a teacher's career.

OUTLINE OF PROPOSALS

The proposals announced by Kenneth Clarke in January 1992 and the proposals published by the Labour Party in December 1991 have several common features. In neither case, we believe, is there both a clear picture of what the system of teacher education will be like by the year 2000 and an equally clear picture of how the transition to the new system will be managed. Building on our assumptions, we advocate a system of ITT that differs from the present system in the following ways.

- The overall responsibility for teacher education belongs to the General Teaching Council.
- The local responsibility for ITT is given to practising teachers in schools rather than to higher education (colleges and departments of education).
- Most of the training takes place in schools which are designated training schools.
- To become a training school, a school or consortium of schools must meet specified criteria.
- The funding for training is paid on a per capita basis to the training school.
- In the training school each trainee works under the supervision of a practising teacher, called a mentor.
- The mentors are trained for their work.
- In every training school the team of mentors is led by a professional tutor, who also has responsibility for induction, appraisal and the further professional development of all teachers.
- The mentors and professional tutor are provided with the time in which to engage in their training activities.
- All training schools are regularly inspected to maintain training standards.

- Where higher education is involved in ITT it is at the invitation of the training school, which acts as the senior partner.
- Higher education staff who work with a training school normally have substantial experience of teaching and mentoring in school.
- The selection and admission of a trainee is the responsibility of the training school.
- Trainee teachers normally choose a training school of a type and in an area similar to those where the trainee expects to secure a first teaching appointment as a qualified teacher.
- Training schools admit trainees at several points in the year.
- Trainees are treated by the qualified teachers as fellow professionals at the novice stage rather than as students.
- Trainees work in teams composed of fellow trainees and their mentors; they also work within the team (or 'firm') of the department of their subject specialism.
- Trainees are paid as instructors, and the grant for student teachers is abolished.
- The competences (knowledge, skills and understanding) to be achieved by trainees are determined by the General Teaching Council.
- The length of ITT is variable, depending upon the relevance of prior training and experience of the trainee and the pace at which the competences can be achieved.
- On attaining the competences or outcomes of training, a trainee is awarded a National Teaching Certificate, which is a licence to teach without supervision.
- The National Teaching Certificate may be counted as one third of a Master's degree in Education for those teachers who wish to pursue higher level academic studies.
- All schools have a scheme for the induction of new members of staff.
- All schools have a scheme for the continuing professional development of all members of staff.

WHAT HAPPENS IN A TRAINING SCHOOL?

- In the training school each trainee works under the supervision of a practising teacher, called a mentor.
- The mentors are trained for their work.
- In every training school the team of mentors is led by a professional tutor, who also has responsibility for induction, appraisal and the further professional development of all teachers.
- The mentors and professional tutor are provided with the time in which to engage in their training activities.

- Trainees work in teams composed of fellow trainees and their mentors; they also work within the team (or 'firm') of the department of their subject specialism.
- Higher education staff who work with a training school normally have substantial experience of teaching and mentoring in school.

Fundamental to our proposal is the notion that trainees acquire a battery of skills for successful teaching. It is, of course, obvious that successful teaching requires more than a range of skills. Teaching is also about the values which underpin the decisions teachers make and about the wisdom which guides professional thought and action. The colleges and departments of education have always seen the transmission of values as an important part of their role. The lecturers regard this process as a way of promoting in students an approach to teaching which transcends what they regard as outmoded or deficient pedagogy – and it is exactly this which has been condemned by critics of ITT as a dangerous indoctrination into a particular set of values. We take neither side on this dispute, but believe that the most important feature of the trainees' world is the mastery of the basic skills of classroom organization. This is not to say that such skills are free of values. But it is to say that only when trainees have achieved the confidence that goes with the mastery of basic skills are they in the best position to examine and, if appropriate, reject the values that lie behind them. This process of becoming a 'reflective practitioner' cannot be fully achieved in initial training, but is an inherent part of the professional development of all teachers after ITT.

In the early stages trainees are at risk of being overwhelmed by the multiplicity of skills involved in successful teaching. Precisely which skills are learnt first depends in part upon individual trainees and in part on the tasks assigned to the trainee by the mentor. The rate of progress also varies considerably from trainee to trainee. Nevertheless, some skills are of a very basic kind and form a core of early learning by trainees.

Our studies of training in other professions have impressed upon us the value of team work in helping trainees towards a rapid mastery of skills. By a mixture of imitation, discussion and deliberation, each trainee working with fellow trainees and mentors should gradually acquire basic skills such as:

- managing and organizing classrooms,
- starting and ending lessons,
- planning and preparing work for pupils,
- explaining and demonstrating to pupils,
- questioning and listening to pupils,
- teaching individual pupils, groups and whole classes as appropriate,

- matching set work to pupils' abilities and achievements,
- motivating pupils,
- diagnosing pupils' strengths and difficulties in learning,
- ensuring continuity and progression,
- marking pupils' work, assessing and recording progress,
- organizing practical work.

Experienced teachers know how stretched they are to provide sufficient attention to individual pupils and small groups. Trainees working with the mentor in the classroom would benefit pupils who would receive more than the usual attention and support. At the same time, the constant supervision provided by the mentor would promote the professional growth of the trainees.

Only after a period of successful co-teaching with a mentor would the trainee be given responsibility for teaching the whole class, with the mentor working with small groups and individual pupils – a progressive reversal of mentor and trainee roles, within a shared responsibility for the class, as the trainees develop skills and confidence.

By this means trainees work towards the National Teaching Certificate. They would not, of course, need to spend all their time in schools; to do so would in most cases make too many demands on the mentors. The training school would be free to 'buy in' expertise where this was lacking in the training school staff and where it might be in any event more cost-effective to do so. Colleges and departments of education, LEA staff and consultants could provide a wide range of relevant expertise to training schools.

For the mentors to carry out their work successfully two essential requirements must be met. First, they must be trained for their work, both in the generic skills of mentoring and in those which are unique to each subject and how it is best taught. A very successful teacher does not necessarily make the best mentor, for teaching trainees is by no means the same as teaching pupils. Trainees are adults, not children, and the content of their training is not at all like the curriculum that is taught to pupils. Much of what successful teachers know is intuitive and taken for granted and so is not always easily talked about in discussion with trainees. Although some teachers make better mentors than others, all mentors can gain from training for the role.

We believe mentors should have the following knowledge and skills:

- a first-class knowledge of their specialist subject(s),
- an outstanding record as a teacher,
- a thorough understanding of and ability to talk about successful classroom practice,

- the ability to debrief trainees after observing them at work and to help them to reflect on what they observe and do,
- an insight into the nature of professional development and how to counsel trainees on it,
- an understanding of how initial training fits into the structure of teacher education as a whole.

The second requirement for a system of mentoring is that the mentors have the necessary time to undertake their work. Mentors need to spend time talking with their trainees and this simply cannot be squeezed into the normal day of a teacher. Mentors need extra time, and some of resources given to training schools will be spent on additional staff or cover arrangements to provide for this.

The staff of the colleges and department of education who work in or with training schools will for the most part themselves be qualified teachers who are also experienced and qualified mentors. The same applies to the training school's professional tutor who takes an overall responsibility for professional development, including ITT. The professional tutor should guide the school in drawing up a policy for professional development, including appraisal, and would then be responsible for implementing this policy in relation to the school's development plan. This evidently would require a senior member of staff to be the professional tutor, since the role entails linking together the demands of the school's development plan to the professional needs of all the staff as well as supervising ITT arrangements.

WHAT IS THE CONTENT OF TRAINING?

- The competences (knowledge, skills and understanding) to be achieved by trainees are determined by the General Teaching Council.
- On attaining the competences or outcomes of training, a trainee is awarded a National Teaching Certificate, which is a licence to teach without supervision.
- The length of ITT is variable, depending upon the relevance of prior training and experience of the trainee and the pace at which the competences can be achieved.

We see the content of training for secondary teachers as being determined by the intended outcomes and consisting of two elements. The first would be subject-specific and concerned with the skills involved in teaching the subject, one in which the trainee is normally a graduate, to pupils. The second element would be concerned with general professional knowledge and skills across all subject specialisms. The GTC would set the unexpected outcomes of training in terms of the knowledge, skills and understanding required in both elements to reach the necessary standard for the award by the GTC of the National Teaching Certificate, which would replace the PGCE.

The aspects of teaching competence to be assessed would be listed under broad generic headings such as:

- establish and maintain discipline and classroom management,
- plan lessons,
- teach classes effectively,
- diagnose and meet individual learning needs,
- assess, mark and record pupil achievement,
- evaluate and modify own teaching,
- set and maintain appropriate standards of professional behaviour.

Such lists of competences are relatively brief and it is emphasized that they do not contain a vast number of separate skills that can be or indeed are assessed in isolation, but rather exemplify different aspects of what is involved under a generic heading. Training schools would be encouraged by the GTC to add to the generic headings to reflect the training needed in particular local circumstances. To teach effectively in a real situation a teacher must integrate separate skills into an holistic performance, responding appropriately and decisively without undue hesitation. The key test for the status of qualified teacher would be the accomplishment of this holistic performance.

Trainees would keep a record of training by means of files of materials prepared for teaching, lesson plans, analyses of and reflection upon training experiences, and assignments completed. Such files and the records and reports of mentors would contribute to the National Teaching Certificate, which would then serve as a 'profile' of strengths and weaknesses which trainees would carry with them to their first appointment. This ITT profile would become the first step in the teacher's professional development record, to be used in appraisal and the design of further training.

The length of training would not be fixed, as with the PGCE, but would end as soon as the trainee met the standards of outcome required by the GTC.

Chapter 6

The effectiveness and role of the mentor in school

The students' view

Martin Booth

There is now an increasing literature on school-based training (Furlong *et al.* 1988; Wilkin 1992; Shaw 1992); the mentor's conception of his or her role (Booth *et al.* 1990; Feiman-Nemser *et al.* 1990; McIntyre *et al.* 1993); the relationship of the mentor to the training institution (Zeichner 1990); and the knowledge basis needed for effective teaching (Gudmundsdottir *et al.* 1985; Shulman 1986). Yet what is lacking is research data from the point of view of the trainee teacher. Where his or her voice is heard, it tends to be there to illustrate the actions or knowledge base of the mentor (for example, Feiman-Nemser *et al.* 1990). It was to remedy this situation that the evaluation project which is the subject of this paper was undertaken.

THE RESEARCH PROJECT

Our evaluation project was based on a group of forty-five English, geography and history students who were training as secondary-phase teachers on the one-year PGCE course at the University of Cambridge Department of Education. The majority of them had taken at least a year off after leaving school: twenty-seven were aged more than 23. Nearly all seem to have had some experience of paid employment; a number had held jobs of considerable responsibility (for example, sales executive; assistant curator, National Sound Museum; station auditor at RAF base). Nineteen of the forty-five had been educated at all-ability (comprehensive) state maintained secondary schools.

The course they were following was 36 weeks in duration. The first term of 13 weeks involved a two-week period of structured experience in a primary school, followed by 11 weeks in the training institution. The programme here consisted of one day a week spent in a subject department in a local secondary school with a further one and a half days of training institution subject-based methodology. The remaining two and a half days a week were spent in the training institution studying broader professional issues such as assessment procedures, grouping arrangements or relationships between parents, governors and schools. The emphasis here was on the practical, with the theoretical issues being teased out of specific situations. Interdisciplinary groups of students met for two hours twice a week to look at videos or to read transcripts focusing on particular incidents and to discuss the wider issues which such situations posed. Discussion was reinforced by a range of readings, read before the seminar; ideas were substantiated or modified by post-session readings. The students' block of teaching practice took place during the second term in forty-four secondary schools, all but two of which were state maintained comprehensive (all-ability) schools. All the subject teachers responsible for the students were well-known to their subject counterparts in the training institution; the teachers were familiar with the training institution programmes and the expectations of the tutors. The tutors, for their part, knew the schools and subject departments and the teaching styles and syllabuses the teachers delivered.

Within this context, we wanted to find out what the students' perceptions and views were on the mentoring they received during their block of teaching practice (the practicum) in the spring term, 1990, and to determine how far, in their eyes, their mentors had proved effective in developing the students' professional skills. Our data were derived from two questionnaires. The first, completed by the students at the end of the first, largely institution-based term of the course (December 1989), attempted to determine how well-prepared the students felt for the term's school-based teaching practice which lay ahead. The intention here was to provide data against which the students' perceptions and views of their work with their mentors during the block teaching practice in the spring term 1990 could be compared. There were two main sections to the December questionnaire. The first asked students to rate on a five-point scale ('Very well prepared' to 'Badly prepared' – with a fifth category of 'not covered') criteria which related to the main subject in which they were training. These criteria were derived from the National Curriculum in the case of English (DES 1989b) or the National Criteria for the General Certificate of Secondary Education in the case of geography and history (DES 1985 a and b).

The second section, which was common to all forty-five students, listed eighteen general professional and classroom skills which the students had to rate in the same way. These included the ability to 'prepare lessons and teaching materials', 'assess pupils' progress', 'discipline and control pupils effectively', 'teach pupils with different cultural backgrounds', 'teach mixed ability groups', 'teach pupils with special educational needs' and 'use information technology (IT) effectively in the classroom'. The list was largely derived from the criteria laid down by the DES for the approval of courses of initial training (DES 1989a). The questionnaire also asked students to list the things they were most and least confident about as they looked ahead to teaching their main subject during the teaching practice term.

The second questionnaire, which was completed in April 1990, was concerned with the students' evaluation of their block practice. This questionnaire asked the students to rate their confidence in both subject-specific and general teaching skills, using the same criteria as in the first questionnaire. We made the assumption that 'confidence' included 'preparedness' (the word we had used in the first question-naire) and that some comparison between the two questionnaires was legitimate. It then went on to determine the extent and nature of the mentoring the students received. Did the mentor hold regular, weekly debriefing and counselling sessions? Did he or she regularly go through lesson plans? How frequently did mentors discuss the subject-specific and general criteria with the students during meetings (students rated responses here on a five-point scale ranging from 'frequently' to 'never'). In general terms, how successful were the mentors (students rated them on a four-point scale ranging from 'very successful' to 'unsuccessful')? Students were then given the opportunity to explain their answers to this question. If mentors were to be given training, what sorts of things did students think should be covered in such a course? Finally, students were asked to list the things they felt most and least confident about as they looked ahead to full-time teaching.

STUDENT VIEWS OF THEIR PREPAREDNESS
FOR TEACHING PRACTICE

At the end of the first, largely institution-based term of the year-long course the majority of students (77 per cent) faced the block teaching practice feeling themselves to have been very well or quite well-prepared to teach their subject specialisms. By subject, the percentages were: English 74 per cent; geography 77 per cent; history 80 per cent. The majority of students, therefore, after only one term of the course embarked on their block teaching practice with considerable con-fidence as far as the teaching of their own subject was concerned.

How well-prepared did they feel for the general aspects of teaching? Here, not surprisingly, given the range of competences listed and the immediate concerns of students with classroom management and subject-specific teaching, students claimed a far greater degree of uncertainty. On average, only 33 per cent of students felt very well or quite well-prepared to prepare schemes of work for an extended period of time; only 22 per cent to assess their pupils' progress (the debate and uncertainties about National Curriculum assessment undoubtedly contributed to this view); only 23 per cent to teach mixed ability groups. There were similar low percentages in the 'very well' or 'quite well' categories in response to competences dealing with pupils of different cultural backgrounds and with children with special educational needs, liaising with support services and parents and giving specialist advice to colleagues.

On the other hand, students felt confident about preparing lessons and teaching materials and considered themselves well equipped with a range of teaching methods. Discipline and conducting oral work seem to have been well covered; so do classroom organization and the use of IT.

Students tend to be utilitarian in their requirements in the early stages of learning to teach, focusing on the issues of immediate concern: classroom management and subject-specific teaching. The responses to the first questionnaire make clear that the students consider that the institution had provided the latter and had dealt well with some of the immediate issues of classroom management and control ready for the coming block teaching practice.

STUDENT VIEWS ON THEIR PROFESSIONAL DEVELOPMENT AND THEIR WORK WITH THEIR MENTORS DURING THE BLOCK TEACHING PRACTICE

At the end of the teaching practice term (April 1990), the students were asked about their confidence to teach their main subjects; the same criteria were used as in the first questionnaire. The percentages of geographers and historians ticking the 'very confident' and 'quite confident' responses showed marked increases; only the English students seemed less confident (74 per cent in December; 71 per cent in April).

Similar increases were shown in the students' confidence in their general teaching skills. By the end of the term's block teaching practice 77 per cent of all students felt very or quite confident to plan schemes of work over an extended period of time and 70 per cent to teach mixed ability groups. Confidence with assessment had risen from 22 per cent to 43 per cent, and 88 per cent felt very or quite confident in their ability to discipline and control pupils effectively. Not surprisingly, confidence in liaising with the support services and parents and giving specialist advice to colleagues was low; more worrying was the lack of confidence among students to deal with pupils with special educational needs. There was a marked fall in the percentage of students feeling confident about using IT in the classroom (from 78 per cent at the start of the teaching practice to 34 per cent at the end) – a reflection perhaps that IT is still not widely used in humanities teaching; 28 per cent of students claimed there was no opportunity to use it.

In general, however, the great majority of students claimed that they were more confident and better prepared both in subject-specific and general teaching skills than they were at the start of the block teaching practice term. A claim of confidence may not of course be the same as proficiency nor can such claims necessarily be attributed to anything other than having had more practice. But data from the questionnaire implies that the mentors may have played a key part in the development of this professional confidence. This is suggested by the association between the extent to which particular aspects of classroom practice, both subject-specific and general, were discussed during the students' meetings with their mentors and the students' claims to greater confidence in these areas. The correlation between low confidence in particular areas and little discussion is a further indication of the importance of the mentor. The students were of course assessing their experiences with their mentors retrospectively and care must be taken not to place too much weight on claims of frequency; nor were the students asked to give any details of the nature or content of the discussion on a particular issue; discussion could, conceivably, have been a condemnation of the issue in question.

Nevertheless, the evidence does point to the key role of the mentor in the professional development of the student. First, the great majority of students (81 per cent) claimed that they had regular, weekly meetings with their mentors; smaller, but not insubstantial numbers (48 per cent), indicated they had regular discussion about specific lesson plans prior to the teaching of a topic. The extent to which the mentor is now playing an important part in the training process is underlined by looking back to a survey of university postgraduate training which was undertaken in 1979–80 (Patrick *et al.* 1982). Then only 11 per cent of the students claimed they had regular weekly meetings with the teacher designated to supervise them.

Our data moreover indicated that for a majority of students discussion in these meetings focused 'frequently' or 'quite often' on the subject-specific issues they had already rated in terms of their teaching confidence. Here there seems to be a marked contrast between the English and geography students and the historians. Whereas, on average, only half the English and 54 per cent of the geographers claimed that subject-specific issues were 'frequently' or 'quite often' discussed during supervision times, 82 per cent of the historians claimed frequency of discussion of the subject criteria. This may reflect the fairly widespread consensus among history teachers as to the nature of their subject and the way in which it should be taught. It may well be, therefore, that the very high percentage of history students claiming to be very confident or quite confident in the teaching of their subject by the end of their block practice (92 per cent) is partly a product of the emphasis which the twelve history mentors gave to subject-specific discussions.

The students also rated for frequency of discussion at supervision times the general teaching skills and issues they had already rated in terms of their confidence. Not surprisingly a large majority of students claimed that preparation of lessons and teaching materials got emphasis in discussion; the development of schemes of work over an extended period of time was also a frequent or quite frequent topic for discussion, reflected in the marked increase in confidence which students claimed to have by the end of the teaching practice. Their confidence, too, with discipline and control of pupils may also partly be a product of the emphasis which mentors gave to this issue in discussion at supervision times. The link between increased confidence and supervision discussion is indicated in mixed ability teaching (only 23 per cent claimed some confidence/preparedness at the beginning, 70 per cent at the end of teaching practice), teaching less able pupils and, less markedly, with oral work.

On the other hand, the link between an increase in confidence and supervision discussion is emphasized negatively by looking at those issues where students showed marked lack of confidence by the end of teaching practice. Only 37 per cent of students felt confident to teach pupils with different cultural backgrounds; yet only 12 per cent of students indicated that this was a topic of frequent discussion. Only a quarter of the students felt confident to deal with pupils with special educational needs; yet only 20 per cent of students claimed that this was an issue emphasized in supervision. Liaison with support services and parents, and specialist advice to colleagues got similar low ratings on both counts. Particularly interesting is the very marked drop in confidence to deal with IT. Whereas at the beginning of the block practice 78 per cent of students felt very well or quite well-prepared to use IT, by the end that had dropped to 34 per cent. Yet only 23 per cent of students claimed that IT capability had been emphasized in discussion with mentors.

Mentors, therefore, according to the students, were in the main effectively building on the subject-specific pedagogy they had received in the first term of the course; some of the more general skills of lesson preparation and classroom management were also being explored and developed. There were, however, a number of crucial issues where mentors, according to the students, seemed either to lack the confidence or expertise to help students develop their wider professional role and competency or were simply unaware of the need to address such matters. Many of the students, of course, were in schools where there are few, if any, children from different ethnic groups; others were placed in schools where children with special needs or links with parents and support services do not assume a particularly high profile. A number of the subject departments the students worked in did not give IT emphasis. This suggests that mentors are both constrained by the framework of the school and by the immediate concerns of the student; they find it difficult (and perhaps consider it unnecessary at this stage of the student's training) to address a wider frame of reference. Yet it is precisely these wider issues which the training institution can deal with in the last part of the course, building on and extending the classroom and subject competences that the student has developed during the block practice; those who would argue that all student training should take place in the school (for example, Lawlor 1990) might well be consigning the trainee to a narrowly utilitarian apprenticeship.

The students were asked to rate on a four-point scale the overall success of their mentors in providing help and guidance. A high proportion (88 per cent) was satisfied with the mentoring they had received, rating their mentors 'very successful' or 'quite successful'. What then did they see as the characteristics of successful mentoring? Students in their comments on the questionnaires emphasized three areas. The most important of these was the general support they received from the mentor, described in terms of the accessibility of the mentor and the sympathetic and positive support that was given. Phrases such as 'encouraged me', 'highly approachable', 'supported me fully', 'tact and sympathy', 'made me feel welcome and useful' occurred time and again in comments from students who felt they had been well mentored and who claimed teaching confidence at the end of block practice.

In this context of general support, the time given to the student was also seen as important. Many of the students referred to the frequent meetings they had with their mentors. 'We used to talk for hours', wrote one; 'she provided a lot of extra support when I had difficulties with her second-year group [12-year-olds]', commented another; 'always available . . . my best friend', wrote a third.

The second area that students highlighted in their comments about the mentoring they had received was the extent to which mentors aided their professional development. A number of comments indicated that students valued mentors who treated them as professionals and who adopted a style of counselling which was not too directive and where they had the opportunity to set at least part of the agenda for discussion.

Above all, [the mentor] and the rest of the department treated me like an equal and made me feel welcome and useful. (English student)

> . . . he did not oversupervise. The psychology he adopted allowed me to develop at my own pace with good guidance given when necessary. (Geography student)

> He made me evaluate constantly, let me make mistakes and then try to work out why this was so. Supported me fully, let me work to my strengths. (History student)

Yet the students were not simply looking for supportive, caring, listening mentors who had time for their problems and treated them as colleagues and equals; they wanted someone who could focus sharply on the issues and who could articulate his or her practice clearly. A historian commented: 'It was always helpful advice but sometimes I felt that [my mentor]wasn't critical enough.' And an English student commented: 'Helpful and successful in a general way, perhaps not quite detailed enough. Maybe overestimated my ability.' Thus the third area for successful mentoring which students pointed to concerned the subject and general issues which were discussed with their mentors. Here the emphasis was very much on the practicality of the discussion and advice offered. An English student who claimed an increase in confidence by the end of term wrote: '[My mentor – first name used] was both understanding and down to earth – good, solid, practical advice.' And another English student, who stated she felt quite confident to teach her subject by the end of term, commented: 'Everything was related to the work I was doing. He offered constructive criticism . . .'

Other students wrote of their mentors as 'a great source of experience, knowledge and materials' or as a person who 'spent a lot of time ensuring we'd planned thoroughly' and who would suggest ideas and teaching materials.

How much of this discussion and advice of subject-specific and general teaching issues was couched in reflective, theoretical terms as against a more practical emphasis on the nuts and bolts of classroom practice is hard to say. The data suggest that what has been termed 'professional common sense knowledge' was the essence of what the students were wanting and receiving – 'recipe' knowledge which would help them at this early stage in their careers to operate effectively in the classroom. It may be that the concern with the 'reflective practitioner' which is current at the moment (see for example Kemmis 1987; Gore 1987; McNamara 1990) is inappropriate for the beginning student trying to get to grips with classroom practice. Calderhead (1989) lends some support to this view and Richerts' research (1990) indicates the 'reluctance of novice teachers to look back on their work with a critical eye'.

Some thirty-six of the forty-five students in our sample claimed that there was a senior teacher in their school with overall responsibility for trainee students. Many of these senior co-ordinators seemed to have organized fairly regular meetings for the trainees but in the main they were not considered very helpful. There was indeed more than a suggestion from the students' questionnaires that most schools have yet to develop an overall school policy as far as trainee students are concerned and that successful mentoring at the moment is largely dependent on the efforts of individual subject teachers creating a mentoring culture or climate within their own departments.

CONCLUSION

This small-scale research project provides some evidence for the crucial importance of the mentor in the development of the trainee student's professional skills and confidence. It gives weight to the view that simply placing students in schools without adequate mentoring support would give students little chance to develop their classroom and subject teaching skills and understanding (Booth *et al.* 1990). It also indicates that in the early stages of their work in schools, students are principally looking for support which is positive, unthreatening and readily available. Students at this stage also want mentoring advice which centres on the immediate, practical issues of subject-specific teaching and classroom management and control, and which builds on the experiences they have already gained. Given student pre-occupation with what they often consider to be the most important and worthwhile aspect of their training – the work they do with practising teachers in schools – it seems logical to start from this point and to reconsider ITT in the light of the experiences students receive in schools.

But the responses of students in this research project clearly indicate that there are crucial areas of professional competence and under-standing which the schools are not covering at the moment; and Furlong's research (1990) indicates that though students in the first instance want a training that is 'strongly practical in its orientation', they also want time to consider the broader issues. It may well be, therefore, that such matters are better tackled once the student has acquired a degree of classroom and subject confidence. Once this has been achieved, the training institution will have the key role in ensuring that the broader issues are addressed.

REFERENCES

Booth, M., Shawyer, G. and Brown, R. (1990) Partnership and the training of student history teachers, in: M. Booth, J. Furlong and M. Wilkin (eds) *Partnership in Initial Teacher Training*, London: Cassell.

Calderhead, J. (1989) Reflective teaching and teacher education, *Teaching and Teacher Education*, 5, 43–51.

Department of Education and Science (1985a) *General Certificate of Secondary Education. The National Criteria. Geography*, London: HMSO.

Department of Education and Science (1985b) *General Certificate of Secondary Education. The National Criteria. History*, London: HMSO.

Department of Education and Science (DES) (1989a) *Initial Teacher Training: approval of courses*, London, DES Circular No. 24/89.

Department of Education and Science (1989b) *English in the National Curriculum*, London: HMSO.

Felman-Nemser, S., Parker, M. and Zeichner, K. (1990) Are mentors teacher educators? Paper presented at the Annual Meeting of the American Educational Research Association, Boston, MA.

Furlong, V., Hirst, P., Pocklington, K. and Miles, S. (1988) *Initial Teacher Training and the Role of the Schools*, Milton Keynes: Open University Press.

Furlong, J. (1990) School-based training: the students' views, in: M. Booth, J. Furlong and M. Wilkin (eds) *Partnership in Initial Teacher Training*, London: Cassell.

Gore, J. (1987) Reflecting on reflective teaching, *Journal of Teacher Education*, March–April, 33–38.

Gudmundsdottir, S., Carey, N. and Wilson, S. (1985) Role of prior subject matter knowledge in learning to teach social studies, paper presented at the Annual Meeting of the American Educational Research Association, Chicago, IL.

Kemmis, S. (1987) Critical reflection, in: M. Wideen and A. Andrews (eds) *Staff Development for School Improvement: a focus on the teacher*, Lewes: Falmer Press.

Lawlor, S. (1990) *Teachers Mistaught. Training in Theories or Education in Subjects?* London: Centre for Policy Studies.

McIntyre, D. (1990) The Oxford Internship Scheme and the Cambridge Analytical Framework: models of partnership in initial teacher education, in: M. Booth, J. Furlong and M. Wilkin (eds) *Partnership in Initial Teacher Training*, London: Cassell.

McIntyre, D., Hagger, H. and Wilkin, M. (eds) (1993) *Mentoring Perspectives on School-Based Teacher Education*, London: Kogan Page.

McNamara, D. (1990) Research on teachers' thinking: its contribution to educating student teachers to think critically, *Journal of Education for Teaching*, 16, 147–160.

Patrick, H., Bernbaum, G. and Reid, K. (1982) *The Structure and Process of Initial Teacher Education within England and Wales*, Leicester: University of Leicester.

Richerts, A. (1990) Teaching teachers to reflect: a consideration of programme structure, *Journal of Curriculum Studies*, 22, 509–527.

Shaw, R. (1992) *Teacher Training in Secondary Schools*, London: Kogan Page.

Shulman, L. (1986) Those who understand: knowledge growth in teaching, *Educational Researcher*, 2, 4–14.

Wilkin, M. (ed.) (1992) *Mentoring in Schools*, London: Kogan Page.

Zeichner, K. (1990) Changing directions in the practicum: looking ahead to the 1990s, *Journal of Education for Teaching*, 16, 105–127.

Chapter 7

The role of subject mentor in further education

Maurice Rothera, Stephanie Howkins and James Hendry

THE CONCEPT OF SUBJECT MENTOR

Systems of mentorship have been introduced on an increasing number of CNAA approved courses of in-service training for teachers in further and higher education during the last decade. The CNAA (1985) defines a subject mentor as 'an experienced colleague or critical friend who can help his or her course member to utilise and translate the benefits of the course', such that 'mentorship implies a dialogue between a course member and mentor about the professional practice of teaching'. Within the East Midlands Scheme, subject mentors function essentially as individuals, 'each chosen uniquely to match student need with mentor expertise and knowledge' (CNAA 1985). Indeed the functions of mentors overlap, but are not identical with, those of course tutors, student counsellors and staff development officers seen as internal consultants and agents of socialization. However in subject mentoring a crucial difference must be appreciated between technical expertise and process skills, since the mentor's repertoire of knowledge, attitudes and skills encompasses both esoteric subject-matter content on the one hand, and teaching and learning method on the other. In other words the 'subject mentor' plays the complementary roles of subject-matter specialist and education consultant.

THE NATURE OF THE RELATIONSHIP

To the extent that the relationship between a subject mentor and his or her course member involves both counselling and imparting of expert knowledge, and is primarily one of confidentiality, such an interaction bears many of the hallmarks of a 'professional–client' relationship (Vollmer and Mills, 1966).

For the client the interaction which takes place between subject mentor and course member over a period of two years constitutes a process of development, based on a succession of learning experiences which are informed by the tenets of Knowles' (1984) adult learning theory and Bandura and Walters' (1963) social learning theory. Hence when the CNAA seeks to promote a 'dialogue' between member and mentor, this consists in all respects in what is a learning dialogue.

In this respect East (1987) goes on to aver that the vital aspect of mentoring 'is the relationship between mentor and protege, a two-way process of mutual affinity', such that the mentor's values, attitudes and accomplishments will eventually be internalized by the course member. Since, according to Kelman (1972), the process of development by which 'internalization' is ultimately achieved also involves stages of 'imitation' and 'identification', the notion of the mentor acting as a role model is not without significance. However, in this connection there is a delicate and important distinction to be made between non-participant role modelling as such ('sitting by Nellie') and the kind of interactions which enable mentor and client to participate fully in a developmental process of problem-solving ('role participation') (East 1987; Badley 1989; Dotan et al. 1986; CNAA 1985).

MODELS OF MENTORING

We are now in a position to posit a 'process model' of mentoring, whereby the client in due course, through experiential learning, internalizes the values of the mentor, participates in problem-solving and eventually becomes independent of the mentor. In similar fashion Badley (1989) identifies three possible models of educational consultancy: the 'colleagual model', where development results from collaboration of peers; the 'counselling model', in which the aim is to facilitate and enable the client to solve or manage his or her own problems (Scott 1989), and the 'professional model', wherein the mentor (or consultant) renders a service to the client in a strictly formal sense.

All three of these models have something in common with the concept of mentoring as denoted by the CNAA, and the first two are actually 'process' or developmental models in themselves.

The present writers have taken a further critical look at the mentor system in the East Midlands, with a view to clarifying what is actually happening in practice. This research was originally undertaken in anticipation of a second revalidation of the Scheme in 1989. Hence our aim is to identify relevant issues for future planning and for the familiarization of mentors, by eliciting definitions of the role of 'subject mentor' from the members themselves, seen here as 'clients' within the system, using a combination of both normative and interpretative techniques in relation to a fairly large and wide-ranging sample. Thus a central issue for a debate that remains is 'the characterisation of the system of mentors or mentorship and the role of mentor' (CNAA, 1985).

METHODOLOGY

The respondents were female and male, mature in-service teachers in further education, all of whom were in the second-year (Level 2) of their Certificate in Education course at Nottingham Polytechnic and who represented an extensive range of experience, length of service and subject-matter specialization.

Two paper-and-pencil instruments were administered to three groups of respondents, comprising two Level 2 groups at Nottingham and one Level 2 group at Lincoln in January 1987 (N = 51) and January 1988 (N = 54). That is, the exercise was replicated in successive years in exactly the same form with regard to content, methodology and type of respondents. Note was also taken of course members' spoken comments about the subject mentor role in discussion after the written responses had been completed and handed in.

The two instruments were:

- a Selection Matrix containing role definition items for the Subject Mentor role, previously elicited from potential (but not actual) respondents;
- a Questionnaire containing both open-ended and closed-ended questions centred on various problem areas to do with the Subject Mentor Role which had been previously delineated by interested parties.

The twenty items contained in the Matrix had previously been elicited from Levels 1 and 2 course members, in response to the incomplete sentence, 'A subject Mentor is . . .' The pro-forma was administered in two consecutive versions: 'ACTUAL' followed by 'IDEAL' corresponding to course members' expectations of their mentors' qualities and behaviours (a) as they actually exist in practice, and (b) as course members would ideally like them to be.

The ten questions which constituted the Questionnaire were derived initially from the set of common themes which had been identified by EMRS in 1983, including 'need for subject matching', advantages/disadvantages of (a) same or different college; (b) being mentored by a 'boss' figure.

These questions were designed to gain factual information about the operation in the field of the subject mentor scheme (closed-ended responses), together with provision of opportunities for respondents to evaluate the effectiveness of the mentoring process and to identify relevant issues (open-ended responses).

It look less than 30 minutes for course members to complete the pro-formas; and feedback from respondents immediately afterwards indicated that the two instruments had been well received.

FINDINGS FROM MATRIX

Definition of subject mentor role

Two prominent features emerge from a preliminary inspection of the results of the matrix analysis:

- Those items which were most frequently selected by course members consisted of 'attribute' (over PERSONAL) items, whereas those least frequently selected referred to 'role' (or POSITIONAL) items. This observation applied equally well to both the ACTUAL and the IDEAL versions of the matrix.
- For all but one of the twenty items of the matrix ('is a friend') the number of endorsements (out of a possible total for the sample as a whole of $N = 105$) for the ACTUAL version fell short of the corresponding number for the IDEAL version.

Points worth noting from the matrix findings (see Table 7.1) are:

- The 'adviser' role, which is the very essence of classical mentorship, precedes all other functions and is actually embedded within the attributes.
- Classical mentorship roles like 'adviser', 'object of trust' and 'role model' take priority in course members' definitions over the instrumental mentorship role of asessor.
- Supportive roles like 'confidant', 'counsellor' and 'friend', although they are inherently classical in nature, are defined by the present respondents as being relatively unimportant.

Findings from questionnaire

The responses to the questionnaire have been presented under a number of headings which allowed responses from particular questions to be analysed in conjunction with one another. The headings include: *location* – whether the subject mentor is located in the same college as the course member or in a different college, and members' preferences regarding this arrangement; *subject area* – dealing with the issue of whether or not the subject mentor works in the same special-subject area as the course member, together with corresponding preferences; *position of assessor* – examines the question of whether or not members consider their mentors to be one of their assessors;

Table 7.1 Classification and ordering of attributes and roles

'Personal' ATTRIBUTES (qualities)		'Positional' ROLES (categories)
Professional competence	Humanistic traits	Functions
Constructively critical comments	Approachable	Adviser
Knowledgeable	Encouragement	Object of trust
Conversant with requirements of subject mentor role	Helpful	Role model
Conscientious	Supportive	Assessor
Explaining subject	Gives time willingly	Confidant
	Sympathetic	Counsellor
	Caring	Friend
Gives praise		
INSTRUMENTAL	EXPRESSIVE	REPERTOIRE OF ROLES
(cognitive)	(affective)	(typology)

interaction – (a) quality of the guidance and assistance received from subject mentors with members' coursework; (b) quality of mentors' Practical Teaching Reports (did members find them constructive and helpful?); (c) mentors acting as role models (whether or not members have had the opportunity to observe subject mentors teaching their own students); *professional development* – the extent to which course members felt that their approach to practical teaching had developed as a result of working with their subject mentors.

Location

The majority of respondents had subject mentors in the same college and preferred it that way (60 out of 101 replies). 'Accessibility for advice' was cited as the principal reason; whilst a further advantage was subject mentors' awareness of the institution and its organization.

Of the 34 respondents who had subject mentors in a different college, 22 expressed a preference for that arrangement. Two strong claims were first that the subject mentor is 'an uninterested party in internal politics, uninfluenced by college personalities, with an 'outside viewpoint'; and second that participants can adopt a more objective approach, and can meet outside the work situation. Similarly the course member has the opportunity to look outside her or his own locality.

There is no easy answer to this problem of location of mentor. The advantages of one arrangement correspond to the disadvantages of the other. In other words, neither situation can ever be entirely satisfactory.

Subject area

There were 84 (out of 105) respondents who had subject mentors in the same subject area and preferred that state of affairs. The predominant reason given was that 'the subject mentor understands and can give guidance on subject-related problems'. Other frequently mentioned factors were mentors' technical experience, awareness of developments in subject knowledge and ability to suggest more appropriate teaching methods. Likewise the course member and subject mentor 'speak the same language'. These factors were considered to be essential in enhancing subject mentors' credibility. Another important facet is that there is an opportunity for subject mentor and course member to share knowledge and experience.

All of this reinforces the notion that a 'subject' mentor must by definition be concerned with giving advice on the content and delivery of a special subject.

It is noteworthy that of the 18 respondents with subject mentors working in a different subject area from themselves, nine preferred that arrangement as it stood. They pointed out that the subject can be viewed from outside, from a different perspective. There may be access to unfamiliar teaching methods; and 'having experienced a mentor not in my subject area, I consider the assessment of my teaching – rather than being overshadowed by content – is more objective'. In addition the view was reiterated that educational (as distinct from subject) skills were of prime importance.

Position of authority

The principal reason given by those course members who preferred their subject mentors to occupy some position of authority (41 out of 99) was that 'mentors further up the scale have had more experience and can be more objective than peers'; and this in turn is seen to be indicative of credibility. Other responses indicated that a person in authority would be more plausible in the role of assessor; would be able to offer practical help in the form of access to resources; have the ability to widen course members' professional experience, including staff development; and have greater commitment to teacher training. Likewise the subject mentor would have a deeper understanding of the politics of Further Education, as well as experience of management.

By contrast a strong claim by the opposing lobby ($n = 58$) is that seniority is of little consequence, whereas knowledge and experience of subject and of classroom are vitally important (evidently 'experience' here is deemed to be independent of authority). Thus, 'a position of authority is not as important as the mentor being held in esteem, i.e. being a good role model'. In similar fashion the personalities and attitudes of both partners are seen as being key factors. 'If the relationship is a personal one, authority is not important.' Furthermore, discussion is held to take place more easily among colleagues of equal status. High-level mentors may be out of touch with the classroom; and status could give rise to distancing between course member and subject mentor. Finally a high-ranking mentor may have little time to devote to his or her client.

Position of assessor

Predominant among the comments made by the majority of respondents ($n = 68$), who considered their subject mentor to be one of their assessors, was acceptance of the fact that 'my mentor completes a sizeable percentage of the teaching practice visits, which are part of the assessed course', and therefore must contribute towards the overall assessment of the members. Similarly a strong connection was perceived between subject-matter expertise and the credibility of assessment by mentors of course members' practical teaching. Importantly it was stressed that 'assessment must be consistent with constructive comment and assistance to course member'; whilst at the same time there was also a tendency to see the mentor as an 'informal' rather than as a strictly formal assessor. In this respect some members asked their mentors to look at coursework prior to submitting it for formal assessment.

A different interpretation was placed upon this situation by those who averred that the mentor should not be seen as an assessor in the official sense ($n = 35$). The emphasis here is wholly upon the informal aspect, whereby 'the mentor is there to guide and advise the student's work where requested, but has no official assessment capacity'. The feeling among course members is that 'although the mentor does assess, this is only to evaluate and give constructive criticism and support', or 'this assessment is more of a helpful nature and is continuous rather than judgemental'. The situation is summed up by one respondent as follows: 'Although I realize that subject mentors' TP reports are not officially assessed, I feel these reports are almost bound to influence or confirm the opinions of the tutor.'

Interaction

Quality of help received with coursework

The most frequent response made by the majority of course members ($n = 87$), who deemed the help received from subject mentors to be useful, was to the effect that constructive comments by mentors and guidance on coursework were highly valued. Encouragement of course members to keep within limitations, and to look for new and different ways of approaching tasks, was pertinent. Thus an objective, problem-solving approach by the subject mentor, involving shaping of the course member's strategies, is seen to be supremely important.

> My mentor helps me to express the ideas I'm trying to introduce into projects or essays, or disciplines my thinking to ensure I've covered the topic with due consideration. This is not to say that he is forcing an opinion on me, but rather I can 'bounce' ideas at him.

Also useful is the subject mentor's willingness to provide materials; and his or her previous experience of the certificate course in terms of knowledge of course members' problems.

Typical of negative sentiments voiced by the minority ($n = 18$) is that course members and subject mentors 'found it difficult to discuss issues like coursework in the everyday working environment' (same college); or that very little help was received from the subject mentor, possibly due to other commitments; or that mentors' comments were too bland. Also some course members recognized that they had 'only approached subject mentors occasionally'.

Quality of Practical Teaching (TP) Reports

By far the greater proportion of respondents ($n = 93$) were appreciative of the quality of mentors' TP reports, as represented by comments like 'the reports are extremely detailed – constructive with criticism, but equally generous with praise', and 'my subject mentor gives helpful and practical suggestions about practical teaching problems'. Indeed, in the opinion of course members, unbiased external observation of teaching is bound to be useful, no matter for how short or long a time the member has been teaching, not least for comparison with self-evaluation. Individual subject mentors' reports were seen as being instrumental in improving course members' methods of teaching, and also in generation of alternative ideas and approaches by given course members, as well as increasing course members' awareness of self and of classroom dynamics. Reference was made in addition to the excellence of individual subject mentors as classroom teachers (role models) and as assessors of practical teaching.

At the same time caveats were entered to the effect that course members did not always agree with the advice given by their mentors; and also that there should be 'less emphasis on positives' and more in the way of constructive criticism as such (in other words bland or vague comments were not acceptable). There was a feeling among the dissenters ($n = 8$) that their TP reports could have been more detailed; and that there was a tendency for mentors to confirm what the client already knows.'Didn't really tell me anything that I hadn't thought of myself (except ways round political constraints).'

Opportunity to observe subject mentor teaching

About half of the sample ($n = 51$), who had enjoyed the opportunity to observe their subject mentor's teaching, felt that this was a salutary experience and one which should be encouraged, since it could lead to changes in course members' appreciation of teaching techniques and student relationships – that is, to development of new insights by members. Additional benefits included reinforcement of course members' own classroom practices and enhancement of self-confidence.

The value of the mentor as a 'role model' was clearly apparent here.

At the same time, by way of a rider, course members need not always be in agreement with subject mentors' techniques; and also not all subject mentors practise what they preach.

The other half of the sample ($n = 53$) predictably cited time-table clashes as a major factor which prevented members from observing their mentors in action. Clearly some subject mentors were reluctant in any case; and in other instances observation took place in contexts and situations other than everyday classroom teaching. Nevertheless it is worth recording that nay-sayers felt that the opportunity would have been a worthwhile experience, had it been available.

Professional development of course members

A majority of respondents ($n = 72$) answered 'yes' when asked whether they felt that their approach to practical teaching had developed as a result of working with their mentors. In fact a wide range of new approaches, techniques, and styles of teaching had been undertaken, which included course members becoming more adventurous (with group work, discussion, and assigned work), moving towards greater risk-taking in a safe environment, and willingness to experiment with new ideas (not least where 'I feel I have the support of my mentor whilst not being assessed'). These experiences led to increase in confidence and flexibility, and to development of a more relaxed style; as well as more thorough preparation by individual members, and management and organization of practical teaching to better effect.

In this connection, opportunity for discussion of actual teaching experience with mentors (in their capacity as fellow-teachers) is seen as being essential in helping members to reflect on their own teaching. This helps in changing course members' techniques with, and attitudes towards, their students. Also there was evidence that course members were now inclined to use student-centred methods; and one new teacher reported that she had learnt to cut down on the amount of work that she gave to the class in any given lesson, and to break the topic down into a few essential points.

Negative comments from the minority ($n = 27$) centred upon insufficient contact with mentors for developments to occur (too few visits); and reluctance in course members' minds to ascribe development solely to mentors' influence, as distinct from that of the course as a whole.

DISCUSSION

Three factors have emerged which are of overriding significance in so far as they underpin, and are crucial to, the effective functioning of the subject mentor scheme as a whole:

- *Legitimacy and credibility of the subject mentor*
  A major theme running throughout course members' responses to the questionnaire, and borne out by the matrix, is that members are continually looking for evidence of their mentors' CREDIBILITY, and are seeking reassurance to this effect. Hence being in a position of authority, though not absolutely necessary, was seen to enhance subject mentors' prestige (cf. Badley 1989); and likewise being in touch with the classroom and in possession of specialist knowledge was deemed to be vital in

connection with the legitimacy of subject mentors' contracts to advise on subject matter and teaching methods. This expertise was also cited in comments related to the credibility of mentors' assessment.

- *Quality of relationship and personality of subject mentor*
  The quality of the relationship between member and mentor is perceived by clients as a pervasive factor which far outweighs all other considerations, even those of 'location' and 'subject area' of the mentor. Central to this relationship is possession by the mentor of appropriate humanistic qualities such as 'being approachable', 'giving encouragement', 'being helpful and supportive', and 'giving time willingly'. This state of affairs was neatly couched by one member who remarked, 'Ultimately it all depends on the personality of the individual mentor.' This finding is in accord with similar conclusions by Wynch (1986), East (1987) and Dotan *et al.* (1986).

- *Constructive criticism by the subject mentor*
  Throughout the investigation it has become apparent that skills like objectivity and balanced appraisal as practised by mentors are of supreme value to clients. That subject mentors should 'make constructively critical comments' about course members' teaching performance and course work is a paramount expectation with regard to mentors' professional competence. This expectation has priority over virtually all other considerations and is a model response in both the questionnaire and the matrix.

REFERENCES

Badley, G. (1989) 'The Staff Development Officer as an Internal Consultant', *Journal of Further and Higher Education*, 13(3), 100–14.

Bandura, A. and Walters, R.H. (1963) *Social Learning and Personality Development*, London: Holt, Rinehart and Winston.

Council for National Academic Awards (CNAA) (1985) Notes on mentorship within CNAA approved courses of in-service training for teachers in further education. Publication 21/27, November.

Dotan, M., Krulik, T., Bergman, R., Eckerling, S. and Shatzman, H. (1986) 'Role Models in Nursing', *Nursing Times*, 82(3), 55–7.

East, P.I. (1987) 'The Mentoring Relationship' MA (Ed) Dissertation, University of Loughborough.

East Midlands Regional Scheme for Further Education Teacher Training (EMRS) (1983) *The Subject Mentor System: A Preliminary Appraisal.*

Kelman, H.C. (1972) 'Processes of Opinion Change', *Public Opinion Quarterly* 25, 57–78.

Knowles, M. (1984) *The Adult Learner*, Houston: Gulf Pubs. Co.

Scott, C. (1989) 'Counsellors as Organisational Consultants: Personal

Tutoring in Further and Higher Education' *British Journal of In-Service Education*, 15(2), 125– 29.

Vollmer, H.M. and Mills, D.L. (eds) (1966) *Professionalisation,* Englewood Cliffs, NJ: Prentice-Hall.

Wynch, J. (1986) 'Mentorship', M.Ed. Dissertation, University of Nottingham.

Chapter 8

Mentoring in initial teacher education

Kate Jacques

While disquiet about the type of school-based or school-centred training persists there is almost no opposition to the principle of mentorship. It is curious that such a critical role which carries with it considerable responsibility and undoubtedly more work has not generated closer scrutiny and more debate.

An attempt is made in this chapter to extend that debate by a review of some of the problems within the role, drawing on the experiences of a small group of mentors who worked on the Articled Teacher Scheme from 1990–92. Over an 18-month period 35 mentors were asked at the end of each term to comment on aspects of their work such as work-load, relationships with other teachers, their views on the training programme, the occurrence of crisis and tension and their views on the future role of mentors. At the end of each term all 35 mentors were asked five rather general open-ended questions and asked to give written replies. The questions were devised after talking to a smaller group of mentors and targeting the areas they wanted to talk about. They were asked about:

- the positive features of becoming a mentor;
- the difficulties encountered in school by being a mentor;
- the level and quality of support needed by a mentor;
- ways in which the school-based scheme could be strengthened; and
- ways in which support for mentors could be strengthened.

Responses to the above provided triggers for further probing by way of interviews with seven mentors individually. Finally, at the end of each training session, normal course evaluations (questionnaires) were conducted by the course director, as well as group feedback sessions in which the author discussed the range of tasks connected with the mentoring role, both anticipated and unanticipated.

The results provide more data than can be dealt with in this paper. Here are presented initial reactions, with particular attention paid to unexpected tensions. First there is an attempt to define the role of mentor and raise questions about the functions and operations of the mentoring task. Second, the day-to-day pressures of doing the job are considered, noting in particular what it is like to deal with one or more students on a daily basis over a long period of time. The third issue addresses training needs. Finally, given the evidence which is being collected nationally, what is the next step? While there is a growing literature on the subject of mentoring which indicates what should be happening little has been written about the stresses and tension the role can create.

The findings of the study are dealt with here under three main headings:

- The mentoring role in school.
- Some conflicts and tensions in the mentoring role.
- Conclusions.

THE MENTORING ROLE IN SCHOOL

The mentors were selected by headteachers, not in response to agreed professional criteria based on the role of the mentor, but largely on the grounds of personal qualities, such as their ability to get on with people and provide a good teaching model.

The original connotation of mentor as a wise, experienced adviser nurturing, supporting, guiding and assessing the naive but eager protégé seems to have been captured by teachers as indeed it has by other professions, and is a significant improvement on the notion of supervisor. The concept of mentorship suggests an expert professional, guiding the apprentice teacher but with the addition of a more precise instructional dimension. The mentor's role involves being an instructor, a teacher, a counsellor and an assessor rather more than simply a craft expert to be copied by a novice. Teachers favour the wider interpretation of the task and wish to have real power and responsibility in the training process. They are now offered control and participation in the training of their own profession and can privilege aspects of the job they judge to be most important. The status of craft knowledge and classroom practice is raised to a level equal to the other aspects of teacher education. This status is extended to the mentor, whose opportunities for promotion may be increased. Some 30 per cent of our first cohort of mentors were promoted in the first year, which created a whole set of other problems. Being selected as a mentor provides endorsement for being a good teacher. What has not yet been tackled fully are the additional strains and tensions generated by a role that is only half understood. Mentoring is more than dealing effectively with practical, craft skills.

Enabling student teachers to grasp the complexity of classroom life and helping *them* to see all the elements is a complicated process. The four categories or levels of training identified by Furlong *et al.* (1988) are useful in helping to set out what has to be done. They are as follows:

- *Level (a) direct practice*
  Practical training through direct experience in schools and classrooms.
- *Level (b) indirect practice*
  'Detached' training in practical matters usually conducted in classes or workshops within training institutions.
- *Level (c) practical principles*
  Critical study of the principles of practice and their use.
- *Level (d) disciplinary theory*
  Critical study of practice and its principles in the light of fundamental theory and research.

Direct practical experience at level (a) in the classroom and school is at the heart of the matter. However other elements of training are required to develop increasingly more informed critical reflection to produce more effective classroom practice. Teachers come to recognize that direct practice in the classroom by itself is insufficient and that they themselves critically analyse, evaluate and theorize both inside and outside the classroom. Indirect practice at level (b) helps provide practice understanding, judgement and skills and can occur in detached contexts. At level (c), acquisition of knowledge of the principles behind different professional practices is needed to promote reflection on their use and justification. At level (d), disciplinary theory, the work is of a different order. Its purpose is to make explicit and critically examine value judgements and theoretical assumptions by reference to the foundation disciplines. Both articled teachers and mentors recognise that levels (c) and (d) are necessary for successful teaching, though they cannot be achieved easily in the classroom.

The mentors began their role with a 3-day residential course followed by two college-based training days each term for five terms. Over this time they formed a supportive, professional bond which assisted the transition from novice to experienced mentor. The mentors in our sample had little difficulty in dealing with the notion of level (a) 'direct practice' during the training sessions. Indeed it became clear that mentors had a very straightforward notion about what student teachers needed to know about classroom practice. In addition they could substantiate and extend their thinking around 'direct practice' to the level of 'indirect practice' (b). They were very comfortable with notions of 'direct practice' and 'indirect practice' and some of the best mentorship training sessions capitalized on contributions made by mentors in passing on and sharing experiences. When it came to 'practical principles', i.e. level (c), it was not that mentors were unable to grapple with principles; simply for many of them critical reflection had not been part of their practice. Having an articled teacher in the classroom increased their appreciation of 'practical principles' and their ability to deal with this increased over time. What they complained of was insufficient time to deal with this aspect of training, although they thought it was essential for articled teachers to have it. In this regard they did feel that professional tutors ought to have a higher profile and that such matters should be shared between mentors and professional tutors. At the final mentorship training day one mentor said: 'This period has seen growth in myself more significant than any other since my initial training 9 years ago. I am beginning to understand the meaning of critical reflection.'

Level (d) was perceived to be more problematic by professional tutors, mentors and articled teachers. All mentors seemed to value the importance of fundamental theory and the contribution research makes to the understanding of teaching and learning. Anxiety was created because the mentors felt that their knowledge of theory and of research was inadequate, although they were quite emphatic that articled teachers ought to know about it. Tutors and mentors recognized the complementary nature of the roles, especially the narrowing of the notorious theory/practice gap.

SOME CONFLICTS AND TENSIONS IN THE MENTORING ROLE

At the outset mentors in our sample recognized that the role would carry additional work. In most instances there was a financial incentive attached to the post. Currently this is paid at the discretion of the LEA; soon the school will be responsible. However, the factors of additional work or more money appeared not to play a significant part in influencing mentors choosing to take on the role. Some felt that the additional pair(s) of hands in the school would be sufficient bonus, alongside the view that the end result would produce the sort of teachers the school wanted. At the start of the project in 1990 there was little doubt in the minds of the mentors and headteachers interviewed that the teachers graduating from a largely school-based course would be better than teachers trained on one of the conventional routes; 18 months on and approaching the completion of the first cohort of articled teachers the message continues to be supportive but different in tone.

Initially mentors were unrealistic about the type of work-load the responsibility would generate. An assumption was that student teachers

would provide additional hands in a busy classroom, bringing with
them fresh ideas and new ways of working. There was a tacit belief
that their own load would be lightened. Most mentors were accus-
tomed to supervising B.Ed. and PGCE students on teaching practice
and were used to leaving these students with the class. While they
desired more responsibility and authority in moulding practical
teaching skills of these students there was a pay-off. What was not
fully appreciated was the different starting point of articled teachers
from conventional students. One-year PGCE students and 4-year B.Ed.
students, while inexperienced in the classroom, normally arrived in
school anxious and keen to practice teaching and try out their carefully
prepared schemes and projects, planned in the security of the college
environment. This group of students were short-stay novices in need
of support and guidance but above all seeking the opportunity to get
on with things. The frustration for supervising teachers was the feeling
of little influence over the practical instruction they perceived the
students needed. The college remains in control and teachers merely
assist. The transition to assuming major responsibility for the practical training, a role they wanted, created shock initially at how much
there was to do. That is not to imply that teachers could not do it,
the shock came with the realization of the range and extent of the
tasks. One mentor declared:

> It was amazing how little my articled teacher knew in the beginning.
> I felt bombarded with really simple questions which I wanted to
> answer but didn't know where to start. I thought everyone knew
> how schools worked. My articled teacher, who helped with hearing
> readers in the past, wanted to know how children's brains grow?
> I do not know, does the college? Now I can see that the question
> was wrong. In the beginning I was frantic for an answer. I was also
> desperately looking for things for her to do.

This statement, and there were many similar, illustrates how much
mentors need to understand the business of inducting adults into a
new work role.

There is little doubt that mentors were surprised by the unexpected
tensions their role generated in the school. Initially some staff showed
hostility due to a belief that the mentor had gained not only assistance
and additional pay but also acquired free time as well. When articled
teachers were placed in other classes the class teacher not infrequently
felt that they were now doing the mentor's job. As a result mentors
often felt isolated and misunderstood by colleagues, a position not
helped by some headteachers who, according to mentors, failed to
appreciate all that the job of mentoring involved. A common complaint
was that headteachers resented the amount of time given to the

articled teachers, especially when it interfered with other tasks prioritized by the head. Mentors tended to be recruited from the ranks of senior teachers in the school, and rightly so from the perspective of the student teachers who wanted the expertise of a high ranker within the organization. Therein lies a dilemma. The senior teacher holds status and expertise but frequently neither the time nor the skill to deal with the complex range of training issues. There was a tendency also for some headteachers to want to use articled teachers as supply teachers when 'stuck', placing mentors in a predicament. The articled teachers felt flattered to be given the responsibility, while the mentors felt uncomfortable about 'using' students prematurely in an inappropriate way. Understandably a headteacher conscious of pressures on the school budget may see advantages in having trainee teachers in school; not least that covering for an absent colleague is valuable experience while serving also to incorporate the articled teacher more formally on to the staff.

Most schools had the agreement of all staff before becoming a training school but some mentors felt that neither the college nor the LEA had provided a detailed enough brief about what was involved. Where articled teachers progressed well and integrated successfully there was little overt opposition from staff, but where articled teachers were either not popular or struggling mentors found themselves becoming increasingly stressed by the resulting strained relationships, both with colleagues and with the articled teacher.

After the first three terms one mentor described her mounting frustration as follows:

> I was looking forward to becoming a mentor because I enjoy having students and feel that I have a lot to offer. What I did not expect was just how different the experience would be. It is so much more intrusive than a student on school practice. After a while I found myself wondering, will this person ever go away so that I can have my class back? It wasn't as if she wasn't any good, she was fine but I did feel jealous and annoyed when she tried to assume too much responsibility, and especially when she disciplined my children. I know it was unreasonable and I had to come to terms with it. Next time I shall be better prepared.

Where the articled teacher is not succeeding or there is a clash of personality this tendency can get hopelessly out of hand. Another mentor admitted to not liking the articled teacher very much and was unable to distinguish between judging the teaching performance or judging the personality:

Everything she did irritated me. She snapped at the children, gave them confused instructions and tried to regiment them in a way which is opposed to the way I do things. I would try to discuss it in our weekly meetings and she listened, agreed to change but never did.

What is interesting about this example is that there was nothing recorded in the articled teacher's profile of competencies to indicate how poor the mentor judged the articled teacher to be. Written statements about relationships with children for instance were bland and imprecise, as were comments on control and classroom management. Reports to the college tutor were tentative but encouraging, indicating progress, and it was not until the headteacher intervened and communicated doubts to the higher education institution that the problems were uncovered.

The early identification of a weak student is simply part of the mentoring role but that is not how it is perceived necessarily by mentors, nor indeed by other colleagues in and outside the school. Besides feelings of personal failure when an articled teacher does not succeed the mentor loses out all round. Status and self-esteem is lost, the mentor training is lost and so too is the financial allowance. This unhappy occurrence affected five mentors on the programme, all of whom suffered emotional anguish from the experience. One described it in this way:

Until very recently I was wholeheartedly in favour of the scheme but I do wonder if it is right to force such a deep relationship on to people. Mentors who have had problems, sometimes resulting in articled teachers leaving the scheme, have all felt personally responsible and have suffered a great deal of anguish, a blow to their confidence and a loss of self-esteem. This is poor reward for a lot of time, effort and hard work. I have recently suffered a minor setback and can appreciate how devastating a 'failure' must be.

The temptation to disregard or misinterpret signs that the articled teacher was experiencing difficulties until they could no longer be ignored was very strong. At the outset the mentors assumed that their articled teachers would succeed or at least made the assumption that any problems could be put right given time. The possibility of failure (or even withdrawal for domestic reasons) was not consciously addressed beforehand and became elevated to personal crisis when it occurred.

When difficulties arose the mentors found themselves reluctant to talk about them, convinced that matters would improve. Interestingly, everyone concerned appeared to be collaborators in avoiding the issue.

A conspiracy of silence reigned for a range of confused but quite understandable motives. Beyond the immediate losses mentioned earlier, there was the responsibility the mentor felt for the principle of school-based teacher training. Delivering criticism and assessing students can be more difficult than anticipated, especially when a relationship is close and mutually supportive. Because of this closeness a mentor may not be able to see what is apparent to an outsider. For this reason working with the professional tutor as a critical friend with a detached view was an important element. In this scheme the college-based professional tutor visited mentors and articled teachers twice a term. The professional tutor's role developed into one of giving advice on assessment procedures and of making an assessment of the articled teachers. The support given by the professional tutor to the mentor was therefore restricted by time and by the nature of the role. The balance of the support offered by professional tutors has had to be reconsidered, not because mentors depend on professional tutors but rather because they need a stronger working relationship with a detached outsider, ideally someone with whom they can conduct a training dialogue. Working collaboratively was valued by mentors. The burden of working in isolation was felt keenly.

CONCLUSION AND STRATEGIES FOR THE FUTURE

In the famous North of England speech in January 1992, Kenneth Clarke, the then Secretary of State for Education, claimed to have found 'the concept of the mentor teacher an attractive one' (Clarke, 1992:12). Confident that teachers themselves should be responsible for training future recruits into the profession, the principle of schools taking a leading role in teacher training was repeated several times by Kenneth Clarke in the speech. In a recent Cambridge Education Paper (Beardon *et al.* 1992) an entirely school-based model of teacher training was advocated. Tight focused training needs are set out along with advice on how teachers and mentors should operate the system. Implicit in both these views is the belief that mentoring is straightforward, that training to be a teacher is straightforward because teaching children is straightforward. The mentors in our sample would dismiss these assumptions as too simplistic.

Some of the rhetoric contained in the literature reads as if novice teachers were passive inert receivers of advice and guidance, whereas the mentor/novice–teacher relationship is dynamic and fluid. To reduce the tasks to simply a set of competencies is to underestimate its demanding nature. The mentor training which was perceived as least satisfactory by our group was that which addressed basic lists of skills and competencies only.

If the motive for reforming initial teacher education is really about quality, and the Secretary of State claims that it is, then the move to a more school-based preparation of teachers must actively promote a coherent and convincing model able to bridge the 'gaps' mentioned at the beginning of the paper. To be perceived as either under-resourced or second-rate would be to miss a major opportunity to tackle the structural deficiencies of the current system.

REFERENCES

Beardon, T., Booth, M., Hargreaves, D. and Reiss, M. (1992) *School-led Initial Teacher Training (Cambridge Education Papers No. 2)*, Cambridge, University of Cambridge Department of Education.

Clarke, K. (1992) Speech at the North of England Education Conference, London, DES.

Furlong, V.J., Hirst, P., Pocklington, K. and Miles, S. (1988) *Initial Teacher Training and the Role of the School*, Milton Keynes: Open University Press.

Chapter 9

Mentoring beginner teachers – issues for schools to anticipate and manage

Chris Watkins and Caroline Whalley

The focus of this chapter is the school-based mentoring process which supports the initial training of teachers in any of its present routes. We draw as much from practical application and experience of mentoring as from theoretical frameworks.

ISSUES FOR THE SCHOOL TO ANTICIPATE AND MANAGE

The main issues that have arisen, during the training of beginner teachers are examined under the following headings:

- some whole-school issues;
- communication issues;
- challenges and conflicts;
- resources;
- management of the learning experience;
- multiple mentors;
- the school's learning from the experience.

Whole-school issues

Schools are social organizations which have their own 'feel' or ethos. It is important that we recognize that the whole school ethos can support or undermine many aspects of professional development including that of mentoring (Joyce and Showers 1988).

Mentoring development in any school will be affected by several factors, amongst them the ethos or culture of the organization (Handy and Aitken 1986), the style of management in the school, which may be through teams, political or hierarchical (Bush 1989), the degree of connectedness and communication in the organization which may be open and wide, well supported and resourced or closed, the view of professional development and teachers' learning which may be seen as an essential aspect of school life, a luxury or simply a nuisance,

(O'Sullivan *et al.* 1988), and the view of initial training and trainees, which may be one of processing and socializing people into old ways and maintaining the status quo of the organization, rather than recognizing new and regenerative ideas.

Where each of the above elements manages to generate an atmosphere supporting the opportunity for challenge, change and growth, the development of mentoring is likely to be positive. In such an environment professional progression will be taken as the norm, and there will be an expectation that practice can develop and that ideas can change through a process of study, discussion, demonstration and practice.

In summary then, to best support the process of mentoring the school has to begin to move towards a situation where there is:

- quality of practice within schools, since this is the principal focus of professional experience and sources;
- effective support to enable the processes of reflection and review to take place;
- a whole-school approach to staff development at all levels – initial training, induction and retention of staff;
- an atmosphere in the school conducive to school-based training in the terms of receptive attitudes and willingness to support trainees;
- the presence of suitable experienced teachers as potential mentors;
- the presence of suitable mentor support and training.

In such an organization there may also be additional benefits in that there could be a reduction in the isolation which is often endemic to the lives of teachers (Joyce and Showers 1988).

Communication issues

Communication is needed at many levels and at various times during mentoring. The school can anticipate and ease some of these processes by clarifying what is being communicated to whom and when and then planning a method and means for the various occasions.

One aspect of communication which can be anticipated is the different needs at different stages. By dividing the process into time periods it becomes possible to analyse and begin to address beginner teachers' needs.

Before arrival

What we pass on at this stage can give the first impression, even before the first visit. It can help to build up a picture about the school and about the people in it. It should be appropriate, conveying a welcome and clearly outlining the sort of reception the beginner teacher can expect.

On arrival

At the school the beginner teacher, colleagues and pupils need different information. The school needs to be aware of and link the beginner teacher into networks in the school. These might be formal like departmental and staff meetings but equally important are the informal arrangements like the rites for coffee and seating which may well exist in the staff room and can be the undoing of the uninitiated.

Introduction phase

The beginner teacher is going to be a member of multiple teams and needs to be able to find a reference for himself or herself in relation to these teams. There is a need to recognize the process of role formation and definition as well as the process of team building. An understanding of these dimensions can give insight into some of the needs when introducing new teachers into the school.

Main work phase

The school will need to coordinate the information flow throughout this stage of everyone who is supporting the learner teacher, linking various teachers in school, college lecturers, and the local education authority (LEA). Setting up learning experiences and review sessions, feeding back observations and accounts and transferring information around, are all important.

Later phases and exit

There is still a need to manage the continuous exchange and flow of information between colleagues in the school as well as with outside bodies, possibly colleges or the local education authority. This stage is also likely to include negotiated reviews as well as written reports.

Whatever the stage, the ownership of information must be discussed and agreed so that all relevant information and how it can be used is clear and understandable to all parties. The beginner teacher must be aware of what is confidential and what is to be released. This is particularly pertinent when the beginner teacher is to gain experience from another school.

Challenges and conflicts

Significant learning is likely to be challenging, as enquiry into areas of teaching and school life is not always comfortable. The presence of a beginner teacher can highlight issues in the organization, and examining procedures and practice may trigger a range of reactions causing anxiety and at worst polarization. Identifying these conflicts as organizational or interpersonal may enable schools to pre-empt some of the difficulties.

Organisational conflicts

Purposes and goals can differ in any organization between:

- department–department;
- individual–departments;
- departments–school;
- individual–school.

There may be a view that 'student teachers take up too much time' or affect pupil behaviour and that a department may suffer as a result of the time they take up: 'We're not here to train teachers', 'It's all too disruptive', 'What will parents think?' All of these comments have been heard and indicate the need for discussion and clarification.

The distribution and allocation of resources, time and money, as well as colleagues, which are all needed to support beginner teachers, may be seen by some parties in the school as better used elsewhere. All of these are potential conflict areas and need to be managed. Some may be clarified in advance.

A beginner teacher could be clear about school policy with regard to:

- planning and preparation time;
- when/if they will be used for covering absence;
- when/if ever will they be used for unsupervised class responsibility;
- or exam invigilation.

Interpersonal conflicts

Trainees sometimes get 'owned' by individuals and departments. This can lead to possessiveness about supervision and taking sides in exchanges. The beginner teacher might pose a threat by bringing new ideas and ways of working into departments. There is also a visibility which the beginner teacher brings to the department attracting the attention of outsiders and senior colleagues. A large number of new relationships are being formed and there are likely to be tensions or conflicts in some of them. The school has to acknowledge that potential for conflict exists and that provision of time, space and resources will enable mediation and resolution in many cases.

Resources

We have categorized these in terms of time, space and additional materials.

Time

It is important that schools recognize time as a resource and negotiate clear time for individuals to manage the process of mentoring. Below are some of the activities mentors are likely to be involved in:

- negotiation between college and school and/or outside;
- the process of mentoring;
- communication between various mentors in the school;
- release of the mentors and other staff to observe and feed back;
- planning and review of the programme;
- networking;
- training other mentors.

Schools need to anticipate the extra time needed so that it can be taken into account and built into development planning.

Space

It is likely that staff will have established space for themselves to work in, but a mentoring role is likely to have different requirements. There are a variety of situations that mentors will be in and times when they will need somewhere undisturbed and preferably quiet. For the unestablished and uninitiated beginner teacher finding space is not so easy. The provision of a storage space for exercise books, pigeon-hole for messages and somewhere to work in relative comfort is often neglected and yet can make a real difference to the way they perceive themselves and their standing within the school.

Materials

A budget can remove some of the difficulties that arise when extra demands are placed on departmental resources. It could support the use of the photocopier, sugar paper, card, etc. and enable the beginner teacher to have autonomy from the outset. Also, learning the art of control over scarce resources could be incorporated into their programme.

Management of the learning experience

The way that learning is managed indicates an underlying approach which is being taken to 'learning about teaching'. We identify four (with apologies to anyone named Nellie).

- *Sitting next to Nellie.* This is still common and founded on apprenticeship models of learning. Much energy can be invested in questions of 'placement' – this poses the key question for this model: which Nellie to sit next to?
- *Observing Nellie.* This is popular but doesn't always clarify what to observe. As one aspect it is important but not sufficient as it cannot investigate the non-observable (people's goals, perceptions, etc.) and may not address the question: what is the relation of observation to action?
- *Enquiring about Nellie.* This has developed extensively in some areas. Again it may be important to consider which Nellies to enquire of and what to do with the results.
- *Trying out being your own Nellie.* This is reminiscent of action learning models in which the beginner is supported in their own problem-solving in a structured way at an appropriate pace.

The learning experience of any beginner teacher can be impoverished by:

- offering them only one model or approach to learning about teaching;
- locating them within one section of school, usually the subject-specific area, disregarding other aspects of school life;
- placing them in one area with little or no structured support in the belief, and probably hope, that professional learning is about 'something rubbing off'.

It is our belief that the beginner teacher needs a planned programme of learning activities which offer range, variety and development. The framework below outlines three dimensions, each of which it is important to consider.

- *Variety.* To observe and learn from different approaches; to learn that different groups of pupils respond differently to the same stimulus; to experiment with approaches and styles.

- *Range.* To recognize the fullness of a teacher's role and to avoid devaluing the non-classroom aspects. Deliberately including aspects such as talking to individual pupils, parental links, experiences outside the school and perhaps in other schools.
- *Towards personal practice.* To give some purpose to observation and investigation; to promote the application of learning; to start the process of professional development for their ensuing years.

What follows from this?

- *Choice.* If learning needs can be discussed choice can be managed with the learner and 'placement' does not become the central issue.
- *Negotiation.* Not everything about a learner's programme can be planned in advance and this reminds us of the need to treat beginner teachers as individuals. We need to be able to discuss starting points and learning needs: what the learner feels they have presently achieved and what they feel confident about tackling next. We then can translate needs into appropriate learning experiences offering a variety of situations across the range. Debriefing by different colleagues can all enrich the experience.
- *Progression.* This needs to be planned and discussed instead of 'throwing someone in at the deep end'. Progession can be planned through stages of observation or investigation, reviewing and learning from that experience and subsequently building it into personal action and practice.

The school's learning from the experience

Schools may vary in the degree to which they recognize that they will learn from the experience of working with beginner teachers. This can be reflected in their reasons for having beginner teachers in the first place, and indeed in their reasons for having had them for the last number of years.

You might recognize some of the following categories adapted from Joyce *et al.* (1983):

- 'We like having the young things around' (but we don't intend to change): the superficially accepting school?
- 'We do it because we're asked to': the non-learning school?
- 'We look forward to the work and to learning from them': the receptive school?

- 'They always get put here' (it's a habit): the passive consuming school?
- 'We don't want them in here': the entrenched school?

School   Beginner teacher

It is important to anticipate that learning may be two-way. This is not always recognized, nor even always valued, and when it is recognized it becomes possible to incorporate that learning into the wider life of the school.

Multiple mentors

We have not focused on one person as mentor though one individual may coordinate the experience, retaining an overview of the process and being aware of the time line for development. We recognize that a number of people will become involved and have outlined an approach which suggests a whole-school view of mentoring. In such a view parallels and links are made with further professional development in the school and to other areas of supervision such as supportive appraisal.

The process of learning to teach must involve a variety of planned experiences which should be devised and built upon by many colleagues all of whom are part of a mentoring process and who at various times will be mentors to the beginner teacher. The selection of a coordinator in a senior position is important because there will be a need for communication and review.

A team of mentors can be built from different parts of the school in order to offer the widest possible experiences. We should also recognize that the mentors themselves will have particular strengths, abilities and qualities; in this way we can ensure that the beginner teacher is being offered a range of ways of learning.

REFERENCES

Bush, T. (ed.) (1989) *Managing Education: theory and practice*, Oxford: Oxford University Press.
Handy, C. and Aitken, R. (1986) *Understanding Schools as Organisations*, Harmondsworth: Penguin.
Joyce, B., Hershe, R. and McKibbin, M. (1983) *The Structure of School Improvement*, Harlow: Longman.

Joyce, B. and Showers, B. (1988) *Student Achievement through Staff Development*, Harlow: Longman.

O'Sullivan, F., Jones, K. and Reid, K. (1988) *Staff Development in Secondary Schools*, London: Hodder and Stoughton.

Chapter 10

A neglected source for reflection in the supervision of student teachers

Peter Lucas

MODELS OF SUPERVISION

The traditional model is one in which the supervisor observes a student teaching a class and subsequently makes oral and/or written assessments of the student's competences. Individual supervisors will vary with regard to the sensitivity they show towards supervisees' feelings in giving their judgements. In some cases students may be given a completed check-list at the end of the lesson. Stones' (1984: 40) 'counselling and pedagogical' model envisages 'the learning of the pupil, the student teacher and the supervisor as enquiry-oriented'. The supervisor, setting his or her face against didacticism, plans the initiation of the student teacher before Teaching Practice into theory-directed analysis of teaching by organizing 'discussion and practical activities'. In this way beginners will secure a grasp of the 'pedagogical principles thought important'. Ideally, the supervisor examines a video-recording of the student's classroom performance and 'notes points that seem to merit particular comment'. His or her written scheme should 'cover every step in the counselling process' to guarantee 'that nothing important will be overlooked in the heat of the moment . . .' (p. 112). To reassure the beginner, says Stones, the supervisor uses techniques from counselling and is 'sharp and probing as well as warm and supportive' (p. 121). He/she endeavours 'only to intervene when essential' – the goal is autonomous critiquing by the beginner.

'Partnership supervision' (Rudduck and Sigsworth 1985) is another model inspired by American 'clinical' experience. The decision as to what elements are to be analysed is the student's, although preliminary discussion will enable the 'partners' to agree on what it is they are going to be considering. Also in this preliminary discussion, the supervisor and the student work out what sort of evidence is needed and how it might be gathered. The supervisor 'shapes his/her observation according to the agreed focus' and his or her commentary subsequent to the lesson is ordered and controlled 'by accepting a strict principle of relevance as defined by the focus' (pp. 154, 155). John Smyth (1985) takes a 'critical' stance. He quotes Cogan approvingly:

> the teacher is called on to assume almost all the roles and respon-sibilities of a supervisor in his interaction with the clinical supervisor. He initiates action, proposes hypotheses, analyses his own perform-ance [and] shares responsibilities for devising supervisory strategies.
> (1985:5; from Cogan, 1973:xi)

But, argues Smyth, clinical supervision is too often substantially about improving skills and is thus 'conservative'. He wants to see the 'critical questioning of the ends of teaching'. The critical model of clinical supervision offers 'the capacity to enable us to examine, understand and challenge the institutional conditions and circumstances of our work'. Smith and Tomlinson offer the 'rapping' model of supervision: radio-assisted practice (1984; see also Tomlinson and Smith 1985). Working within 'the modern psychology of skill', they have shown how the radio-microphone can be used by the supervisor to supply advice and assistance, which, together with feedback are crucial if skills are to be acquired (Tomlinson and Smith 1985:115, 116). Rapping enables the supervisor to enjoy secretly 'getting straight through' to the beginner 'with clearly observable effects' (Smith and Tomlinson 1984:127), and 'in natural classroom settings' (p. 126).

Where are the pupils?

These models seem to draw on pupils' perceptions to a limited degree, if at all. The judgemental supervisor may overhear comments made by students in class, but these are likely to be casual, unsystematic episodes.

'AN ESSENTIAL PERSPECTIVE'

There has been increasing research interest in pupils' views (e.g. Meighan 1977; Tucker 1979; Wragg and Wood 1984; McKelvey and Kyriacou 1985; Hull 1985). It seems quite legitimate to believe that pupil judgements on their teachers can be regarded as valid (see McKelvey and Kyriacou 1985:28, 29). A cross-cultural investigation involving Sheffield and Stockholm secondary school pupils, student teachers, teachers and supervisors noted pupils' 'shrewd common-sense' and an 'attitude to actual students (if not to the idea of students)' that mostly 'was down-to-earth, constructive and generous about initial difficulties such as over-anxiety'. The team concluded that 'the pupils' viewpoint, in short, provided an essential perspective from the very centre of teaching practice, the classroom' (Harrison et al. 1990:253).

Hull (1985:3) argues that, 'teaching and learning only synchronise effectively in an act of collaboration', and that a lot of schoolchildren, 'are acutely aware that the reality they inhabit is constructed' but 'that they are conscripts to that reality with no voice in its structuring' (p. 4). He urges that pupils be given 'rights of comment and analysis with respect to their classroom experience' (Ibid.). Whilst suggesting the democratic value of 'a dialogue between pupils and teacher . . . to sound out one's feelings towards the other, to examine issues of mutual concern, to air grievances, to find and lend support and so on', Emmerson, Carter and Lasalle (1981:56) note that participants 'must learn to listen to other opinions and respect the rights and feelings of others'. Their warning that some 'sort of balance needs to be struck between freedom and democracy and discipline and control' should be seen, partly, in the context of a current situation where teachers are being prompted by government policies to wean themselves from what Grace (1987) calls the 'ethic of legitimated professionalism' and to become more politically aware in their reflections. Learning how to establish and maintain such a dialogue could become a significant indicator of successful teaching in the 1990s and beyond. Recent national developments reinforce the argument for attending to pupils' opinions. 'Active learning' has been promoted (e.g. by the Technical and Vocational Education Initiative), featuring collaboration, reconceptualization of the teacher as facilitator and fellow (if more expert) learner, more useful feedback and self-assessment in records of achievement. Her Majesty's Inspectors regularly advise teacher trainers to stress pupil learning and this is the objective of National Curriculum attainment targets and statements of attainment. Pupils' evaluation of how their teachers work seems a natural corollary of such developments, would parallel moves in higher education where the place of student evaluation of courses is being strengthened, and deepen understandings of citizenship (which is a National Curriculum cross-curricular theme).

UNRAVELLING MARCUS'S MYSTERY

How might the gathering of pupils' opinions be incorporated within a supervisory strategy? Criteria such as economy of time and effort, and flexibility in being able to respond quickly, easily, and comfortably to a student teacher's felt needs are important. In my example these criteria are met. Marcus was a lively student teacher, energetic, intelligent and imaginative. Among his concerns during his second and final teaching practice on a postgraduate English university course was that he was not getting on sufficiently well with one of his secondary school classes. Puzzlement made him focus on his personal characteristics rather than what he was doing as a teacher: 'Is it the way I act?' 'Do I have mannerisms that may be putting people off?' Because his supervisor's approach drew on 'partnership', Marcus had been expected to identify in advance the problems to be analysed in post-lesson discussions. Faced with the student's concern, the supervisor was unsure as to what he should look for to provide evidence for analysis. Should he record pupils' non-verbal reactions to the student teacher's questions? Such non-verbal behaviour could, in fact, be very hard for an observer to detect, and even harder to interpret accurately. In the event, Marcus courageously took advantage of an offer his supervisor had made to his students to debrief, during the lesson and in another room, a student-selected group of four to six pupils. The outcome both pleased and surprised Marcus. Pupils' comments focused on him as a teacher, which was the reason for his being with the class – he was not there simply as a 'person' to strike up a 'good' relationship (a point that student teachers sometimes see insufficiently clearly). The comments provided an agenda upon which Marcus could act. The pupils identified what they liked: 'He shows you diagrams' (which was in contrast to teachers who just gave notes); his attempts to introduce discussion; a play. Because the lessons had interest, the pupils could 'take in more like'. In their cross-cultural study, Harrison *et al.* (1990) note that 'in Sheffield, especially, pupils were critical of their usual teacher and welcomed the methods and approaches of the students involved in this enquiry' (p. 253). The pupils also identified what they did not like. The girls were not enthusiastic about the content – the Spanish Armada: 'Boats are for boys.' And Marcus, it seemed, was not doing enough to involve girls in discussion: he 'never comes to girls'. Furthermore, his approach to homework was criticized: he was not explaining it enough (which contrasted with an alleged repetition of instructions for work to be done in class which they implied had been carried to the point of boredom); he did not always give homework; he was not checking sufficiently to see that it had been done; and he was 'not strict enough'. How reliable as evidence were these statements by the pupils to the supervisor? And how did Marcus react? Below the pupils' statements are given with Marcus's reaction following each. (The post-lesson discussion between Marcus and his supervisor had been audio-taped.)

Pupils' statements and Marcus's reactions

- *'Boats are for boys.'*
  (Laugh) I figured that was coming up. . . . I'm going to look at why it [the Armada] happened which gives me a chance to look at Queen Elizabeth and Mary Queen of Scots.

- *'Never comes to the girls.'*
  Now that's weird because I make a conscious effort to [go to] them.
- *'Not always giving homework.'*
  Yes it is something I'm supposed to do but there are times when I sit here and think 'Well I'm just making up homeworks for the sake of making up homeworks.'
- *'Not checking on homeworks.'*
  I only just went round today and did it!
- *'Not explaining homework enough.'*
  That's probably because I'm leaving it. Perhaps not leaving myself enough time to explain it at the end . . . it's just when I'm sitting there I mean I know what the homework is going to be but I don't like to interrupt [what] they're doing in class at the time so I feel it's got to be at the end.

Clearly the pupils had come to a comprehensive appraisal of Marcus's teaching, and the level of intersubjective agreement between their statements and those of the student teacher is high.

OBSERVATIONS

Eliciting pupils' perceptions in this way shows how a supervisor can secure and relay insights not otherwise available. As judges or as partners, supervisors can note only what they perceive as significant in the unfolding complexity of a lesson. They can note only what they see during the particular (and limited) visits they make. Whilst Hull (1985), with classroom management in mind, is right in saying that 'good standing with pupils is an achievement of immense significance to teachers – especially beginning teachers', we have to remember that student teachers are likely to be testing themselves to see what they can do, which may involve approaches the pupils are used to and others to which they are not. McKelvey and Kyriacou say that 'the research overwhelmingly shows that . . . pupils prefer what is known as sound, traditional practice – that is they are essentially conservative in their expectations and these expectations form the rules for the behaviour they expect from their teacher'. Marcus was an innovator, and seen to be so by the pupils. They liked the innovations; they were not conservative about these changes in their routine. Effectively, they signalled: 'Go on with them.' At the same time, Marcus had to behave properly (in their eyes) about homework, which they, not privy to the thought he revealed on this issue to his supervisor, clearly saw as having importance. To get the homework aspect right could only increase his chances of success with his innovations, whose worth was diminished whilst some of his behaviours were seen as inappropriate. Marcus had been aware of female dissatisfaction with content, but he seemed to have perceived the gender issue for him with that class simply as one of content. It was not likely, therefore, that it would have been suggested by him as a focus for the supervision. Had the supervisor stayed in the room throughout the lesson, and continued to write a descriptive record, the sheer force of 'never comes to the girls' might well have been missed. Before the debriefing, his supervisor had recorded that one girl had contributed, on Marcus's request, an oral summary; only boys (a very small number) were subsequently recorded as responding or being prepared to respond. It is possible, then, to suggest that the written record for that episode of oral interaction (had it been the main or only evidence) would have been more likely to point in the direction of a conclusion along the lines of Marcus having to increase overall response rather than for him to try to secure a greater sex balance. Moreover, the contribution of even one girl enables a student teacher to claim he/she is endeavouring to get girls to contribute. Marcus's pupils' comments appeared fair and objective. It may be asked: 'What happens to the relationship between the student teacher and the students if the comments are all negative?' The use of this debriefing strategy is a matter for careful consideration by the supervisor in each particular case. And, of course, it is up to him or her to structure the debriefing so that favourable as well as unfavourable comment is encouraged. The structure might usefully be negotiated with the student. When likes and dislikes of a personal nature are expressed, it is again a matter of judgement by the supervisor as to how they are handled. The example of Marcus can be seen as a tentative but important step towards establishing genuine classroom dialogue between student teachers and pupils (and supervisors) about the ways people are taught and the ways they learn most effectively. To illustrate: suppose a student teacher has learned from his/her supervisor (as in the case we have examined) that the girls do not think they are being involved sufficiently in discussion. He/she can choose to use the opportunity to draw explicit attention to the point in a subsequent lesson and work openly upon it, challenging the girls to respond positively to his/her efforts to respond positively to their wishes. To draw on Schon's terminology (1983, 1987), we would then have an example of 'reflection-in-action' following 'reflection-on-action' as the goals between teacher and learner were more fully shared. Rudduck and Sigsworth (1985) 'question whether a higher education tutor, who sees only isolated episodes in the continuum of a student's experience on teaching practice, can be sensitive to the "fine grain" of a particular student's development in a particular context' (p. 156). However, tutors (as 'outsiders') are better placed than teachers to debrief pupils, because the latter have no need to ingratiate themselves with supervisors and are likely to have less anxiety about identification than if the debriefing was done by teachers.

CONCLUSION

The argument of this paper has been that traditional and substitute models of supervision give no or insufficient attention to ascertaining and using the views of the pupils being taught.

REFERENCES

Cogan, M. (1973) *Clinical Supervision*, Boston: Houghton and Mifflin.
Emmerson, P., Carter, A. and Lasalle, J. (1981) 'Talking about School', *AEP Journal*, 5, 5, 48-57.
Grace, G. (1987) 'Teachers and the State in Britain: A Changing Relation', in Lawn, M.L. and Grace, G. (eds) *Teachers: The Culture and Politics of Work*, Lewes: Falmer.
Harrison, B.T., Deas, R., Henderson, J., Knutton, S., Roberts, M. and Trafford, J. (1990) 'Framework and Process in Teaching Practice: A Suitable Case for Re-modelling?' *Educational Review*, 42, 3, 247-59.
Hull, C. (1985) 'Pupils as Teacher Educators', *Cambridge Journal of Education*, 15, 1, 1-8.
McKelvey, J. and Kyriacou, C. (1985) 'Research on Pupils as Teacher Evaluators', *Educational Studies*, 11, 1, 27-31.
Meighan, R. (1977) 'Pupils' Perceptions of the Classroom Techniques of Postgraduate Student Teachers', *British Journal of Teacher education*, 3, 139-48.
Rudduck, J. and Sigsworth, A. (1985) 'Partnership Supervision (or Goldhammer Revisited)', 153-171, in Hopkins, D. and Reid, K. (eds), *Rethinking Teacher Education*, London: Croom Helm.
Schon, D.A. (1983) *The Reflective Practitioner: How Professionals Think in Action*, London: Temple Smith.
Schon, D. (1987) *Educating the Reflective Practitioner*, San Francisco: Jossey-Bass.
Smith, R. and Tomlinson, P. (1984) 'RAP: Radio-Assisted Practice. Preliminary Investigations of a New Technique in Teacher Education', *Journal of Education for Teaching*, 10, 2, May, 119-34.
Smyth, W.J. (1985) 'Developing a Critical Practice of Clinical Supervision', *Journal of Curriculum Studies*, 17, 1, 1-15.
Stones, E. (1984) *Supervision in Teacher Education: A Counselling and Pedagogical Approach*, London: Methuen.
Tomlinson, P. and Smith, R. (1985) 'Training Intelligently Skilled Teachers', in Francis, H. (ed.), *Learning to Teach: Psychology in Teacher Training*, Lewes: Falmer, 102-18.
Tucker, N. (1979) " 'Could do better': Students Reporting on Teachers', *Where*, 152, 264-66.
Wragg, E.C. and Wood, E.K. (1984) 'Pupil Appraisals of Teaching', in Wragg, E.C. (ed.), *Classroom Teaching Skills: The Research Findings of the Teacher Education Project*, London: Croom Helm, 79-96.

Chapter 11

The mentor connection

Murray Reich

Over the past ten years substantial numbers of women have moved into professional and managerial jobs traditionally held by men. A recent survey of 5,000 alumni of women's colleges showed that 43 per cent are lawyers, physicians, managers or computer specialists. They are making their presence felt in middle management as never before and now demand representation at the senior level. Do mentors play a role in professional and managerial women's climb to the top?

I recently conducted a study of male executives that showed that most had had mentors and had in turn been mentor to an average of four people. Of this group, less than 5 per cent indicated that they had had a female protégé. Not only are women currently a minority in the upper echelons of American management; it seems that precious few are being groomed to maintain that toehold. I proceeded to conduct a study on women executives' experiences with the mentor relationship, compared them with men's experiences, and determined how important mentoring was to their rise in the corporate hierarchy.

This article focuses on the nature and extent of the relationship between female protégés and their mentors.

THE SURVEY

The questionnaires used in this survey were similar to those I used in my study of male mentors but, in addition, they included items on networking and personal problems to determine whether the mentor relationship improved networking and whether the value of the relationship was mitigated by sexual biases. As in my previous study, the forms focused on the whats and the hows – rather than the whys – of the relationships. I asked whether individuals developed strong emotional ties, whether they had similar personal values, and whether they considered the relationship to be a professional, teacher–student, and/or a personal one.

The response rates were high: 32 per cent for 87 members of the Princeton Research Forum, a group of professionals and scholars; 33 per cent for 160 members of the New Jersey Women Networkers who were attending a meeting on 'superwomen'; 51 per cent for a sample of 61 successful female executives in New Jersey industry and government; and 40 per cent for women executives I had met at various conferences. In all, of 353 women surveyed, 37 per cent responded.

Respondents held a variety of positions, such as president of a small firm; marketing manager; senior vice-president of a large state bank; government and corporate counsel. The average age, 41, was comparable to the average age in my study of male executives. About 77 per cent (compared with 90 per cent of male executives) had a mentor who influenced their career development. On average, they – like their male counterparts – become protégés at about 30, while their mentors, over half of whom were their supervisors, were about 43.

The previous study found that top executives must develop high-potential subordinates to replace them as they move up the ladder; if they don't, they are unlikely to be promoted themselves. Yet some women respondents argued that mentors are *not* necessary for advancement, that they can hurt a career, and that they must in any case be chosen with great deliberation. Other women noted that relationships with male mentors sometimes become sexual and warned that some invitations to help may be disguised sexual advances. Many women contended that the 'old boy' networks often control promotions, which can result in the best qualified candidates being passed over for the choice assignments.

By the time they were 37 (about two years older than the men I studied), most of the women had had mentors and were beginning to serve as mentor to others. They were an average of 13 years older than their new protégés; the average age of the men's protégés was 28. Only half of the women directly supervised their protégés, compared with 74 per cent of the men. More significant is that most (90 per cent) were mentors of other females; less than 5 per cent of the men had chosen female protégés. One possible reason is that men still resist helping qualified women because of sex stereotypes. Further, women are more likely to be in mentoring positions *vis-à-vis* other women than men are. Undoubtedly many women felt a responsibility to assist high potential women in advancing their careers.

THE NATURE OF MENTOR ASSISTANCE

From the perspectives of both protégés and mentors, female managers felt that mentors gave valuable concrete aid. The most important aids named – in order – were assignment to special projects, creation of new positions and the granting of autonomy on difficult tasks. Fewer women than men (49 per cent versus 63 per cent) stated that mentors transferred them early in their careers to challenging jobs; consequently, they did not rate the benefit as highly. As one financial manager said,

> My mentor was looking for women to move into management and encouraged me. He eventually became president and I moved with him. Although I have left the company, he still is of help. He will retire soon and I am sure our relationship will continue.

A public administrator said:

> My mentor gve me support in taking risks and listened to my problems. Female mentors are important to women; they prove to us that it can be done. She helped me to view differently job changes, take risks others saw as potential mistakes, and move from viable positions to others of greater challenge. She also gave me the emotional strength to deal with issues facing women in management, such as sexist attitudes, career and family.

Political aid, such as career guidance and counselling on company politics, was considered more important by female than by male protégés. Over half of both male and female mentors applied pressure on others to obtain promotions for their protégés. More women than men, however, reported that they obtained useful career development advice. Overall, women esteemed guidance at least as much as concrete action, possibly because they are relatively new entrants to corporate management and do not have much experience in the politics of large organizations.

BENEFITS OF THE MENTOR RELATIONSHIP

Women, like men, gained from being protégés and mentors. As protégés, women appreciated the increased opportunity to develop their abilities and be creative. More important, 99 per cent (versus 87 per cent of the men) said they gained greater self-confidence through the mentor relationship, that it enhanced their awareness of their strengths.

Both sexes valued the opportunity to make tough decisions, learn management skills, join winning teams, develop useful contacts, and achieve more rapid promotions. More women than men reported that mentors stimulated their thinking (84 per cent versus 77 per cent), gave them feedback about their weaknesses (78 per cent versus 66 per cent), and allowed them to set their own job goals (80 per cent versus 72 per cent). Apparently, more women than men felt that mentors helped them find and use their talents.

Female mentors also benefited from the relationships. Some gains were similar to those for men. For example, when they were supervisor *and* mentor to a protégé, both women and men noted improved performance of their work group (85 per cent and 87 per cent). Women were more likely than men (88 per cent versus 79 per cent) to become aware of the protégé's needs through the relationship, but did not value this as highly as fostering better performance.

Among the differences in opinion between male and female mentors, men more often said they were helped by keeping a top protégé on their work team (78 per cent versus 66 per cent); both sexes, however, prized this factor. Women mentors assigned greater value to making productive use of their experience. A high percentage of both sexes gained satisfaction from helping younger people, and most people felt mentoring improved their managerial talents. But women assigned higher values to these benefits than men did.

Respondents cited other factors, such as appreciating the needs of others and being stimulated by the ideas of bright and creative protégés, as being only moderately important. Like the male mentors, the women gave little value to such factors as a desire to feel connected to the younger generation and a sense of power; some did not feel these factors were involved in the mentor relationship at all. Fewer women than men (44 per cent versus 66 per cent) felt that senior management recognized the worth of mentoring.

DRAWBACKS OF THE MENTOR RELATIONSHIP

Women protégés noted fewer negative aspects of mentor relationships than men did. The disadvantages did not nullify the vast benefits. Half found few or no disadvantages. The major drawbacks listed by both men and women were being too closely identified with the mentor and being marked as his or her 'person'. Other negative factors cited less frequently included: 'Kept from better jobs', 'Received too much protection' and 'Had personal problems.' Some respondents (16 per cent of the women and 22 per cent of the men) said that the association caused a moderate amount of stress and that one or more of the above conditions truly hurt the relationship.

Some women commented on the disadvantages of mentor relationships. The educational director of a small firm said, 'As I outpaced and outgrew the relationship my mentor grew defensive and fearful that I would make him look bad. Now instead of making me look good he calls me a know-it-all.'

A manager stated, 'My company so misuses the supervisory position that I lost a second career. My supervisor wanted a *clone*, not a protégé. "Discipleship" has that problem – independence versus imitation.'

Some women were able to break away from the mentor without harming the relationship between themselves and their mentors. One woman, while serving a one-year law clerkship, was encouraged by her mentor to join the mentor's law firm. For a few years the mentor monitored her progress, and they worked together on many cases until she began to develop her own case-load. The problem was that she was perceived as an adjunct of the mentor by other lawyers. 'Eventually I was forced to wean myself away from her cases to enable myself to work with and for other partners', she said. 'Fortunately this was accomplished without jeopardy to the relationship between my mentor and me.'

Both male and female mentors de-emphasized the drawbacks of mentoring, but women cited slightly fewer major problems (11 per cent versus 17 per cent) than men did. However, women encountered moderate to great difficulty when they recommended their protégés for other positions and when their top people competed for the same job. Comparably small percentages of women and men became disillusioned with protégés. Like the men, they had more trouble with their protégés (11 per cent and 9 per cent) and reported trouble with termination of the relationship (7 per cent and 5 per cent).

Overall, women respondents reported less difficulty than men with their mentors and/or protégés. Like the men, they had more trouble with their protégés than with their mentors. Keep in mind that most women (71 per cent) had had male mentors, and they in turn cited a female as their most important protégé. Data are insufficient to determine whether this difference in gender affected the results.

THE SPECIAL NATURE OF WOMEN'S MENTORING

Female mentor–protégé relationships were different from those involving men only. The affective, or emotional, quality was more vital for women than for men. The office director at a small college said:

> This relationship has continued more than a decade, although we only worked together for four years and she was my immediate supervisor for only two of those years. Most unexpected was the combination of professional and personal aspects mixed together in equal measure and now almost indistinguishable from one another, and the recognition that as friends and colleagues we are quite complementary, having different strengths and weaknesses.

Our results verified these comments. Regardless of gender, mentors cared about the future of their protégés, but female mentors' feelings were stronger. As protégés, more women reported that their mentors viewed their career development as important. Likewise, all female mentors reported caring about their protégés' promotions.

More women than men noted that their relationships with mentors (67 per cent versus 42 per cent) and protégés (63 per cent versus 44 per cent) developed into close friendships. In particular very few men (60 per cent) developed close emotional ties with their mentors. Somewhat more women (69 per cent versus 59 per cent) said they continued to have a close relationship with their mentors.

Most women felt that good 'chemistry' was very important to the success of the relationship. Women rated the emotional factor more highly than men. Both men and women saw their mentors as role models who informed them of their strengths and weaknesses, but the women generally considered this a more important function than men did. Both men and women felt that as mentors, they were more frank with their protégés than their mentors were with them.

Women, like men, emphasize the professional nature of mentoring, but as women they are more likely than men to stress the caring, nurturing and teaching aspects of the relationship. For the women, teaching possibly meant telling their subordinates how to perform a job in addition to providing situations in which protégés learned by themselves on the job.

MENTOR CONTRIBUTIONS TO CAREER ADVANCEMENT

Even though men and women differed on details, they agreed that the mentor relationship contributed to their careers. As key mentors, both men and women rated their influence on their protégés as 'important'. Apparently, Erick Erikson's concept of 'generativity' applies equally to both sexes; and the desire of middle-aged women and men to leave part of themselves to the next generation played a telling part in the mentoring process.

The essence of these relationships was captured in a few of the respondents' statements. A college president said,

My greatest reward comes in watching a talented young person grow and develop both personally and professionally and meet and surpass expectations about their potential, especially if others didn't recognize it.

An administrator of a government agency said:

As a professor I served as the role model for literally hundreds of students in my 12-plus years of teaching. Often I was the only female professor students had. Their feedback was extremely positive; students recognize the need to have mentors.

RECOMMENDATIONS

My research results indicate that under optimum conditions, women benefit from informal mentor relationships. Usually their mentors are their supervisors. The relationship affords them the chance to gain greater self-confidence, learn new skills and develop their abilities. Mentors are caring individuals who derive satisfaction by helping young, bright, energetic women. Both mentors and protégés contribute more to their organization by virtue of these connections. The findings verify that most competent individuals are motivated by exciting jobs in which they can develop their talents – not by power.

Women, more than men, derive intangible benefits as well as concrete aid from a mentor. Another difference is that women are more likely to see the relationships as personal as well as professional. While only a few respondents developed truly close ties with their mentor or protégé, most nevertheless stressed the excellent 'chemistry' of their relationships. Concrete aid is vital to the mentor relationship for both sexes, but women desire more personal benefits as well.

In the face of stiff business competition, corporations must look to their human resources departments to improve management development programmes and motivate a larger proportion of the large number of professional women entering the labour force. Organizations must use all of their resources to help women move into senior positions. One important aspect of this challenge is the mentoring process.

Since mentors are so valuable for women, human resources managers might consider designating competent individuals to work with their women employees. They can sponsor workshops on mentoring, covering its values and limitations, and the types of benefits mentors provide. Workshops should stress that (1) usually supervisors want to help high-potential individuals, (2) women should de-emphasize the personality match of their mentor relationships, (3) top executives set high standards and enjoy developing qualified employees, (4) the mentor relationship is most often the result of outstanding performance, not a prospective protégé's selection of a mentor, and (5) men's and women's approaches to mentoring differ.

Some women have ambivalent feelings about work and family that can interfere with the mentoring process. Women mentors will often discuss with their protégés how to handle career, children, marriage and household duties. Despite increasing equity in other areas, women still often have primary responsibility for the home and bear the nurturing duty of all family members. For men, this problem generally exists less often.

By age 43 the female mentors in my survey had each taken on an average of four protégés. As these protégés in turn assist others, the women will begin to form their own 'old girl' networks that will continue to gather momentum . Human resources managers will do well to observe the mentor relationships in their companies, see to what extent men are mentoring women, coach both female and male managers in the nuances of mentoring protégés of both genders, and reap the synergistic advantages of having more women in the highest echelons of management.

Part C

Mentoring in induction training

Introduction

The previous section examined the political background to school-based training, looked at the role of the mentor in this initial teacher education context and explored how mentors and mentees have responded to the mentoring process. The concept of the mentoring-school has also been introduced. But the value of mentoring does not cease with the initial training phase. It extends into the induction of newly qualified teachers and indeed should be seen as important in the continuum of teacher education (from pre-service to induction and in-service). Part C is directed towards mentoring for induction.

Prior to 1992 in England and Wales initial teachers qualifying to enter the profession had to serve out a year as probationers, at the end of which they were assessed and, if successful, granted qualified status. (The probationary period is still retained in Scotland and Northern Ireland.) The government recently changed the system to that of the 'newly qualified teacher' (NQT); but provided some financial support to local education authorities to establish induction programmes. In the first article in Part C, Mike Turner still uses the language of probation but the principles he identifies apply equally to NQT induction. He sees mentoring as an important means by which beginning teachers are successfully socialized into the school, LEA and profession.

Turner also articulates the links between effective mentoring and 'reflective teaching'. He shows how a focus on 'reflective practice' benefits the mentor as much as the mentee. It is *both* who, ultimately, change and improve their practice. He argues that developing as a 'reflective practitioner' is more appropriate to this induction phase than initial teacher education (ITE) since the beginning teacher is now able to draw on wider experience. From this base of understanding Turner goes on to discuss the management of the induction process, examining the role of each of the players: LEA, headteacher, probationer/NQT, mentor. The central role of the headteacher has implications for whole school involvement: a return to the idea of the mentoring-school; and the need for mentor training is established. Turner also adds an important insight: that a key skill in being a mentor is the ability to observe lessons analytically – a skill to be seen alongside Elliott and Calderhead's note that mentors need a professional language through which to communicate their insights (Part A), and the view of students that successful mentors identify teaching points and draw out professional learning (see Booth in Part B).

Ann Waterhouse's article examines the ideals and reality of induction. She uses two imaginary case studies to articulate a programme of competences for all teachers in the current, rapidly changing, educational environment. By contrast, the pithy extract from Kay Kinder and Peter Earley describes the range of strategies actually employed in schools and LEAs in induction support programmes. Together, these two articles help focus on the need for appropriate strategies for induction, while earlier debates in Part A and in the Turner article in this part, provide the basis for a theoretical model of the required mentor role in induction.

The work of Peter Earley in investigating the realities of induction programmes is continued in the next extract. Induction is firmly positioned as part of the continuum of teacher education, as is the beginning teacher's entitlement to an induction year in which individual professional development needs are addressed. The close relationship between skills and objectives of mentoring and appraisal are offered as one such link in the continuum of professional development. The article concentrates on investigating the extent to which the intentions of government through its funding agencies have been realized in the practices of local authorities to whom the money is delegated. The future role of local authorities is raised: a topic open to debate in a climate of political change which is tending to diminish their powers and spheres of influence. It is worth considering how feasible it would be to place the entire, or the main, responsibility for induction in the hands of schools, and to consider who else might be involved.

Chapter 12

The role of mentors and teacher tutors in school-based teacher education and induction

Mike Turner

In a discussion of professional development across a range of professions Eraut (1985) identifies one of the key dilemmas for new teachers as the need for professional autonomy in tension with feelings of isolation. Stone (1987) reported on the success of having a teacher tutor as a 'buddy' and this view is supported by Marson and Pigge (1987) who reported clear indications of the success of induction programmes which included 'mentor type' teachers. Blair and Bercik (1987) went even further in stating that mentors were essential to successful induction and declaring that in order to achieve success mentors needed more than their present superficial level of training. They suggest that mentors need training in demonstrating teaching, observing teaching and coaching teachers and they should also study teacher development, new teacher needs, effective teaching, supervision skills and professional development.

Godley (1987), compared his own observations of mentor effectiveness with how mentors perceived their roles. He found that they saw themselves as being most successful in being resource persons, problem-solvers, evaluators and providers. In his observation Andrews (1987: 150-1) also took the viewpoint of mentors when he proposed five ways in which they would benefit from undertaking their role as providers of probationer induction within schools. These can be summarized as:

- modelling different instructional methodologies (gaining constructive feedback on own teaching);
- providing regular observation and feedback (thus experiencing peer supervision);
- working jointly on the introduction of new curriculum materials (thus gaining from new teachers' recent studies and gaining curriculum management expertise);
- engaging in classroom research (taking part in and encouraging critical reflection in teaching);
- acting as a resource and consultant (gaining experience in educational consultancy).

The mentor's view of the process is also examined by Crawley (1990:125–6) in an interesting overview which encompasses her own induction and her role as teacher tutor. She says of her role and training as teacher tutor that:

> The consultancy aspect of the teacher tutor role was enjoyable, talking things through with the probationer and planning and organising their release times. . . . We formed good relationships and I found the role sometimes required me to act as go-between for the head and probationers. . . . My own position in the school as an experienced member of staff who the head respected, but nonetheless a class teacher alongside the newcomers was ideal for a teacher tutor . . .

REFLECTIVE MENTORS: REFLECTIVE TEACHERS

Although the idea of the 'reflective teacher' had been widely discussed in the literature (e.g. Schon 1983; Pollard and Tann 1987) the first discussion of any significance of the concept as it applied to beginning teachers and their mentors was in a paper by Goodman (1987). She proposed that, however good their initial training as pro-active and reflective practitioners, beginning teachers: 'may not be able to act upon many of their decisions until they have gained more experience' (p. 212) and went on to propose a role for improved induction and mentoring: 'perhaps most novice teachers could become reflective decision makers given the right type of pre-service education and school based induction programme' (p. 226).

This theme of the reflective teacher is picked up by Tickle (1988) who expounds on the need for reflective mentors to be part of a research-based induction programme.

In a later paper (Tickle 1989) he proposes a clear role for the reflective mentor when he claims that probationary teacher success is linked with: 'capacity for reflection-in-action [being] recognised and developed with support from colleagues who are themselves reflective practitioners' (p. 284).

Wildman and Niles (1989) reporting on the Chesterfield Beginning Mentor Programme (USA) wrote of the advantages the mentors felt they received from their role:

- opportunities to work and talk with other teachers during mentor training;
- participation in beginning teachers' success and progress;
- and having the opportunity to reflect on their own teaching.

These mentors helped beginners:

- to learn about teaching;
- to feel good about teaching;
- to manage their workloads;
- to become part of the school community; and
- they were often friends who gave personal support.

The importance of choosing reflective teachers as mentors is emphasized by Tickle (1989) who asserts that it is the only way to ensure that new teachers themselves become reflective. There is a need for deliberate socialization – where new teachers were left to socialize themselves within the profession through trial and error there was a tendency for them to develop idiosyncratic coping strategies which led to anxiety, frustration and even failure.

Heath-Camp and Camp (1990) emphasized the importance of a deliberate policy of induction support for new teachers when they suggested assigning a mentor to each new teacher who was preferably a veteran teacher in the same field. Once this relationship was established mutual observation was recommended and a pro-active role for the mentor in regularly seeking out and offering help and advice to the new teacher. Heath-Camp and Camp were quite clear in their opinions on the dilemma of using the mentor as the new teacher's evaluator and warned that it should never be done.

THE MANAGEMENT OF THE PROBATION AND INDUCTION OF NEW TEACHERS IN PRIMARY SCHOOLS

My own research (Turner 1992) has been on the management of probation and induction in primary schools in five LEAs and mainly reinforces the above findings. The research examined the roles of LEAs and their officers in providing probation assessment and support as well as their provision of centre-based induction courses. School-based support and induction and the role of the heads and designated teacher mentors in providing structured induction courses was looked at over the period of the induction year. The pivotal role of the head teacher and the importance of their establishing empathic relationships within the school were established as important factors in effective induction for the new teacher. Case studies of the most successful probationers and their less successful colleagues when analysed suggested that reasons for some teachers' relative levels of success were to do with their personal cognitive style and the level of support they received in their placement. Another key finding was that placement itself is a major factor in individual success in the first year of teaching – inappropriate or unsympathetic schools made coping with the first year of teaching even more difficult. The participants in the research recognized the essential dilemma inherent in attempting to provide a new teacher with professional respect at the same time as supporting them in the classroom and socializing them into the school, the LEA and the profession.

The research arrives at a grounded theory derived from the views of all the stakeholders (that is to say, all those parties in the interview data who had a stake as participants or in the management of probation and induction in the primary sector). This theory asserts that it is only through empathic and professional induction that new teachers can both deliver their best performances as teachers and become contributing members of a developing professional community. The ongoing three-phase nature of teacher education and professional development (pre-service, induction and in-service) depends on mutual professional support and understanding (supporting the conclusions of the James Report (DES 1972)) the Bolam *et al.* TIPs survey (1979) and more recently the recommendations of Andrews (1986)).

In this article I will concentrate on my findings concerned with the school-based professional tutor, designated support teacher or mentor. The research pointed up the need for a more clearly defined role for mentors within schools – one for which they have been trained, have been given time and are recognized within the staff development programme. *The New Teacher in School* (DES 1982, 1988) suggested that the role of designated teacher (mentor) should not be undertaken by heads except where there was no reasonable alternative because of the clash between line management responsibilities and the more collegial role preferable for training and supporting a new teacher.

There was evidence in my survey however that where the head was committed to the system of designated teachers, as well as a close supporter and contributor to the process, induction was most successful and where heads were less committed to the idea of designated teachers and played very little part it was less successsful.

An interesting recent suggestion in the research literature (e.g. Godley 1987; Tickle 1989; Crawley 1990) is that mentors should be required to be not only supportive but pro-active trainers demonstrating their qualities as reflective practitioners as well as encouraging reflection in their beginning teacher charges. Recent evidence (Eraut 1985) suggests that providing these mid-career professionals with a new role in the school and with training to enable them to carry it out gives them a new lease of life and the recognition of their new role gives them new esteem within the profession. The support that mentors give to new teachers varies but where it is appropriate, empathic and effective there is little doubt that it not only helps the retention of staff but helps to build staff loyalty and teamwork for the future.

For every new teacher the personality of their mentor is highly significant. The relationship is one which can make or break new teachers. My interviews and case studies revealed that new teachers who had problems and who achieved a low level of success in their probationary year often had ineffective support teachers (or an unproductive relationship with them). Personality differences were one factor – Keiran (the least successful of my sample of 22) had quite strongly differing views from his designated teacher who lectured him rather than helping him and Ken (another low-achieving probationer) had a similar personality clash with his mentor who was more concerned to tell him how to teach than to listen to his problems. Rose (a rather shy new teacher who achieved poorly in an unsuitable school placement) had a designated teacher who was most successful with another new teacher but could not relate to her. Four others of the sample probationers did not rate their designated support teachers highly. On the whole they received little actual help from them apart from sympathetic enquiries and assistance with planning. Laura had a designated teacher with whom she could relate and from whom she received some help but felt she needed more active and positive support.

At the opposite extreme all of the new teachers who had very good relationships with their mentors reported a high level of support and were high achievers. Nita worked very closely with the teacher of the parallel Infant class who was her designated teacher and the interaction was on a daily basis – though the head (also an Infant specialist) undertook to deliver any training and assessment. Diane and Sally both worked in open plan schools and shared a teaching space with their designated teachers which enabled observation, feedback and even active training to be carried out in an unthreatening everyday context. Wendy and Olive were both mentored by the deputy head who made a point of seeing them every day, observing them, allowing them to observe her, working jointly with them and have regular detailed feedback discussions with them. She monitored their planning and evaluations and praised their every achievement whilst suggesting new methods and approaches to extend their skills.

Where relationships with designated teachers were good, the school atmosphere was welcoming and expectations were high (without being over-demanding) new teachers made the most progress in becoming accepted and settled professionals.

A most important caveat needs to be added here. All of the designated teacher mentors, however successful, had the same feelings about their role. They would have liked their jobs to have been more clearly defined, they would have liked training to enable them to undertake the work more effectively and they would have liked release time in order to be able to carry it out properly. These needs expressed by designated teacher mentors are amply supported by research findings: Bolam (1976) found that teacher tutors were most successful if they were trained in their role and Cobban (1976), in finding that the greatest help a probationer could be given was to get helpful feedback on lessons, added that the observer needed to be trained in order to give objective and helpful feedback. McCabe (1982) describes a possible pattern for a course for teacher tutors and Blair and Bercik (1987) suggest a core curriculum for such a training course. Crawley (1990) reported that her training as a teacher tutor greatly enhanced her understanding of her role and helped her to maximize her effectiveness. Wubbels, Creton and Hooymayers (1987) suggested that training was an essential factor in the effectiveness of teacher tutors and that it should be carried out by teacher training institutions.

Some heads in my sample made it quite clear that although they were unable to provide release time for induction designated teachers they had directed the number of hours to be devoted to the task and indicated that they would use any time provided by the LEA to increase designated teachers' involvement in induction. Only one of the designated teachers reported having been on mentor training (this was minimal – as part of the LEA system she had accompanied the head to one probationary year briefing session). In another LEA the Inspector reported that there was an element of mentor training in some areas (though not in the area studied in the research) with an intention to introduce it to all districts in the near future and two of the other four LEAs intended to have at least one early induction session jointly with designated teachers and their probationer charges. Although one LEA was intending to expand schools' roles in taking responsibility for professional development – within the terms of its school development plan – there was no clear policy for making the role of designated tutor a broader staff development role. One school in the sample of eleven had indicated that in future they would be asking their staff development teacher to undertake a mentoring role with initial teaching students and new teachers. Eraut's (1985) suggestion that taking on a staff development role 're-awakens' mid-career professionals provides a rationale for developing the role of staff development tutor with induction as part of the role.

Where the head delegated the responsibility for induction to another teacher – the deputy head or another appropriately experienced colleague – it was apparent that it was necessary for it to be monitored delegation. All concerned needed to know that the head had a clear and informed interest and that it was the head's responsibility to see that the job was done properly. The role of the head is always crucial to the success of induction programmes – whether they are actively involved or ensuring that the programme is effectively delivered.

The role of teacher tutor (designated teacher or mentor) is a highly significant one. The evidence is that where the relationship and the role are well managed it is one of the most effective ways of helping to socialize, train and realize the potential of the beginner teacher. Evidence from research from several different countries (Huling-Austin 1986; Huffman and Leak 1986; Goodman 1987; Heath-Camp and Camp 1990) suggests that the most appropriate teacher tutor is an experienced colleague, not too distant in age from the probationer, who is teaching a class of roughly the same age group the same kind of syllabus and within a similar philosophy. If the teacher tutor's class is close to, connected to or even (in an open plan school) in the same space as the beginner's it is even more satisfactory.

Once the right teacher tutor has been found there is a need for them to be briefed and, where possible, trained in their role. At the very least teacher tutors need to have some idea of the new teacher's induction programme, to be involved in their orientation and to be given details of any assessment procedures that the school and the LEA will be carrying out. In several of the schools I visited the designated teachers only knew that they were 'to look out for' the probationer and to be ready to give them advice if necessary. Research reports over the past twenty years (e.g. Conner *et al.* 1975; Tisher, 1982 and Vonk, 1983) have revealed that where teacher mentors have been designated to help probationers they have seen their role as reactive and pastoral. The most effective designated teachers in my sample, and reported in a range of research, have been pro-active and involved in training the new teachers as well as acting pastorally. There has nearly always been a willingness too, in the best teacher tutors, to learn from the recent and relevant expertise that the new teacher brings to the school in terms of techniques and knowledge.

Training for the tutor is necessary because few teachers have had the experience of observing other teachers at work and commenting on their technique and achievements. Possible patterns for training courses for teacher mentors have been proposed by many researchers including McCabe (1982), Blair and Bercik (1987), and by several contributors to Wilkin (1992). Very few teacher mentors have had experience in training and counselling adults. The ability to give ongoing support and advice without offending or appearing to be patronizing is not available to all and some training can help develop skills in a neutral setting. Skills in planning and evaluating are important as is the ability to assess the other person's work and be able to give advice that will enable them to improve and these can best be revised and developed in training sessions.

In order to be able to undertake their own training and in order to work with the new teachers on school-based induction the teacher tutors will need release time. If the new teacher's release time is divided equally between centre-based courses, school-based induction and time for their own use for preparation and evaluation it might only mean two or three half days a term release for the teacher tutor. These half days however, if used skilfully, should enable the teacher tutor to assess the new teacher's needs, demonstrate ideas and techniques and deliver specific training on particular aspects of teaching which are requested or observed needs. Where new teacher and teacher tutors have the opportunity to make visits to other schools together the learning is seen to be much greater – between them they notice more and subsequent discussion enables adaptation and adoption of ideas and techniques more effectively.

Schools which invest release time in training teacher tutors will soon realize that – if the tutors are effective – they will have developed skills which are useful across the school. As appraisal comes into schools teacher tutors will be experienced and will be able to advise colleagues on techniques. Schools which are designing staff development plans will have a colleague who has already been involved in planning a course for individuals and who has contacts with training establishments and the LEA teachers' centre and advisers. In the ILEA the teacher tutor and induction coordinator were seen as prime candidates for promotion because of their experience in working with other staff and their knowledge of other schools and LEA procedures.

REFERENCES

Andrews, I.H. (1986) *Five Paradigms of Induction Programmes in Teacher Education*, University of Bradford, unpublished PhD Thesis.

Andrews, I. (1987) 'Induction Programmes – Staff Development Opportunities for Beginning and Experienced Teachers', in Wideen, M. and Andrews, H. *Staff Development for Staff Improvement*, Lewes: Falmer Press.

Blair, S. and Bercik, J. (1987) 'Teacher Induction – A Survey of Experienced Teachers', ERIC document ED 303 405.

Bolam, R. (1976) 'Resources for INSET' *British Journal of In-Service Education*, 2, 3, 4–7.

Bolam, R., Baker, K. and McMahon, A. (1979) *The Teacher Induction Pilot Schemes – TIPS Project – National Evaluation Report*, Bristol, University of Bristol School of Education.

Cobban, I. (1976) 'A Training Model for the Teacher Tutor Role', *British Journal of In-Service Education*, 2, 3.

Conner, K., Conner, S. and Jennings, M. (1975) 'The New Teacher's Problems', *London Educational Review*, 4, 1, Spring.

Crawley, F. (1990) 'ILEA and the Induction of New Staff: A Co-ordinator's View', *Primary Teaching Studies*, 5, 2, Feb.

Department of Education and Science (1972) *Teacher Education and Training* (The James Report), London: HMSO.

Eraut, M. (1985) 'Knowledge Creation and Knowledge Use in Professional Contexts', *Studies in Higher Education*, 10, 2.

Godley, L.B. (1987) 'The Teacher Consultant Role: Impact on the Profession', *Action in Teacher Education*, 16, 1.

Goodman, J. (1987) 'Factors in Becoming a Pro-active Elementary School Teacher. A preliminary study of selected novices', *Journal of Education for Teaching*, 13, 3.

Heath-Camp, B. and Camp, W. (1990) 'What New Teachers Need to Succeed', *Vocational Education Journal*, 65, 4.

Huffman, G. and Leak, S. (1986) 'Beginning Teachers' Perceptions of Mentors', *Journal of Teacher Education*, 37, 1, Jan–Feb.

Huling-Austin, L. (1986) 'What Can and Cannot be Reasonably Expected from Teacher Induction Programmes', *Journal of Teacher Education*, 37, 1, Jan–Feb.

Marson, R.N. and Pigge, F.L. (1988) 'The Differences between Self-Perceived Job Expectations and Job Realities of Beginning Teachers', *Journal of Teacher Education*, 38, 6.

McCabe, J.J.C. (1982) 'Attitudes, Personality and Induction: A Research Note', *British Journal of Teacher Education*, 4, 2.

Pollard, A. and Tann, S. (1987) *Reflective Teaching in the Primary School*, London: Cassell.

Schon, D. (1983) *The Reflective Practitioner*, London, Temple Smith.

Stone, B. (1987) 'Why Beginning Teachers Fail', *Principal*, September.

Tickle, L. (1988) 'New Teachers and the Development of Professionalism', in Holly, M.L. and McLoughlin, C.S. (1988) *Perspectives on Teacher Professional Development*, Lewes: Falmer.

Tickle, L. (1989) 'On Probation, Preparation for Professionalism', *Cambridge Journal of Education*, 19, 3.

Tisher, R.P. (1982) 'Teacher Induction: An International Perspective on Research Programmes', New York, paper given to American Education Research Association.

Turner, M.A. (1992) *The Management of the Probation and Induction of Teachers in Primary Schools*, University of Sussex unpublished D.Phil thesis.

Vonk, J.H.C. (1983) 'Problems of the Beginning Teacher', *European Journal of Teacher Education*, 6, 2.

Wildman, T.M. and Niles, J. (1989) 'Teaching and Learning to Teach: The Two Roles of the Elementary School Teacher', *The Elementary School Journal*, 89, 4.

Wilkin, M. (ed.) (1992) *Mentoring in Schools*, London: Kogan Page.

Wubbels, T., Cretton, H.A. and Hooymayers, P.H. (1987) 'A School-based Teacher Induction Programme', *European Journal of Teacher Education*, 10, 1.

Chapter 13

Mirror, mirror on the wall, what is the fairest scheme of all? Reflections on the induction needs of newly qualified teachers

Anne Waterhouse

The two following models, illustrating the provision of induction, illustrate *the ideal*, to enable teachers to function successfully, and *the reality* which can be expected in the present climate prevailing in our schools. *The possible* is discussed later. In the ideal model the new teacher would take up her first appointment having achieved success working through the appropriate levels of a National Curriculum or similar for pre-service teachers:

A NATIONAL CURRICULUM FOR PRE-SERVICE TEACHERS

AT   1 Personal and professional qualities and commitment;
AT   2 knowledge of institutional, social, educational and economic contexts;
AT   3 knowledge of child development;
AT   4 knowledge of curriculum and subject content;
AT   5 classroom management and control;
AT   6 curriculum development and delivery;
AT   7 teaching and learning strategies;
AT   8 communications with pupils, colleagues, parents and professional support staff;
AT   9 use and organisation of resources;
AT   10 assessment, record keeping and reporting.

(Waterhouse 1992)

The school would operate on the basis of collaborative decision-making with all staff contributing to policy decisions and planning and record-keeping strategies. There would be whole-school strategies for dealing with stress with all members of the school community sharing their concerns and coping strategies (Cole and Walker 1989: 131). The school would have clear induction strategies for all teachers moving into a new role or taking up new responsibilities. The new teacher would feel assured that the school was following the DFE

Administrative Memorandum of *Guidance on Induction of Newly Qualified Teachers* (DFE 1992) and the GTC *Recommendations for Good Practice in the Induction of Newly Appointed Teachers* (GTC 1992). There would have been opportunities for her to visit the school both before her interview and following her appointment, on a permanent contract, to a post which matches the subject and age group to which she has been trained. On her visits to the school she would have been given a copy of a comprehensive staff handbook containing information about school and curriculum policies, staffing structures, resources and financial information, legal responsibilities and information about the professional support available, within school and within the LEA, to enable her to be clear about what is expected of her and what she should expect from her pupils.

A senior member of staff, with appropriate training, would have been introduced to her as her mentor and would be available whenever our new teacher needed help and guidance. The school would be sufficiently well staffed to allow the allocation of a reduced daily timetable giving her time to observe and work alongside her colleagues, visit other schools and attend regular induction meetings and courses provided by the LEA to enable her to meet with other new teachers and share experiences. Such meetings would also enable the LEA advisory service to establish positive relationships with the next generation of teachers. Additional school staffing would enable the mentor to undertake all his or her responsibilities towards the new teacher. The advisory service would also be augmented to enable headteachers and mentors to benefit from their support and also to ensure that the within-school support and provision was adequate for, and meeting the needs of, the new teacher.

The new teacher would not be subject to formal appraisal during her induction period but would be entitled to regular monitoring and assessment with appropriate feedback. Regular observation and support of her work in the classroom, by her mentor, head of department and headteacher, would be the norm and as such would not be threatening or negative. Her mentor would have quickly established a positive and supportive relationship with her and would be able to provide sensitive advice both when asked and when appropriate. Colleagues would be aware of her possible loneliness and self-doubts about her own capabilities and would respond accordingly. There would be no question of our new teacher being unsuccessful, due to the adequate pre-service training and school experience she had already gained and the quality of the support offered to her, particularly during her first year.

Would that all fairy tales were the norm but in reality of course it is impossible to offer the new teacher everything she needs and the induction period, as with all other initiatives taking place in English schools in the 1990s, is a compromise. The new teacher is highly likely to be offered a temporary contract, possibly only for one or two terms, with no guarantee of continuity. There are many schools which are currently employing newly qualified teachers in preference to experienced teachers because of the pressures on headteachers and governors to keep within the budget and pre-determined staffing costs. Consequently there may not be sufficient experienced teachers to act as mentors and, particularly in primary schools, the headteacher or deputy may nominally add the role to their many others. The growing tendency to replace experienced staff with newly qualified staff is likely to have an effect on the collective teaching competence of the school and the whole-school climate may not be able to set appropriate expectations either for staff or for pupils.

The interview may well have taken place during the summer holiday with no opportunity for the new teacher to visit the school and see it working either before the interview or before starting work. Not all schools have compiled a comprehensive staff handbook and the new teacher may only have a copy of her timetable and, if she is lucky, copies of the schemes of work and the National Curriculum ringfiles. Although the situation may be different in secondary schools the majority of new teachers appointed to primary schools have to take immediate full responsibilities for a class, with a growing and worrying tendency for this to be oversized. Staffing levels generally do not allow for the provision of non-teaching time for any staff and in the small schools the headteacher also has class teaching duties. There is therefore little possibility of the new teacher being given a lightened timetable nor for the mentor to have time to undertake observation and support. Opportunities to observe and work alongside experienced colleagues will be few and far between.

Many schools will be unable to provide supply cover to enable the new teacher to go out of school due to difficulties in covering INSET for any teachers. The advisory service, if it still exists at all, will continue to be under considerable pressure from their responsibilities for inspection, monitoring and appraisal. Newly qualified teachers will be lucky to receive one visit per term and more likely will only be observed once during their first year. Although the current models of appraisal are not required to include new teachers, future regulations may prescribe their inclusion adding to the pressures and stress new teachers are already experiencing.

Fairy stories are often based on caricatures of real life and although it would be rare to find either of the above models in practice the true picture of induction in the majority of schools reflects elements of them both. The last five years have seen an unprecedented number of changes introduced at a rapid pace. Newly qualified teachers are beginning their careers at a time when the statutory requirements of the National Curriculum alone embody the need for experienced teachers to modify their working practices. For many teachers this also includes the need for them to alter personal and deeply held values and attitudes about the nature of their own work. Teaching has traditionally been a solitary and private activity with teachers having freedom and autonomy over their own classroom practice and performance (Nias 1989:17; Alexander 1984:154). Change implies the development of new skills for teachers and also threatens established routines and relationships (Shipman *et al*. 1974:176). The Secretary of State acknowledged that 'Teachers are the key resource in any school' in the introduction into his enquiry into primary education in December 1991 (DES 1992: para.2) following goverment recognition that 'legislation alone will not raise standards' without the 'imaginative application of professional skills at all levels of the education service' (DES 1987: para. 10). Ideally these skills would include the following range of competences for all teachers:

REQUIRED COMPETENCES FOR TEACHERS

- AWARENESS
  - teaching styles
  - learning styles

  Equal Opportunities School Culture/Ethos Special Educational Needs

- PLANNING
  - use of theory
  - evaluation
  - coherence/consistency
  - differentiation
  - identification of resource needs

- RESOURCE PREPARATION
  - use of learning environment
  - organization
  - access and retrieval
  - appropriate materials

- CLASSROOM MANAGEMENT
  - differing teaching/ learning styles
  - clear expectations
  - organizational routines

- RELATIONSHIPS   – children   – individuals
  - groups
  - class
  - school
  - staff/colleagues
  - parents
  - governors
- CURRICULUM   – specific leadership expertise
  - flexibility
  - willingness to learn
- ASSESSMENT   – planning
  AND TESTING   – observation
  - variety of strategies/ resources
  - record keeping/reporting
- PROFESSIONAL   – developing expertise
  DEVELOPMENT   – personal philosophy
  - positive relationships
  - commitment/clarity of conviction

(Waterhouse 1992)

Some experienced teachers are finding it difficult to accept the relevance and need for the above competences in the face of externally imposed change to their established working practices. The newly qualified teacher is therefore taking up her first appointment at a time of dramatic change. Her experienced colleagues will be able to draw upon 'withitness, the term coined by Kounin (1970) to describe the ability to be aware of the wide variety of things which are simultaneously going on in a classroom' (Pollard and Tann 1987:122) and other class management skills but may well be experiencing difficulties with the increased subject knowledge requirements of the National Curriculum. Alexander (1992) concluded that schools need to consider their strategies for classroom and curriculum management as well as ensuring that teachers have 'the range of specialist expertise required to sustain all the subjects of the national curriculum and to deploy such expertise in more flexible ways than hitherto, considering a variety of teaching roles from generalist to specialist' (DES 1992: para.186). Within this context the new teacher has a contribution to make to the professional development of her colleagues as well as securing her own needs.

Even where schools are unable to fulfil ideal-world induction requirements there are strategies which can be employed which will be of benefit to all staff and thereby increase the effectiveness of what is offered to the pupils. The first years of teaching consolidate the new teacher's attitudes and the organizational health of the school has a vital role to play.

There are five essential requirements for teachers:

1   They should be able to influence the decisions which affect them at work.
2   In a healthy school they will have a sense of purpose and direction.
3   They should have a strong sense of acceptance and support from their colleagues.
4   Their work enables them to feel competent.
5   They have a rewarding awareness of their own development.

(Cole and Walker 1989:131)

REFERENCES

Alexander, R. (1984) *Primary Teaching*, Holt, Rinehart and Winston.
Alexander, R. (1992) *Policy and Practice in Primary Education*, Routledge.
Cole, M. and Walker, S. (1988) *Teaching and Stress*, Open University.
DES (1982) *The New Teacher in School: Matters for Discussion*, HMSO.
DES (1987) *The National Curriculum From 5–16, A Consultation Document*, HMSO.
DES (1988) *The New Teacher in School: A Survey by H.M. Inspectors in England and Wales*, HMSO.
DES (1992) *Curriculum organisation and Classroom Practice*, HMSO.
DFE (1992) *Guidance on Induction of Newly Qualified Teachers (NQTs)*, Administrative Memorandum, HMSO.
GTC (1992) *The Induction of Newly Appointed Teachers, Recommendations for Good Practice*, NFER for General Teaching Council Initiative for England and Wales.
Nias, J. (1989) 'Teaching and the Self' in Holly, M.L. and McLoughlin, C.S. (1989) *Perspectives on Teacher Professional Development*, Falmer Press.
Pollard, A. and Tann, S. (1987) *Reflective Teaching in the Primary School*, Cassell.
Shipman, M., Bolam, D. and Jenkins, D. (1974) *Inside a Curriculum Project*, Methuen.
Waterhouse, M.A. (1992) *Teaching Children And/Or Training Teachers*, paper presented to SCETT Annual Conference, November.

Chapter 14

Key issues emerging from an NFER study of NQTs

Models of induction support

Kay Kinder and Peter Earley

The NFER has just completed an 18-months research project, funded under its Membership Programme, investigating the role of local education authorities in the professional development of newly qualified teachers. The research has consisted of two main phases. The first, a questionnaire survey of all LEAs in England and Wales, took place in the summer of 1992 and examined *inter alia* induction policies and guidance; LEA induction programmes; the assessment of new entrants; links with HEIs; continuing professional development; conditions of service and professional entitlements and other issues and concerns. An interim report based on this survey was published last year (Earley 1992) and the data re-presented in the light of the Department for Education's objectives in supporting expenditure on induction training through its GEST scheme (Earley 1993). The second phase of the project was completed in summer 1993 and consisted of case studies of induction practices in thirty schools in six LEAs which had been identified for the researchers as 'good practice' schools. Termly visits were made to the eighteen primary and twelve secondary case study schools and on each occasion interviews undertaken with NQTs, induction coordinators, mentors, headteachers and other personnel involved in the induction process.

The research identified a number of key issues and concerns: these are listed in Figure 14.1 and form the basis of the project report which will be available in the near future (Earley and Kinder 1994). For the purposes of this paper, we would like to attempt an overview of our work by outlining several models of induction support. These models were found to varying degrees in the participating schools and LEAs. It is not intended, however, to do much more than present the models in this paper; hopefully they will provide a useful conceptual framework for further refinement and analysis, whilst also enabling us to focus on what we see as the key issues, especially with regard to the possible future contributions of HEIs to effective induction practices.

- importance of summer period (preparation, documentation, etc.)
- mentor relationship and collective mentoring
- term 1 support and release time
- need for external contacts with other NQTs
- importance of observation and school visits
- individually tailored support programmes
- school induction programme
- LEA induction programme
- assessment ambiguities
- SMT commitment to staff development (policy on induction?)

Figure 14.1 Key issues arising from NFER research

An attempt to identify models of induction training was made by the Teacher Induction Project evaluation team in the late 1970s (Bolam *et al.* 1979). On the basis of the data gathered the evaluators described five models of induction training. The fifth – the most complex – was called the White Paper Model and drew heavily on the James Report notion of the professional tutor, with a co-ordinated programme of internal and external support facilitated by the guaranteed release of new teachers (probationers). The NFER research schools and LEAs could have been analysed using the TIPS categories, but it was felt there was a need to provide a framework which could accommodate the full range and complexity of the various structural arrangements and interpersonal processes found in the case study schools and LEAs.

MODELS OF SUPPORT FOR NEW TEACHERS

NQTs potentially have a wide range of support/development contacts. First, the LEA may provide a central programme of induction – though the amount and timing of this varied considerably. In some LEAs, NQTs received induction sessions for two terms, in others a programme ran throughout the year. Some met once per term, others considerably more. Induction which was subject-specific rather than dealing with general issues ranked highly with secondary NQTs and, in primary, options (age-specific or subject-focus) within an LEA programme were particularly appreciated. This arena for interaction with other NQTs was seen as a crucial part of the induction year by virtually all respondents. It was an opportunity for peer support in working through issues, needs and concerns pertaining to the first year of teaching.

A second LEA contribution to induction for the NQT was the adviser's classroom visit. A corollary of the demise of the LEA adviser role generally, this input was not a feature in all LEAs. The visit may be from school/patch or subject adviser (or advisory teacher), and was usually, but not always, connected to quality assurance/assessment of the NQT. In some cases, it related to schools' serious concerns about their NQT's teaching performance. These visits were often valued by NQTs for the 'neutral outsider' role, as well as for insights into teaching performance and foci for development. Senior managers in schools also rated the fall-back position which an LEA adviser's observation offered them in the case of 'problem' NQTS.

Within schools, NQTs may also experience a central induction programme – meetings held with (or arranged by) senior staff covering a range of issues from the macro-level of school contextualization to the micro-level of pupil–teacher interaction. Headteachers (in primary), deputy heads or senior teachers usually took responsibility for this aspect of induction support.

The amount and frequency of the school central induction programme meetings again varied: weekly, fortnightly, monthly; in or out of school time (e.g. lunchtimes or after school); throughout the year, or first and second terms only. Such formalized meetings were not generally a feature of primary induction programmes, except in one or two of the larger schools (with more than one NQT). However, meetings organized with subject coordinators did figure in some smaller schools.

Opportunities for observation of practice by the NQT – within and outside schools – could also be included in the school's programme at both primary and secondary level. In many instances (though notably less frequently in primary), school induction programmes also included procedures for easing the workload of NQTs. Extra non-contact time, guaranteed no cover arrangements and no or co-form tutoring (in secondary) were all deliberate management strategies (though cover and form tutoring may be instituted later in the year). Staff responsible for induction often had an assessment function.

School induction programmes may also begin in the summer term prior to the NQT taking up their teaching post – with considerable variation in the amount of structured support offered to the NQT at that time, the kinds of information relayed and how much time the NQT spent in school. Payment for summer induction was sometimes a feature.

A further dimension to the support systems for NQT was invariably that of the 'mentor'; someone within the school offering one-to-one support relating to classroom practice, curriculum planning and/or administration. Mentors could be of varying status, usually middle management, though heads, deputies and ex-probationers might also carry the nomenclature. Mentor involvement with NQT assessment was another variable. In some cases, a second 'mentor' was instituted, often of lower status who operated in non-judgemental mode. The relationship might be formalized by regular and timetabled tutorials, or mentors might operate in responsive mode. It may follow the procedure and agenda of LEA profiles (usually competence-based) and developed, using GEST funds, in conjunction with HEIs.

Put together, the NQT's arenas of support can be illustrated as Figure 14.2:

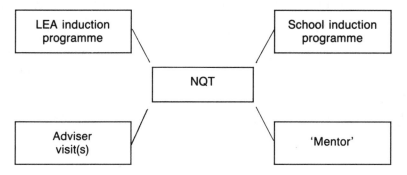

Figure 14.2 Sources of support for NQTs

However, two further networks were possible. LEAs could offer mentor training and/or support groups, most often to those with responsibility for induction, though sometimes to middle managers with mentoring responsibilities. Alternatively, or as well, written guidance in the form of handbooks, guidelines to the profile, etc. were made available. Equally (though this was rare), school induction coordinators could offer training/support to their own staff in cases where a number of mentors were operating in the school.

Four main models of induction support emerged within the case study schools:

Mono-support systems

In this system, responsibility for an NQT's induction was officially undertaken by a single person, usually in a senior management role. No other person from within the school had a formal or official input into induction. However, informal support might be offered or sought from other personnel (e.g. headteachers, year colleague) and official assessment functions undertaken by the headteacher or another senior staff member. This system more usually operated where a single NQT was appointed.

Bi-support systems

In this system, the school offered support from a mentor (usually middle management status) in addition to a central induction programme involving the provision of information on school procedures and/or opportunities for discourse on teaching and learning issues. The latter was operated by senior management in the role of coordinator of induction; the central programme may also involve individual tutorial support.

The pre-eminence of one or other of these two arenas of support was a significant variable. Thus, the mentor relationship might have formal prominence – usually signalled by timetabled meetings and/or the following of profile procedures. Sometimes, the mentor's strong personal commitment to the NQT's development was evident without these formal accoutrements. In some other examples of bi-support systems, the school's central programme emerged as the main source of induction support; with a less defined, committed or consistent role for the mentor. In these cases, the induction coordinator might make a strong pastoral commitment to the NQT. Alternatively, both levels of support might be a particularly strong feature.

Tri-support systems

Tri-support systems usually offered a combination of central meetings and/or supervision (involving senior staff), middle management mentor support (academic and/or pastoral) and, as well, another official designated personnel of similar or near similar status, such as a 'buddy', a 'critical friend', a second in charge or year leader. This extension to the support system was being formally instituted in more than one school for the following academic year as the overlap of assessment and support functions for official mentors sometimes proved problematic.

Multi-support systems

Multi-support systems referred to those school induction programmes which offered support at a number of levels (either as bi- or tri-support systems), but in addition had evidence of coordination between the levels. Thus, secondary induction coordinators running training/information sessions for mentors in secondary schools would be an example of a multi-support system or, in primary, a headteacher (in charge of induction) attending the planning meetings of the NQT's year group. Again, there was evidence of some schools adapting their induction procedures to a multi-support system, as the need for consistency between mentors emerged. However, there were no examples of mentors contributing to central programmes. Joint training of mentors/NQTs featured in one LEA but appeared not to be adopted in schools, despite several assertions by mentors and NQTs of the value – and logic – of this.

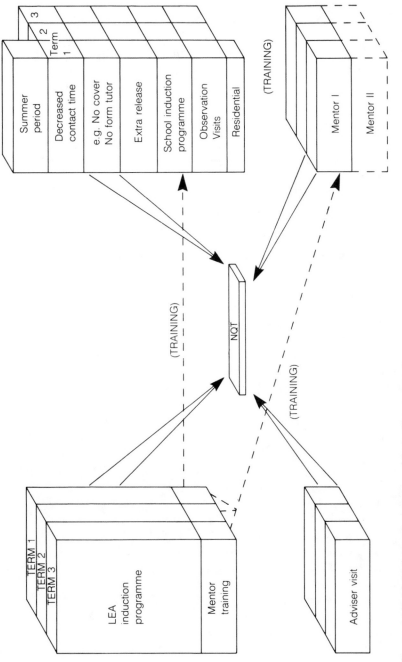

Figure 14.3 **Multi-support systems of induction support**

The final report of the project provides further details and gives specific examples of schools operating within each of the four main models of induction support. A three-dimensional representation of the multi-support system for the induction of NQTs has been attempted in Figure 14.3. The contributions that HEIs could make within such a system are many and varied, especially at a time when the role of the LEA in relation to induction has changed and, most likely, will continue to change in the light of recent legislation and other initiatives.

REFERENCES

Bolam, R., Baker, K. and McMahon, A. (1979) *The Teacher Induction Pilot Schemes Project: National Evaluation Report*, School of Education: University of Bristol.

Earley, P. (1992) *Beyond Initial Teacher Training: Induction and the Role of the LEA*, Slough: NFER.

Earley, P. (1993) 'Initiation Rights? Beginning teachers professional development and the objectives of induction training,' *British Journal of In-Service Education*, 19.

Earley, P. and Kinder, K. (1994) *Effective Induction Practices for New Teachers*, (Provisional title) Slough: NFER.

Chapter 15

Initiation rights? Beginning teachers' professional development and the objectives of induction training

Peter Earley

The significance of the induction period for beginning teachers has recently been highlighted by Her Majesty's Inspectorate (HMI 1992) and by the publication of an important document from the General Teaching Council for England and Wales (GTC 1992). In addition, since 1992 the Department for Education, through its Grants for Education Support and Training (GEST) scheme, has helped stimulate improvements in induction and supported LEAs in the training of their newly-qualified teachers (NQTs). In the first year of the grant forty-three authorities were successful in their bids for funds, whereas in 1993–94 all LEAs submitting satisfactory bids were supported. The Department has also made funds available directly to grant-maintained schools and some are allocating certain monies (e.g. £2,000) to each NQT specifically for induction purposes. The DFE's objectives in supporting expenditure by LEAs and GM schools on induction training are five-fold. They are to:

- improve the links between initial teacher training, induction of NQTs and INSET during the early years of teachers' careers, particularly through the development of profiling and competence-based approaches to professional development;
- improve coordination between the induction activities of LEAs and those of schools;
- encourage provision which is carefully differentiated to meet the particular needs of individual teachers and groups of teachers who will have obtained qualified teacher status through a variety of different routes;
- help to ensure that those responsible for induction training are effectively prepared for this role;
- help to improve the quality of written guidance and other materials used in the induction of NQTs.

(DFE 1992)

An NFER research project, funded by its Membership programme, is focusing on the role of the LEA in the professional development and induction of new teachers. It consists of two distinct phases. The first phase of the research involved a questionnaire survey of all LEAs in England and Wales and resulted in the publication of an interim report documenting current practices and future concerns (Earley 1992). The second phase of the project consists of more detailed case study work in six LEAs and over thirty schools to investigate induction *practices* within both schools and LEAs. As part of this wider study into the professional development of beginning teachers, data have been gathered on all of the aforementioned DFE objectives and it is the intention of this article to illuminate the extent to which these are said to be met by school and LEA practices. Most attention, however, will be given to the first objective of improving links between initial teacher training, induction and continuing professional development. In conclusion, a few comments concerning induction in the 1990s and the future role of LEAs are offered which have implications for the rights and entitlements of teachers new to the profession.

LINKS BETWEEN ITT, INDUCTION AND INSET

The first DFE objective is to improve the links between initial teacher training (ITT), induction and INSET, particularly through profiling and competence-based approaches to professional development. The NFER survey found that the partnership between the LEA (and its schools) and local ITT establishments was at various stages of development, in relation to both initial training and the induction of new entrants. For just under half of the seventy-two LEA respondents the partnership in relation to initial training was said to be 'beginning to develop', whereas for four out of ten LEAs it was described as 'quite well' or 'well developed', with as many as one-fifth regarding it as 'not at all developed'. It was usually the case that LEAs with developed partnerships in relation to initial training were similarly placed in relation to induction.

Respondents were asked to describe the attempts, if any, that were being made in the LEA to ensure that closer links existed between schools, ITT institutions and the authority. Several remarked that the future of any partnerships with higher education providers looked grim, that the LEA would have no role (except in the articled teachers scheme) and that with the new developments in the secondary PGCE, any links would be with the schools and not with LEAs. One respondent remarked that they were collaborating over the selection of 'training schools' but for others the LEA's role is aborted now that HE can approach schools directly'.

Others replied to this question by making reference to the existence of various planning and steering groups, the involvement of heads, teachers and LEA personnel on PGCE programmes, teacher recruitment and returner courses and the links that had been forged by licensed and overseas teacher schemes. As discussed later, LEAs were also working with HE to produce induction support materials. In one authority the GEST funds were being used to liaise with ITT institutions when graduates were experiencing problems in order that advisers, mentors and schools could ascertain whether the problems had been foreseen and what corrective action needed to be taken. Another LEA was involved in a pilot scheme with a college (from where most of its NQTs were recruited) to follow a sample of students into their first post. GEST funds had also been allocated for mentor training which was being offered by local establishments and, in one LEA, an initial teacher training and induction coordinator post had been funded in conjunction with a university department of education.

Respondents were also asked to describe any attempts that were being made in the LEA to ensure that there was a logical progression in professional development experiences. Reference was often made to the development of competence-based profiles; a continuous record of the new teacher's development which is an aid to professional learning. Many pilot schemes were reported to be operating and induction was conceived as part of an ongoing development programme. A small number of authorities were involving ITT institutions in the actual delivery of induction. One LEA used different institutions to run its secondary and primary induction programmes, whilst several others were planning to have theirs accredited. One authority, however, was not sure whether to proceed further on the accreditation front as: 'Our NQTs tell us that accredited induction would be best begun at year two, including a profile/portfolio.'

For others, the appraisal process would encourage individuals to identify strengths and weaknesses and to be more specific in identifying needs. There was a close relationship between the objectives and skills of mentoring and teacher appraisal, and the latter (as part of the professional development process) should chart any progression. Continuing professional development and the accreditation of INSET experiences was being encouraged and one LEA made specific reference to a five-year career development programme for teachers.

Records of achievement or professional development profiles for teachers were seen as eventually forming part of appraisal systems and some of these were reported to be well developed, after having been successfully trialled. They were being used with new entrants and, in some cases, NQT handbooks contained a sample personal development plan which was to be used in schools for the first year, prior to full appraisal. Other authorities had built on or adapted some of the management development profiles funded by the School

Management Task Force, or suggested that when funds were available such a profile could be produced 'linked closely with teacher appraisal, Circular 9/92, licensed teacher and NQT competences, plus [the emerging set of] school management competences'. For others, however, development work on such initiatives was unrealistic in the current climate and had been shelved as a result of personnel reductions and development of funds to schools. Any further work in this area would therefore have to be done by the schools themselves.

Respondents were asked to comment on how any plans they may have had for developing teacher profiles and portfolios linked into other INSET developments. Again, for some this was in internal matter for schools, or it was a key issue still to be addressed. For others, the emerging profiles were to form the basis of INSET content and would help identify needs and personal target setting. Records of achievement were being offered to schools which were intended to become integral to all professional development and form a career profile for all teachers: 'It would be a means of identifying and prioritizing the ongoing development needs of staff' or 'a log for each teacher to record appraisal, professional development and career management'. Profiles were seen as playing a key bridging role and would encourage 'a more holistic approach to appraisal, whole-school review and staff development'. Accreditation options were also being considered or were already in place.

There is currently much debate about the competences required for teaching and whether or not there is a need for a *nationally* agreed profile of skills or competences. A recent document from the National Curriculum Council (NCC 1991), for example, talks of initial teacher training as being unable to equip new entrants with all the knowledge, understanding and skills they will need during their career and argues for 'clearer, agreed statements of the competences new teachers are expected to achieve'. It also suggests that a set of national expectations (or standards of competence in NVQ terms) 'will bring more coherence to the first stages in the professional development of teachers and ease the transition from initial training to induction and beyond' (NCC 1991). In a similar vein, the recent government enquiry into primary education makes reference to the 'division of labour between the initial, induction and INSET, stages' and discusses the need to think in terms of three sets of teacher competences – those needed before commencing teaching, those that can be deferred until the induction period, and those that become part of ongoing INSET or professional development (Alexander *et al.* 1992). Indeed, twenty years ago another government commissioned enquiry – the James Report – made a similar point and suggested some areas of competence were best developed after initial training and 'are better left until they can be built on school experience and personal maturity' (DES 1972).

The NFER research sought views on this issue and asked respondents if, in principle, they were in favour of a nationally agreed profile of skills or competences for teachers on the completion of training (regardless of route to QTS), at the end of the first year in post, and at the end of the early phase of a teacher's career (e.g. after 2–5 years). Approximately three-quarters of all LEAs were in favour of such a profile at each of these career stages. (The proportion of those in favour was even higher when the relatively high number of non-responses was removed from the calculations.) There was much agreement that if national standards of competence were to be specified for teachers, then these should be devised by the profession itself. Local authorities, in conjunction with schools and higher education establishments and the professional associations, all had a role to play. Several respondents referred to the need for this task to be undertaken by a representative national *independent* body (with 'any proposals put out for proper consultation') or a General Teaching Council which would 'establish a framework flexible enough to accommodate local needs'. References were also made to other bodies such as HMI, CATE, the DFE, NCC, even NCVQ was mentioned by one respondent!

COORDINATING SCHOOL AND LEA INDUCTION ACTIVITIES

The NFER research sought details on the availability and value of induction programmes – whether provided by the school or the LEA – and these are discussed in the interim report (Earley 1992). HMI in its recent report also looks at induction programmes and is critical of the unnecessary overlap between school-initiated and LEA-provided induction. Similarly, the Memorandum 2/92 states that 'arrangements made by LEAs for the training and support of NQTs should supplement not duplicate provision by schools, to provide maximum benefit for the NQT' (DFE 1992: Annex A).

In the NFER survey, nearly eight out of ten respondents claimed that there were arrangements in place within the authority to avoid any such duplication. This was usually achieved in a number of ways. Schools would often know well in advance what the LEA induction programme consisted of and could thus use it as a guide and plan accordingly. Duplication was avoided, or at least minimized, by regular review and evaluation and by consulting headteacher representatives, professional tutors and INSET coordinators. In some cases there was close liaison between NQTs and the organizing member of the LEA programme, whilst in several authorities induction teams and groups of school-based mentors planned LEA programmes. Regular meetings of mentors also meant that they were made aware of the details of LEA programmes and thus could give consideration to how these might best fit or reinforce those offered by the schools. Steering groups, usually consisting of senior school staff, LEA personnel and teachers recently having completed probation, planned the LEA's central programme and requested each school to submit details of its own programme. Some authorities admitted that the arrangements to avoid duplication were fairly loose or that LEA information was not always read by senior management teams. One LEA was, in fact, using part of its GEST funds to support a research team to examine and make recommendations regarding the continuity of school–LEA induction. For others, this was less of a problem as induction coordinators advised schools to base their programmes on certain issues and to focus on particular NQT interests and needs, whilst the LEA provision was more general, concentrating on broader themes or offering a number of options.

MEETING INDIVIDUAL NEEDS

The specific grant from the DFE for induction wishes to support induction programmes that encourage carefully differentiated provision to meet the needs of individual teachers and groups of teachers (see list of DFE objectives above). The NFER research sought information on the matching of school and LEA induction programmes to the needs of individual NQTs and on any special provisions that were made for particular categories of new entrants. Very few respondents thought that the school-initiated or central induction programme did not match the needs of individual new teachers. Nearly a quarter stated that they did match NQTs' needs, whilst seven out of ten thought they 'partly' met such needs. When asked how this matching of needs was achieved, reference was made to a number of factors.

Planning groups or working parties – usually consisting of LEA personnel, heads, mentors and NQTs – were sometimes found or new teachers surveyed to discover their main concerns or difficulties and what they would like the induction programme to provide. Individual needs were identified and met through regular contacts with LEA advisors, the NQT, his or her mentor and headteachers. Advisory teachers and induction coordinators were said to have a key role in providing support tailored to each new entrant, as well as monitoring and evaluating progress. Differentiated programmes to meet individual needs would often result from a needs identification exercise, all the more important, it was suggested, because of the wide age-range of new entrants (e.g. 21–56 years) and the differing routes to qualified teacher status (QTS). In a few LEAs, reference was made to termly personal career interviews or 'personal development plans with targets and review dates'. Profiles were offered to encourage NQTs and their mentors to plan a programme.

In one authority the professional tutor discussed the NQT's profile (which had been completed during initial training) and together they were responsible for devising a personal development plan for the induction year. This was reviewed in the third term of the programme. The LEA's induction programme offered, on several separate occasions, a number of options from which the new entrant could choose. The last term's central programme, however, was totally negotiated. Other LEAs offered a 'menu' of training opportunities from which specialist choices could be made or there was total flexibility in content for part of the programme in order that individual needs might be addressed. One respondent remarked how the school's induction programme, via the mentor, considered the needs of individuals, whilst in the LEA's programme, individual NQT's needs were addressed collectively. Another remarked 'how "the process" of the centrally organized sessions allow individual needs to be addressed, i.e. few formal inputs, lots of small groups, participatory, problem-solving work'.

Over two-thirds of local authorities reported making special provision for the induction of different categories of new entrants who had reached QTS by a variety of different routes. Special provisions were made for licensed and articled teachers and in most cases they were encouraged to participate in LEA induction programmes and subject specialist sessions, as and when appropriate to their own needs. In some cases, new entrants from overseas or from ethnic minority backgrounds were targeted within each institution for extra support. In one LEA an extended programme from the multi-cultural support team was offered in addition to 'normal' induction, whilst in another 'equal opportunity issues are explored with all new entrants but teachers from ethnic minorities are offered a separate session where issues of stereotyping and bias can be addressed from their perspective'.

PREPARATION FOR INDUCTION

There was a general recognition by respondents that as school-initiated induction became more important, the LEA would be less directly involved in the provision of in-service training other than to school-based mentors. The role of mentors or professional tutors was seen as crucial and it was suggested that there would be a greater focus on their preparation, training and possible accreditation. A school-based mentor or professional tutor system was likely to replace or be given greater importance than regular adviser and advisory teacher support visits. The LEA's main thrust in the future would be 'to train mentors to be aware of ways in which they can provide meaningful induction programmes'.

As a result of the growing importance attached to the school-based professional tutor or mentor, an attempt was made to discover the extent to which authorities were currently offering training and preparation for those individuals performing this key role. Just over seven out of every ten LEAs who provided information offered such training and many of those who currently did not, had plans to do so in the future, particularly if their next GEST submission was successful. Respondents were also asked to estimate the percentage of teachers currently responsible for the tutoring or mentoring of new entrants who had been trained for this role. (This training need not necessarily have been provided by the LEA.) About half of the respondents were unable to answer this question. For those that did there was a wide distribution between LEAs and between the primary and secondary sectors within the same LEA. Secondary mentors had a greater chance of having been trained than their primary counter-parts. Eleven authorities reported that 90 per cent or more of their secondary mentors had received preparation, whereas only five LEAs said this was the case for primary schools. (Only two authorities reported having trained 90 per cent plus of both their primary and secondary mentors.) Conversely, nine LEAs stated that to their know-ledge none of their mentors had received any preparation for the role. (For three of these nine authorities this was true for both primary and secondary sectors.)

The amount of mentor training made available also varied, with most LEAs offering only a few days or several half-day sessions. A few offered longer periods and were encouraging or sponsoring mentors to enrol on award-bearing courses. In one LEA, for example, five days release was made available and an 'induction development plan' was to be produced, assessed and accredited by the local university. Certificates or Diplomas in Professional Studies were to be awarded to those who successfully completed the assignments. Alternatively, they counted as one module towards a higher degree. The training – whether delivered by the LEA or HE – usually consisted of devising school-based induction programmes, observation, counselling and mentoring skills. One authority was currently looking at a number of areas that were all closely related in terms of training needs, (e.g. new headteacher mentoring, professional review skills, mentoring for initial teacher trainees) with a view to providing a generic programme that could be applied to a particular context. Others were producing distance-learning materials or support packs for mentors, whilst at least one example was given of how trained mentors were involved in the training of others within schools who had responsibility for NQTs. Training for middle managers – heads of department, curriculum coordinators and heads of year – was seen as particularly important.

IMPROVING THE QUALITY OF DOCUMENTATION

The final DFE objective in supporting expenditure on induction training is to help to improve the quality of written guidance and other materials used for induction purposes. An earlier HMI report suggested that all schools should have the benefit of written guidelines for induction from their LEAs (HMI 1988). The NFER survey showed that virtually all LEAs provided these in some form or other. Respondents were asked to stipulate to whom guidance was offered and this was usually made available to new teachers, headteachers and mentors/ professional tutors. It was quite common for there to be a single handbook with minor modifications made according to the needs of those involved in the induction and assessment of NQTs. In a few cases separate handbooks were also available for advisers and inspectors, and governors.

The quality of the handbooks varied with the best providing information on such matters as the LEA's policy and arrangements for induction, the relationship between induction and assessment, the respective roles of those involved, suggestions for a school-based induction programme and information regarding conditions of employment and resources available within the authority. Many also contained helpful hints and advice on key areas, such as classroom management and control. A large number of LEA handbooks included extracts from or, more commonly, the entire DES Administrative Memorandum 1/90 on the treatment and assessment of probationary teachers. The more recent handbooks contained the latest DFE guidance on the induction of newly-qualified teachers (DFE 1992).

Several LEAs had been involved, either individually or in consortia, in developing detailed written guidelines and support materials for school staff. In Wales, for example, GEST funding had been deployed by four authorities to establish working parties of school, LEA and higher education personnel to produce handbooks for primary and secondary schools. The guidelines, which were piloted in the academic year 1992–93, were a product of practitioners' current experiences of both providing and receiving support in the first year of teaching. They were developed in order to improve the induction of NQTs following the abolition of the probationary year, whilst paying particular attention to induction in small rural schools and Welsh medium schools. The handbooks were to be used by anyone involved in the induction process, although the materials were primarily aimed at headteachers, mentors and new staff. Information was provided on the needs of NQTs, the management and organization of induction programmes, induction roles and tasks, examples of current (effective) practice and guidance on particular areas (e.g. school-based programmes, classroom observation, conducting review meetings). The support pack also provided the reader with some background materials and extracts from recent research findings.

INDUCTION IN THE 1990s

The NFER survey attempted to document the role of LEAs in the professional development of newly qualified teachers with particular reference to the induction period. It provides basic data about the support, training and assessment of NQTs as well as citing the views and opinions of the LEA personnel directly responsible for these activities. As such, much of what is recorded should be perceived as 'a view from the LEAs'. It comes at a time, however, when the role of the LEA is changing and its functions contracting. Unsurprisingly, the key findings of the survey reflect this period of transition and uncertainty.

Similarly, teachers entering the profession are doing so at a time of unprecedented change, especially in relation to the curriculum and its assessment. They are also commencing their careers when the traditional forms of support, monitoring and assessment associated with probation have disappeared. Understandably, respondents expressed concerns about the current phase of transition; it was not always clear what the future arrangements for NQTs would look like or if they would be an improvement on existing practices. There was general agreement that the initial year in teaching was critical and that new entrants' 'experiences of the first term were likely to colour all subsequent attitudes to the job'. A study of probationers in Scotland found that the first year's experience was most formative and would either 'turn them on or turn them off' (Draper et al. 1992). As a result there was 'a need to set high expectations and standards at this stage when there is greatest receptiveness and willingness to learn and develop'. The first year of teaching was generally recognized to be of considerable significance to the professional development of NQTs. Induction was seen as the first stage in a comprehensive programme of professional support available throughout a teacher's career. In the words of an LEA handbook, an effective induction programme meant 'never having to say you're sorry you got the damned job!'

The key question that needs to be addressed, however, is should LEAs continue to play a significant role in the professional development of NQTs? The answer to this partly depends on whether LEAs are seen as 'adding value' to the process and the NFER interim report indicates clearly the various areas in which LEAs see themselves as making major contributions. It documents the views of LEA personnel on how the arrangements could be improved and it suggests that LEAs be advised to concentrate their resources in the future in four key areas: mentor training; developing links with ITT establishments; supporting and monitoring school induction practices; and providing central induction programmes.

Most LEAs saw an important future role for themselves in some or all of the above four areas and expected schools to welcome their involvement in the provision of induction services. Many respondents believed the quality of provision was such that the schools would continue to use their services either directly (e.g. buying into central programmes or observation time) or indirectly (e.g. the purchase of support materials or mentor training). For some there was a need to give serious consideration to ascertain where their strengths lay and where to concentrate their efforts to improve. There was a commonly-held view that LEAs should provide NQTs with the support and training that was either beyond the reach of individual schools or uneconomical for them to attempt to provide. The expertise, experience and wider perspective of LEA personnel should be seen as a resource for schools to use.

It could be argued that the quality of the induction process during the all-important first year of teaching should not be totally dependent upon the school and the degree of importance it attaches to induction. A professional development entitlement or the right to support and training for beginning teachers is an idea which has existed for many years. LEAs, in partnership with schools, can support NQTs and the management of school-initiated induction.

REFERENCES

Alexander, R. *et al.* (1992) *Curriculum Organization and Classroom Practice in Primary Schools: A Discussion Paper*, London: Department of Education and Science.

Department for Education (1992) 'Induction of newly-qualified teachers', *Administrative Memorandum* 2/92.

Department of Education and Science (1972) *Teacher Education and Training* (James Report), London: HMSO.

Draper, J. *et al.* (1992) *A Study of Probationers*, Edinburgh: Scottish Office Education Department.

Earley, P. (1992) *Beyond Initial Teacher Training: Induction and the Role of the LEA*, Slough: NFER.

General Teaching Council (1992) *The Induction of Newly-Appointed Teachers: Recommendations for Good Practice*. GTC, England and Wales: NFER.

Her Majesty's Inspectorate (1988) *The New Teacher in School*, Department of Education and Science, London: HMSO.

Her Majesty's Inspectorate (1992) *The Induction and Probation of New Teachers: A Report by HMI*. Department of Education and Science.

National Curriculum Council (1991) *The National Curriculum and the Initial Training of Students, Articled and Licensed Teachers*, York: NCC.

Part D

Mentoring and assessment

Introduction

In earlier parts of this book, the issue has been raised of the relationship between mentoring and assessment. Clearly, mentors monitor the progress of mentees: they watch them at work, give advice and offer constructive criticism. To do these things implies that mentors carry out an assessment role, where they make judgements and in doing so apply assessment criteria. But what criteria? How are they arrived at? How valid are they? How consistent across mentors and institutions? Above all, what model of the teacher is implicit within a particular set of criteria and is this universally accepted?

Part D of this book focuses on these issues, and in particular examines the use of competences in teacher education. Competences have been used in teacher education in the USA since the 1970s and were introduced to the FE sector in the UK in the early 1980s. However, the major sphere of influence derives from the work of the National Council for Vocational Qualifications (NCVQ) with the award of NVQs based upon the demonstration of competences. Since 1992 competences have been part of the national regulations for initial teacher education in England and Wales (DES 1992; DFE 1993). The inclusion of competences as outcome criteria for awarding qualified teacher status (QTS) has been controversial. For example the list of competences has been strongly criticized for confusing criteria for judging standards for performance outcomes with behavioural descriptions of such outcomes (BERA 1992). But the criticism of using competences as a means of assessing teachers goes much deeper than this and seems to arise from a concern that competences can only be narrowly defined. This, it is feared, will lead to a limited skills-based interpretation of the teachers role, bereft of a dimension which involves values or beliefs. Others see the competence movement as having evolved some distance from its behaviourist roots in the USA of the 1970s to a broader approach which can embrace concepts such as the 'reflective practitioner' (Hextall *et al.* 1991).

The range of chapters included here sets out the views of the various protagonists both on the use of competences and more broadly in the area of standards and quality in teacher education. It is clearly a debate that will rage for some time and as the British Education Research Association (BERA 1992) has suggested, one that requires extensive research before a consensus can be developed.

Richard Pring's chapter which opens this part, lays the political and philosophical groundwork by probing questions of standards and quality. He argues that competences which have developed in a vocational context cannot be imported into an academic context; and that judgements in an academic context depend on the authority of experts rather than the analysis of task.

Pring's chapter should be read alongside Geoff Whitty's response in the next chapter, which explores the concept of quality in teacher education and argues for an explicit model of assessment, such as that offered by competences, where the criteria for judging outcomes are open to student and tutor. These two articles set out a broad canvas of issues for those involved in designing teacher assessment models to consider.

The next chapter by Geoff Whitty and Elizabeth Willmott analyses some of the advantages of using a competence approach to assessment. Whitty and Willmott point to: the demystification of teacher education; the clearer definition of role for both schools and colleges; the improved confidence from employers in the outcomes; and the clarity of goals for students. But they are also realistic about the potential drawback (see p. 214) and are alert to the potential for reductionism if the competences are too narrowly defined. This, however, is not a problem inherent in the use of competences but with the particular models developed by teacher educators.

The disadvantages of the competence model lead Terry Hyland to argue against it in favour of what he calls the 'professional expertise' model for further and adult education. He believes reduction to competences trivializes professional skill and that teaching is too sophisticated a process to be caricatured in this way. This view is also explored in the short chapter by John Furlong, which is a response to the government's 1992 circular.

Furlong's analysis of circular 9/92 leads to some interesting conclusions. He argues that the circular itself does not demand a narrow mechanistic approach and could be valuable in teacher education programmes in the following ways: establishing a common minimum curriculum entitlement; recognizing systematic training as one of several appropriate pedagogical strategies; and helping to structure the professional judgements of those involved in assessment.

One of the issues in assessing teaching using a competence model is that while teaching is a value-laden activity, values are hard to impart, absorb or demonstrate through a competence model. This was a problem which exercised the minds of the Open University's PGCE team when it established its competence-based model of assessment. In the chapter by Bob Moon and Ann Shelton Mayes, a solution is proposed: one where professional qualities are seen as a dimension of the competences. In setting out professional qualities as an explicit part of the assessment framework, students, mentors and tutors explore this aspect of the teacher's role at every stage of the teacher education programme. The professional qualities dimension ensures judgements on competences are made within a broad professional framework.

Whatever one's views of the competence model it is becoming widespread; and in the final chapter Sue Gifford describes the model at work for induction teachers in Surrey. Gifford's chapter asks how competence can be tracked, and comes out in favour of the developmental portfolio. The portfolio has become a common – and many would argue an effective – learning tool, which can be used to provide evidence of professional learning at any stage of a teacher's career.

REFERENCES

BERA (1992) *Reform of initial teacher training*. Report of Task Group, Research Intelligence, Spring.

DES (1992) Circular 9/92 *Initial Teacher Training (Secondary Phase)*.

DFE (1993) Circular 14/93 *The Initial Training of Primary School Teachers*.

Hextall, I., Lawn, M., Menter, I., Sidgwick, S. and Walker, S. (1991) *Imaginative Projects: Arguments for a New Teacher Education*, London, Goldsmiths' College.

Chapter 16

Standards and quality in education

Richard Pring

In this chapter I shall limit myself to the following main points.

First, I shall rehearse the political arguments about falling standards and about the need of the educational system to do something about them – and of the government, therefore, to do something about the educational system.

Second, I shall then say a little about the consequence of this – the ways of putting this concern into operation.

Third, I shall move into the more theoretical and critical domain, and place the prevailing notion of standards within the wider context of different educational traditions. The arguments about standards cannot be divorced from a much larger ethical debate about the purpose and the control of education.

Fourth, I shall reflect on all this in a more philosophical way, trying to clarify what by now (in the argument) appears more and more to be an 'essentially contestable' concept.

Finally, I shall draw all these points together very inconclusively.

POLITICAL CONTEXT

There has in the last fifteen years been a steady flow of warnings from government about 'declining standards'. The 1977 consultative document *Education in Schools* commented on Callaghan's Ruskin speech in the following way:

> [it] was made against a background of strongly critical comment in the press and elsewhere on education and educational standards. Children's standards of performance in their school work was said to have declined. The curriculum, it was argued, paid too little attention to the basic skills of reading, writing and arithmetic, and was overloaded with fringe subjects.
>
> (DES 1977)

Already we see two kinds of decline in standards – poor performance in the basic skills (children not writing, reading, adding and subtracting as well as a similar cohort of children would have done in a previous age) and the neglect of more traditional subjects as these were usurped by fringe subjects (no doubt peace studies and other forms of integrated studies). But the document goes on to mention poor discipline and behaviour and the neglect of economic relevance.

The consultative document was produced by a Labour government, but one which was reacting, first, to well-orchestrated populist appeals from the political Right and, second, to the concerns of commerce and industry which argued that the output of the educational system – yes, even those who came up to traditional standards – were ill-prepared for the economic world they were entering into. Therefore, there were four areas of quality concern – basic skills, traditional learning, discipline and economic relevance. 'Quality' is reflected in the standards, explicit or implicit, to which reference is made when performance is judged. In that sense quality and standards are logically related concepts, and therefore the four areas of quality concern picked out in Callaghan's speech reflect four different kinds of standard – which kinds may not always be compatible with each other.

Mr. Eggar, in addressing the fifth annual conference of the Joint Council for the GCSE, said that 'many of the challenges which have to be faced have to do with standards. There is the need for adequate differentiation, particularly for more able pupils' (Eggar 1991). This requires the introduction of level 10 in National Assessment 'which is demonstrably more demanding than the existing Grade A of GCSE'. It is the job of schools, therefore, to make sure that the performance of pupils, in each of these general standards areas, improves in the sense of measuring up to standards further up the hierarchy. Thus presumably the standard expressed in 'can read fluently most words with four syllables' is higher than the standard expressed in 'can read fluently most words with three syllables' because the one would seem to subsume the other (but this is not necessarily true).

Two questions therefore seem to be appropriate: why choose a particular objective of performance as *the* standard of measurement? and why choose one level, in the hierarchy of levels, rather than another as the appropriate standard for a particular age group? The first question would itself seem to raise two subsidiary questions: why are these particular statements of objectives chosen out of an infinite number of possible statements (that is, is there anything in the nature of historical enquiry or economic relevance which makes these rather than those the appropriate standard bearers) and who has the authority for deciding which, amongst many competitors, are to be the appropriate standards? The National Curriculum and the subsequent reports on the Foundation Subjects do not, on the whole, address these questions.

At the post-16 stage of education, ministers have identified a different sort of problem. They seem to be more satisfied with the standards that have been set by 'A' level boards, less satisfied with the number of those who 'measure up' to those standards. Thus, again and again, attempts to reform 'A' level examinations have foundered on the confidence that those in power have placed in the 'A' levels. Mark Carlisle, when in office, argued for the retention of 'A' levels as guarantees of high standards. They have been variously described by ministers subsequently as the 'gold standard', the 'flagship' and 'the jewel in the crown'.

There is something odd and inconsistent in this, because pre-16 standards of GCSE and of national assessment are the kinds of things which can be expressed in statements – or at least, that is what is intended in the GCSE and national assessment reform. They are the objectives against which performance can be measured; performance either does or does not meet these explicitly stated objectives. However, this is quite clearly not the case in 'A' levels where such explicit objectives are rarely provided and where grades therefore refer not to 'absolutes' but to relative places within the overall distribution of marks.

Higher education has not escaped the concern over standards – not that standards are said to be declining (which institution would admit to that?) but that standards will inevitably decline if numbers are increased without a parallel increase in resources.

MONITORING OF STANDARDS

We have seen therefore that, in meeting the public concern over standards, the government has pursued several courses of action. It has established 'absolute standards', hierarchically related, in areas of traditional learning. It has re-asserted the 'flagship role' of 'A' levels. It has expressed confidence in the standards set by the degree awards of higher education, despite the decline in the unit of resource.

Nonetheless, it is one thing to assert these things. It is quite another to check that the assertions are correct – to monitor what is in fact the case. Monitoring standards in schools and in higher education has been of several different kinds.

First, this has been a central role of HMI (and of local advisers). It would be argued that the accumulation of experience, the corporate awareness of what is good work, the sense of judgement established through constant critical discussion in the context of widely observed practice – that such professional activity gives insight and judgement that escapes others.

Second, there are the results of public examinations. Thus, the examinations at GCSE , or at 'A' level are graded; grades are totted up or averaged; league tables are produced in the Good School Guides.

Third, there have been, in the last fifteen years, the attempts by the Assessment of Performance Unit to provide longitudinal comparisons of performance across the curriculum and, on a very light sampling basis, across the country at different ages. The reports on languages, on science and on mathematics have provided us with the very best evidence available on what pupils can or cannot do.

Fourth, the educational system has been monitored by the occasional evaluation study – the in-depth probe by researchers.

The major weakness in these ways of monitoring standards, pointed to by critics, is the lack of explicit and detailed criteria by which judgements are made. Just as a knife is judged good or bad according to how well it cuts – and the criteria for cutting well can be established beforehand (does it slice through this tomato without the juice spitting out?) – so too might any performance be judged by its 'fitness for purpose'. That being so, then the purpose of the activity needs to be clearly spelt out, and the criteria for successfully achieving that purpose established.

Therefore, quality is now to be 'assured' through the application of 'performance indicators', and such indicators are to permeate the system of education at every level. Each institution should have such indicators. One performance indicator will be examination results, but these examination results in turn will arise from the application of performance indicators to the students. Furthermore, these performance indicators will be explicit and justified against the purposes that the institution or examined subject are trying to serve – and, hence, the importance of 'mission statements', a mixture of ethical judgements (about what is worthwhile) and specific goals, which pin that worthwhileness down to attainable objectives.

This quality assurance requires a system – a mechanism for establishing the purposes, for deciding upon the criteria which demonstrate the achievement of those purposes, and for checking whether those criteria have been applied. Such a mechanism is increasingly modelled on that of industry. Thus, distinctions are made between quality control and quality assurance. 'Quality' is seen in terms of fitness for purpose, that purpose being established partly by the customers of the service but mainly by the government as the custodian of the interests of the customer. 'Quality control' refers to the particular procedures for ensuring that those purposes are established and that the performances conform to specifications (that, for example, x number of students obtain the grades in different subjects which indicate that the learning objectives have been met). Quality control (and thus quality assurance) needs constantly to monitor the 'value addedness' of the institution. There have to be measurements, and measurements of performance both before and afterwards (both at the input and at the output stages) should be provided under the quality control system. Quality requires therefore the adoption of business practice – and business language: fitness for purpose, quality control and assurance, mission statements and performance indicators, value addedness and audits.

DIFFERENT CONTEXTS

Academic

The contrast is frequently drawn between the academic and the vocational. This distinction over-simplifies reality but it nonetheless permeates our thinking about the aims of education – and thus about our conception of 'standards'. The academic tradition lays stress upon intellectual discipline and upon the high standards of thinking, arguing, enquiring, experimenting, speculating that are part and parcel of an intellectual discipline. Such disciplines are characterised by their own distinctive logical structures – by the concepts that must be mastered if one is to think in a disciplined way, by the exacting methods of enquiry, by the special demands of proof and of evidence. To learn to think in a disciplined way is to grasp certain rules of procedure, concepts, ways of testing the truth or correctness of what is being said. It is to learn to experience the world from a particular perspective.

Such disciplined ways of thinking develop over time. They are sustained by social arrangements partly recognized in learned societies and professional associations, partly reflected in traditions of criticisms and in power structures and authorities recognized by people with similar interests. Academic disciplines therefore have both a logical and a social dimension. They are ways of identifying and of exploring problems which, through criticism and through the identification of new problems, are constantly evolving, establishing new standards, new criteria of good performance.

The acquisition of different academic disciplines is often seen as a hallmark of 'liberal education' – the liberation from ignorance, from mere common sense, and from narrowness of vision.

Characteristic of this initiation into those different forms of knowledge is a lack of clarity about ends and standards, although there are recognised authorities who are able to recognise high standard work when they see it and who are able to show the apprentice (through example very often) what counts as meeting the standard. This might be shown though not stated – the manifestation of the universal in particular. Moreover, the apprentice learner comes to see this for himself as he struggles to improve the style of an essay or to render more elegant a piece of poetry or to make more incisive an argument; such a struggle only has meaning in the context of implicit standards in reference to which one feels dissatisfied with one's efforts and motivated to do better.

There is a dominant academic tradition which sees quality of intellectual endeavour (and the implicit standards of good or bad performance) to lie within specific traditions of disciplined enquiry. Such traditions are defined partly in terms of the relevant concepts, procedures, problems, tests of validity. And these concepts etc. can be used more or less effectively, more or less correctly. Thus there *are* standards but these, though acknowledged in one's intellectual efforts, are more often than not unspoken. Though recognized in judgements made, they cannot often be anticipated. And the application of these standards does not entail the explicit formulation of them. Hence, the importance of the 'judgement' of those who are authorities within the subject (the HMI, the academics, the professional teachers). And, hence, the importance, too, of a period of initiation – the gradual recognition by the learned of the many standards which are acknowledged within the exercise of intellectual disciplines.

Vocational

By contrast, vocational learning has come to stress not tradition, but job-relatedness. It requires the acquisition of those skills and understandings which are required for doing specific jobs. Successful learning signifies fitness for purpose; one first identifies the requirements of the job and then one specifies the 'can do's', the competences that enable one to do the job. The competences, revealed in the undertaking of standardized, job-related tasks, constitute the standards. They are tested out in 'on the job performances', which thus become the indicators that the person is competent and thus has met the explicitly stated standard. Performance indicators are not the same as standards – it is always logically possible that a particular performance might be a fluke and might not demonstrate the mastery of a particular competence. But, nonetheless, the description of the indicators, of the competence and of the tasks on which the competence is to be demonstrated, must be sufficiently close for several successful performances to be conclusive evidence that the standard has been reached.

The development of national vocational qualifications (NVQs) presupposes this connection between standards, competences, and performance indicators. Thus, an NVQ is defined as

> a statement of competence clearly relevant to work. . . . The statement of competence should incorporate specified standards in
> – the ability to perform in a range of work related activities; and
> – the underpinning skills, knowledge and understanding required for performance in employment.
>
> (Jessup 1990)

To be competent (i.e. fit for the specified purpose such as hairdressing or welding) can be broken down into various units which in turn can be analysed in terms of a coherent range of elements: thus, no doubt the competent hairdresser will be competent in several aspects (or 'units') – washing the hair, styling it, etc. And each of these units (styling, for example) can be analysed into interrelated but distinguishable elements (for example, cutting fringes, shaping the hair at the nape of the neck, covering bald patches). Competence in each element can be verified through performance, and overall competence at a defined level ascertained. Essential to the whole enterprise is the precision with which competences are stated and the performance indicators made explicit. Unlike the standards implicit within academic studies, the standards of vocational competence are quite explicit, and the performance criteria so clear that there can be little doubt about what the successful learner can do.

Unlike academic standards, vocational ones are not mysterious entities slowly internalized, requiring a gradual apprenticeship, possessed 'more or less' and in varying degrees. Rather, one either is or is not competent. One can either do the job as it is analysed in terms of a range of performances or (as performance indicators show) one cannot. The hairdresser can either shape the hair as requested at the nape of the neck or s/he cannot. In that sense, standards are absolute.

Moreover, the competence is demonstrated in the performance. Courses might or might not be necessary for the achievement of competence – the end is logically disconnected from the means. And therefore courses (where they exist) are assessment led. They are but a means to an end. They, unlike the context of academic standards, do not require, as intrinsically necessary, the apprenticeship, the participation in the very activities through which the standards come to be recognized.

It is the aim of the National Council for Vocational Qualifications eventually to produce a list of competences relevant to all the jobs in every aspect of industry and commerce, and to mark these competences (or clusters of competences) with qualifications pitched at five different levels. According to Jessup, 'the specification of competence [in each of these 1,000 or so qualifications] plus performance criteria provide the operational realisation of the new kind of standard' (Jessup 1990:17).

The apparent advantage of this conception is that it eliminates the subjectivity, the dependence on authority which is so often associated with judgement of quality within the academic tradition. For, in the case of vocational standards, these are the explicitly stated competences defined in terms of the observable performances which the competent person can be expected to do. They depend not on the authority of experts, but on the analysis of tasks. They reflect, quite objectively, a fitness for purpose.

This rather seductive vision of standards and explicitly stated competences can, so it is believed, so easily be transformed into a model for general and academic education, too. Cannot one analyse competent philosophizing into a range (a wide range, maybe) of sub-competences each with its performance indicators (for example, the ability to employ 'modus ponens' in the presentation of an argument or the ability to rehearse the main tenets of logical positivism)? And, in so doing, might one not reduce the length of philosophy courses for some as one checks out beforehand (and regularly throughout a course) the number of competences that the potential philosopher already has and that he or she no longer needs to be introduced to? Performances, indicating competence, can be given in specially constructed workshops or in answer to multi-choice questions. One ought to be able to accredit prior learning, even amongst aspiring philosophers.

There are, however, difficulties. NCVQ has not felt able to reduce all competences to those which can be narrowly and unambiguously related to a limited set of performance indicators. There has recently been discovered the need for general competences (manifest in the newly invented GNVQs – or General National Vocational Qualifications). Moreover, a lot has been written about 'core skills' (of communication, problem-solving, numeracy and personal effectiveness). Such core skills must be taught through the academic subjects and the vocationally oriented learning tasks.

Other difficulties there are, too, which those who wish to equate standards with criteria of competence or 'fitness for purpose' fail to recognize. In particular, there are the problems of 'absoluteness' which, for example, NVQs aim to reflect – either you can or you cannot turn a piece of wood at level 2. You either are or are not competent. There is no room for shades of competence – or at least, where there are such shades they are thought to be a defect in the analysis, not a reflection of things as they are. And yet quality is often reflected in such adverbial qualifications of competence (or 'can do's') as 'elegantly', 'gracefully', 'imaginatively', 'intelligently', 'creatively'. Such adverbs imply judgement which is irreducible to the application of pre-conceived performance indicators.

Learning to be capable

Disagreement is not simply between those within an academic tradition (who see standards to be logically tied to achievement within distinctive disciplines of enquiry and of scholarship) and those who tie standards to 'fitness for purpose', where purpose is analysed into fairly specific job-related requirements. There is disillusion with both conceptions of education and training and with the perceived relationship between them, for there are capabilities or core skills or transferable qualities which are sufficiently general and generic as to apply to a wide range of often unpredictable situations. Such capabilities are seen to be more important than job-related competences (for these might soon be out of date as the economic climate changes) or than the concepts and understandings of particular academic disciplines (for these, without regular use, will soon be forgotten).

Responding to the market

In each of the three contexts outlined above, quality, and thereby the standards implicit within our assessment of quality, presupposes some objective basis for judgement – some base from which might be evaluated the achievement of the learner. Indeed, the very word 'achievement' has built into it the idea of standard, of good or bad performance, of *mastery* of something which is worthwhile, of improvement, and often of struggle as one feels dissatisfied with one's performance (in painting, say, or in playing a game). It is not clear what sense can be given to achievement, to improvement, to dissatisfaction, to struggle, to effort without the implicit recognition of standards against which one judges what one has done or produced. Part of being educated is to come to recognize these standards and to internalize them – to apply them to oneself. In that sense, standards imply an objectivity, a comparative dimension to one's own performance that cannot be simply the product of whim, of one's own wishes, of what lies in one's own self-interest. This may seem a rather exiguous sense of objectivity, but it is important. It indicates that the standards implicit in all judgement cannot simply be created at one's convenience. One's performance has to measure up to standards which are inseparable from the activity as one perceives it and these perceptions have themselves been internalized from participation in a form of life shared with others.

The academic, vocational and pre-vocational traditions agree on this general point about the objectivity of judgement – and *therefore* on the objectivity (in this sense) of standards.

There is, however, a competing tradition which seeks to place standards in a very different context – a context which embraces relativism as the only rational position to adopt on matters of value. Thus, it would be argued, there is no rational base for saying that one area of learning is more worthwhile than another, or that one activity is superior to another, or that one form of understanding is more valuable than another. In that case, there are no standards, objectively speaking, to be maintained by the masters of those standards, by those who are authorities within the educational world. In a strange and contradictory way, that seems to be partly the position of this government despite its frequent concern for standards.

Frequent reference is now made to consumer choice as that which will ensure the raising of standards. It is assumed that, as the consumers hunt around for 'the best' service, so the competition for selling what is offered will result in greater efficiency, more effective teaching. But the corollary of market forces operating in a world of moral scepticism is that market forces define as well as promote standards, for the consumer always knows best. Quality is that which pleases the consumer – whether it be the top ten in music or Harold Robbins in literature. There are no authorities of what is good in education; only competent technicians in delivering that which the consumer wants.

To conclude this section, I have placed the debate on standards, and thus on the quality of education, within the context of different traditions concerning the aims and values of education and training.

The academic tradition understands standards as the measures, certainly, of correctness, appropriateness, stylishness, validity, within distinctive disciplines of enquiry, but measures which more often than not are implicit only within these enquiries, teased out, not by politicians and civil servants, but by philosophers of science or of history as they reflect on the processes of science and the process of thinking historically. They can be applied without being explicitly acknowledged; they are acquired slowly over a period of time and always are only more or less understood; they are passed on to the next generation of students through example, through the correction of the particular, not through the definition of the universal.

The vocational tradition, which, when properly restricted, can sit happily alongside the academic tradition, is concerned with 'fitness for purpose' where those purposes are clear and specific. They are derived from an analysis of the economic task. Standards concern the competences which demonstrably are the means for achieving those purposes. In theory, there should be nothing controversial about such standards – or in ascertaining whether they have been reached, for they are spelt out in terms of performance indicators, and performances, on standardized tasks, can easily be observed.

However, this task has not proved to be easy, and there is a third and importantly different tradition which trades on the vocational but wants to expand into the academic, thereby transforming it into something different. This tradition speaks of more general competences – not those specific to plumbing or to hairdressing, but those specific to life in general.

Fourth, however, we see a more radical interpretation of standards explicitly embraced only by those who have been marginalized within the political debate. That interpretation ultimately is distrustful of standards – or at least of any values other than those which the consumer wishes to adopt.

CONCEPT OF STANDARDS

In this final section, I want briefly to pull together various strands of the argument, for, in pointing to these competing traditions, I have failed to say exactly what standards are or what is meant by standards. That, of course, must be the case because the meaning of any word is related logically to its use within a language or within a field of discourse. Hence the importance of locating 'standards' within different traditions and wide discourses – including the dominant metaphors of each one.

Nonetheless, there are certain logical features of the word and certain philosophical considerations about human action which help us decide between different traditions – or at least the limitation of each.

First, there is something odd about standards going up or down. The *performance* of pupils, as measured by standards, go up or down, but not the standards themselves. If standards were to rise or fall, that rise or fall could only be judged to be so against a different type of standard – viz. those standards whereby one assesses the standard of standards, and thus one is into an infinite regress.

Second, however, one might see 'standards declining' as meaning that *performance* is not coming up to a standard to the extent that it once did or that performance is coming up to a standard which is different from that which once it came up to – and different in the sense that it is less demanding than the other standards. Levels of standard, as in the National Curriculum, must mean something of this kind – that is, the same kind of activity envisaged at various levels of difficulty and thus differentiated in some norm-referenced way. For example, one can see how long division presupposes a range of arithmetical activities, such that there is some logical progression from simple addition and subtraction to the more complex operation. Each level represents a different standard, but the standards are logically related in so far as success in one presupposes success in the others. In this way one has differentiated, hierarchically related standards.

Third, however, standards are bench marks, they are criteria whereby one assesses or evaluates the quality of a particular activity or process. And that quality must depend upon the identification and the purpose of the activity – upon the values that are embodied within it. Strictly speaking, there are as many standards as there are activities; there are as many activities as there are intentions and purposes that drive people on. There are standards peculiar to house cleaning, painting landscapes, writing Shakespearian sonnets, appreciating the impact of science on the environment. Moreover, as purposes and values change, so too must the standards whereby we assess those activities. As mathematicians reflect on the nature of mathematics, as employers require different sorts of mathematics in order to meet a changing technological world, so does the value that we attach to mathematics change and so does the nature of the activity – and so, too, therefore, do the standards whereby we judge achievement within mathematics. Similarly, just as society comes to value different forms of life, just as we come to embrace different virtues (enterprise rather than modesty, autonomy rather than obedience), so do our moral purposes change, and so too do the standards whereby we assess moral worth. Standards have neither gone up nor come down. They have simply changed. Such considerations make nonsense of the aggregate of marks whereby we talk of the standard in mathematics or *the* standard of morals. And it makes it logically impossible to make sensible comparisons of standards across the generations – or, indeed, across cultures unless those cultures and those generations share a common set of values with regard to that activity.

CONCLUSION

The difficulty in talking about standards is that the concept is, like 'truth', or 'goodness', or 'beauty', both logically indispensable and yet impossible to define without considerable philosophical elaboration. That worries those with a narrow conception of rationalism who believe that all concepts can be operationally defined and their use made clear and unambiguous. Governments whether to the Right or Left who seek to control outcomes – to bureaucratize education and turn it into something else, to transform teacher into deliverers of a curriculum – will no doubt be seduced by this temptation. They will ignore the complexity of these notions and treat them as though they can be reduced to simple definitions.

But that is to abstract them from the wider social and educational traditions in which they have their meaning. I have simply articulated a little those different traditions. To ignore these differences can so easily distort what teachers have traditionally been about, namely, to introduce the next generation to those ideas and skills and beliefs that have survived critical scrutiny. And to be aware of this is important for, in failing to be aware, there are attempts to change our educational institutions out of all recognition.

REFERENCES

Department of Education and Science (1977) *Education in Schools*, London: HMSO.
Eggar, T. (1991) Address to the Joint Board for GCSE, 27 September.
Jessup, G. (1992) *National Vocational Qualifications: Outcomes*, Lewes: Falmer.

Chapter 17

Quality control in teacher education

Geoff Whitty

CONCEPTIONS OF QUALITY

Polytechnic directors argue that, in higher education generally, there should be considerable flexibility in interpretation of the concepts of quality and academic standards rather than imposing one arbitrary standard. They argue that assessment of quality needs to be related to an institution's own mission and declared intentions (MacGregor 1990). However, part of the problem is that higher education as a whole is increasingly being asked to pursue multiple, and sometimes contradictory, missions. In activities that span the academic/vocational divide, such as teacher education, this is especially the case. Arising from this, I want to consider the relevance to teacher education of the four 'contexts' identified by Richard Pring (Chapter 16 this volume) and the different sorts of quality indicators they seem to imply. In doing so, I will explore how far it is appropriate for quality in teacher education to be assessed by academic criteria, vocational criteria, capability criteria or market criteria, and whether we should be assessing quality of intake, process, content or output.

Academic

In teacher education academic criteria were increasingly used during the 1960s and 1970s, partly in order to enhance its status. This applied both to subject studies within the emergent Bachelor of Education (B.Ed.) degree, but also to the theory of education. There are those who argue that academic conceptions of quality are not applicable to teacher education at all, but there is a rather stronger argument that different criteria should apply to different elements of teacher education. This might seem to imply that, in the B.Ed. course, academic criteria of quality should be applied to subject studies and vocational ones to professional preparation. But what standards should we then apply to what were traditionally called educational studies?

And would it mean that only criteria of vocational competence should be applied to the Postgraduate Certificate in Education (PGCE) course?

In the past, most courses have avoided these issues. But, in the face of an apparent, though not unambiguous, official shift in the direction of entirely vocational criteria for teacher education (though probably not subject studies), the prevailing view within higher education will almost certainly be a defensive one. Most academic teacher educators would want to support Pring in defending the place of traditional academic criteria, even if not their dominance. Thus, there would probably be general agreement with CNAA's insistence (1900–91) that all courses leading to its awards, whether academic or vocational, must be concerned with:

> the development of students' intellectual and imaginative powers; their understanding and judgement; their problem solving skills; their ability to communicate; their ability to see relationships within what they have learned and to perceive their field of study in a broader perspective. Each student's programme of study must stimulate an enquiring, analytical and creative approach, encouraging independent judgement and critical self-awareness.

However, CNAA does ask us to be explicit about academic criteria, as well as vocational ones, and, while Pring's defence of academic criteria in education is well taken, I have some misgivings if this involves resort to the argument that implicitness is the very essence of academic judgement. He suggests that standards in the academic tradition are implicit, while those of vocational competence are quite explicit. In that context, we should heed the words of the French sociologist Pierre Bourdieu (1976) who criticizes educationists for finding 'democratic' excuses for maintaining traditional implicit approaches to education by denouncing possible alternatives as 'technocratic'. For Bourdieu, implicit pedagogies and modes of assessment reflect an 'aristocratic' culture and are thus class-biased.

Pring also seems to regret that moves towards credit accumulation and accreditation of prior learning and experience are potentially undermining some of the features that embody quality in academic courses. I share some of his concerns, especially over the fact that quality criteria relating to coherence and progression, once the touchstones of CNAA validations, now seem much less in evidence. Appropriate quality criteria for modular and credit accumulation programmes certainly need urgent attention. However, these very same developments are also opening up opportunities for higher education amongst groups previously denied them and that might in itself be used as an indicator of quality provision. The number of people entering teacher education by what the Department of Education and

Science (DES) still calls 'non-standard routes' may be as important as the numbers with high 'A' level grades, and especially so if their end results are comparable.

Vocational

Under this heading, Pring concentrates largely on the National Council for Vocational Qualifications (NCVQ)-inspired move towards competence-based assessment which makes the quality of outcomes both paramount and explicit. Higher education in general is having difficulty in adapting to a shift towards an emphasis on the quality of outcomes beyond examination results. A letter in the *Times Higher Education Supplement* (29 March 1991) suggested that quality control in industry was 'Does the car work?', but in higher education the equivalent was 'Does the lecturer turn up to his classes?' Yet, in teacher education at any rate, we also do surely have to ask the question 'Can the new teacher teach?' If the competence-based approach to training quality places an undue emphasis on such outcomes, there can be no harm in reminding higher education of the importance of this measure of quality, especially in an activity like teacher education.

In fact, in the last few years, there has been considerable official interest in the idea of competence-based teacher education. I have written at length about this elsewhere and will not dwell on it here (Whitty and Willmott 1991) (see Chapter 18). However, while there are a lot of problems about competence-based approaches, it is important to recognize that they can be rather more flexible and adaptable than at first sight appears. We can all cite horror stories about reductionism in American examples and even some schemes of Further Education (FE) teacher education over here, but outright rejection of competence-based quality criteria may be too hasty. Indeed, teacher educators need to consider whether, as Eric Tuxworth, one of the earliest British writers on the subject suggested, our suspicions derive from the fact that such approaches 'remove some of the mystique and institutional restrictions that surround teacher education' (Tuxworth 1982). It could just be that 'producer interests' are at work here, as the government might put it.

There are, though, legitimate concerns about the extent to which this approach can undermine the importance of a coherent programme of study, often seen as a necessary part of teacher education. But specifying more explicit exit criteria certainly encourages us to ask questions about fitness for purpose rather than just assuming it. It is also not yet clear what the limits to the use of competence-based approaches are, and the B.Ed course would actually be an ideal testbed for exploring how far competences can be applied to general and academic education as well as vocational training. Certainly competence-based standards developed for routine jobs in industry will not be applicable even to professional training. However, if they recognize the importance of underpinning knowledge and understanding, and generic professional competences as well as specific classroom skills, competence-based criteria may be worthy of far more exploration than is sometimes assumed.

Learning to be capable

I have argued on other occasions that even courses based around the fashionable concept of the reflective practitioner may not be as incompatible with a competence-based approach as is sometimes suggested. Having told us that 'teaching is not reducible to a set of technical operations', the authors of a recent pamphlet go on to say they are 'not running away from the issue of the systematic appraisal of teaching competence' and they argue that even the quality of reflectivity can be formulated as a series of competences that can be monitored. Two of their examples are:

- A reflective practitioner can articulate and defend his/her own purpose as a teacher and relate this to other professional opinion
- A reflective teacher treats teaching as an experimental process, recognizing the necessity of turning reflection into action, choosing between alternatives, and critically evaluating the process.

(Hextall *et al.* 1991)

In the light of the problems Pring identifies with the term 'competences', it might even be preferable to argue that these sorts of competences are examples of what he and others describe as learning to be capable, or the 'core skills' of professional education.

I suspect that in learning to be capable the quality of the experience and quality of the outcome are extremely difficult to disentangle in practice, whatever the theory of an outcome-led approach to education and training as expounded by NCVQ. On the other hand, if there are good grounds for requiring people to take courses, rather than merely demonstrating their capability, we surely owe it them (especially if they are mature students) to make explicit why the particular learning experience of being on a course is an essential facet of quality. While there may be a firm philosophical basis for what critics dismiss as the mystique of teacher education, both the competence movement and the capability movement offer positive scope for its demystification. But to recognize that is by no means tantamount to suggesting that quality should be measured, and funding allocated purely on the basis of the number of competences demonstrated by students.

The market

With regard to the market approach to quality, there is a problem about who counts as the consumer in the case of teacher education. The student's interest in whether the lecturer turns up to lectures is one test of consumer satisfaction, but the future employer is likely to be most interested in the quality of the output in relation to its affordability. Thus there is confusion about whose consumer choice is assumed to constitute the guarantor of quality within the market model of education and training. If there are multiple consumers with different interests, then this also implies a need to recognize multiple dimensions and multiple measures of quality. As for the paradox in government thinking to which Pring points, it will be interesting to see how far the neo-liberal commitment to the market will outweigh the neo-conservative concern to ensure the maintenance of traditional values through the control of curriculum content (Whitty 1989).

QUALITY CONTROL AND QUALITY ASSURANCE

It appears then that all the views of quality identified by Pring have some relevance to the assessment of quality in teacher education. I now want to focus on notions of quality control and quality assurance. The Academic Unit Audit (AAU) established by the Committee of Vice-Chancellors and Principals (GVCP) defines terms in this way:

- Quality control is an operational function applied at all levels by an institution to its teaching activities and is concerned in detail with the way these are organised, undertaken and evaluated, in order to ensure fitness for purpose, an optimised use of resources, and the achievement of their identified goals.
- Quality assurance is concerned with the way in which an institution, in discharging its corporate responsibility for the courses and qualifications it offers, satisfies itself that it has effective structures and mechanisms in place to monitor the quality control procedures employed, and that these promote the enhancement of existing standards.
- Quality audit is the monitoring of those structures and mechanisms to ask of institutions how they themselves make sure that their own standards are adequate.

While there is considerable confusion in the use of these terms within institutions, I will try to follow Pring's usage. His use of the term 'quality control' is broadly consistent with the Unit's definition, while he uses the term 'quality assurance' to cover the concepts of quality assurance and quality audit.

It should be clear from what I have already said that, in introducing more explicit quality control procedures, we do not actually have to choose between conceptions of quality traditionally employed in either academic or vocational contexts. Although there are those who argue that the only thing that matters is where you get to rather than how you get there, the notion that stressing exit criteria and competences inevitably involves the abandonment of a concern with the quality of input, process and content variables is a false one. Even Gilbert Jessup (1991), whom Pring identifies as the high-priest of the outcome-led approach, argues that the whole point of specifying outcomes is to promote learning, presumably by improving the quality of the learning experience. A concern with quality must therefore inform the whole process of education and training. Furthermore, it is important to be able to compare the quality of different ways of reaching the same outcome, as well as different outcomes. It is therefore entirely appropriate to employ a whole variety of perform-ance and quality indicators. These will almost certainly need to embrace input, process, content and output indicators along a variety of dimensions, as well as multiple measures of efficiency and effective-ness, such as how much value is added at what cost.

One way in which the different emphases of the different tradi-tions that Pring identified might be brought together is under the currently fashionable concept of Total Quality Management or TQM (Marsh 1991). Although often rejected because of its provenance in the world of business and industry, its emphasis is on the whole culture of an organization becoming committed to customer satisfaction through continuous improvement, and with providing all employees with practical techniques to measure, test and improve standard operating techniques and develop innovative solutions to complex problems. One piece of advice offered to managers moving in this direction is: 'No longer put your best and most reliable people in inspection. Rather re-orientate the whole organization to start thinking about the prevention of problems rather than their detection' (Cook 1990).

There are certainly some problems about applying this approach to education, especially given the need to attend to multiple concep-tions as well as multiple dimensions of quality (Williams 1991), and the language employed would clearly need to be adapted for the educa-tion context. Nevertheless, it is an approach that argues that all workers should be treated as professionals, a stark contrast to the government's tendency to want to deskill professionals and make them subject to models of control that are now regarded as outmoded in much of business and industry. Interestingly, a Green Paper produced by the CVCP (Elton and Partington 1991) argues that TQM is an approach to quality control particularly well-suited to collegial cultures such as those found in universities. It might thus provide a more positive basis for moving forward than the mere defence of past academic practice, while its emphasis on the whole culture of the enterprise might serve to recapture the holistic notion of quality I think Pring is struggling for and which he rightly fears might be lost in some of the more reductionist competence-based approaches to quality.

One of the reasons why TQM is highly controversial is that discussion of its applicability is often linked to discussion of the use of BS5750 as a kitemark for training quality. While some people argue that the two should go hand in hand, a Bristol University specialist in quality in manufacturing has dismissed BS5750 as 'a nasty and insidious attempt to impose bureaucratic standards derived from industry on academic departments' (quoted in Tysome and O'Neill 1991). Nevertheless, the interest by some institutions offering FE teacher training in the possible adoption of BS5750 demonstrates a willingness at least to consider how far quality control and assurance procedures from other fields are applicable to us.

An effective quality assurance mechanism requires commitment from those whose quality it seeks to assure. We therefore probably need a representative version of CATE or a General Teaching Council (GTC) rather than an appointed committee. The ideal is an approach that generates internal commitment and external confidence and one in which the external elements of quality assurance stimulate a real concern with quality control within institutions.

In my experience, the mature CNAA model for quality assurance began to do this, not least in teacher education.

CONCLUSION

Although reading Pring's paper on standards has certainly made me reflect carefully on my own position about quality control in teacher education, I would still argue (Whitty 1991), that, among other things, quality teacher education requires:

- A genuine partnership between the various stakeholders (training institutions, schools, LEAs, etc.) in all routes to Qualified Teacher Status.

- A clearer definition of the competences (or core professional skills) required by teachers as reflective practitioners.
- Monitoring of academic validation through a quality assurance system, based on the best practice developed under CNAA.
- Administration of professional accreditation through a reconstituted and representative version of CATE or through a GTC, with strong extra-professional representation to ensure public accountability.
- Sensitivity to local and sectional needs within this national framework.

REFERENCES

Bourdieu, P. (1976) 'The School as a Conservative Force: Scholastic and Cultural Inequalities', in Dale, R., Esland, G. and Macdonald, M. (eds.) *Schooling and Capitalism*, London: Routledge and Kegan Paul.

Council for National Academic Awards (CNAA) (1990–91) *Handbook 1990–91*, London, Council for National Academic Awards.

Cook, D. (1990) 'Total Quality Management – Fine Talk or Real Improvement?' *Total Quality Management*, 1 (1), 13–21.

Department of Education and Science (1984) *Initial Teacher Training: Approval of Courses* (Circular 3/84), London, Department of Education and Science.

Elton, I. and Partington, P. (1991) *Teaching Standards and Excellence in Higher Education: Developing a Culture for Quality*, Sheffield, Committee of Vice-Chancellors and Principals.

Griffiths, S. (1991) 'Aberystwyth objects to quality audit', *Times Higher Education Supplement*, 17 May.

Jessup, G. (1991) *Outcomes: NVQs and the Emerging Model of Education and Training*, London: Falmer Press.

Hextall, I., Lawn, M., Menter, I., Sidgwick, S. and Walker, S. (1991) *Imaginative Projects: Arguments for a New Teacher Education*, London, Goldsmiths' College.

MacGregor, K. (1990) 'Polys Welcome Hands-off Performance and Audit Line', *Times Higher Education Supplement*, 11 May.

Marsh, P. (1991) 'Bounce in the showroom', *The Higher*, 1 November.

Tuxworth, E. (1982) *Competency in Teaching: a review of competency and performance-based staff development*, London, Further Education Unit.

Tyesome, T. and O'Neill, S. (1991) 'Ministers Warned Off "Kitemark" for Colleges', *Times Higher Education Supplement*, 12 July.

Whitty, G. (1989) 'The New Right and the National Curriculum: State Control or Market Forces?' *Journal of Education Policy*, 4(4), 329–41.

Whitty, G. (1991) 'Next in Line for the Treatment? Education Reform and Teacher Education in the 1990s', Inaugural Lecture, Goldsmiths' College, University of London, 14 May.

Whitty, G. and Willmott, E. (1991) 'Competence-based Teacher Education: Approaches and Issues', *Cambridge Journal of Education*, 21(3), 309–18.

Williams, G. (1991) 'Identifying and Developing a Quality Ethos for Teaching in Higher Education', *Newsletter One*, Department of Policy Studies, Institute of Education, University of London.

Chapter 18

Competence-based teacher education
Approaches and issues

Geoff Whitty and Elizabeth Willmott

INTRODUCTION

Competence-based and performance-based approaches to teacher education are by no means new. They were popular in the USA in the 1970s and began to have some impact in the further education (FE) sector in the UK in the early 1980s (Tuxworth 1982). During the 1980s, they were given fresh impetus by the influence of the National Council for Vocational Qualifications (NCVQ) on the work of that sector and by the wider debate about quality in education and training. The award of NVQs is based upon the achievement of competences and is not dependent upon a particular programme of learning or period of time as a prerequisite (Jessup 1991). While these developments were not centrally concerned with teacher education, their potential relevance was soon recognized. A number of Cert.Ed. (FE) courses adopt significant elements of a competence-based approach to teacher education.

The use of a competence-based approach to teacher education for the school sector is rather less developed, although Eraut (1989) has pointed to its potential and a few B.Ed. and PGCE courses are beginning to show signs of its influence. Meanwhile, critiques of conventional approaches to initial teacher education have led to growing demands that it be both school-based and more directly linked to the competences required of the beginning teacher. Circular 24/89 (DES 1989b) contains exit criteria for certain activities within courses of initial teacher education, while a similar list has been circulated to LEAs engaged in the training of licensed teachers (DES 1989a). The recent NCC document on initial training has tried to bring these together (NCC 1991).

The apparent official interest in linking qualified teacher status (QTS) to the achievement of certain specified competences has initiated a flurry of activity on the part of various agencies and institutions to explore the potential of competence-based approaches to teacher education. Even so, no consensus has yet emerged about the meaning of 'competences', let alone agreement about the specific competences that should be engendered by initial teacher education or INSET courses. As long ago as 1977, competence-based education was described as 'a bandwagon in search of a definition' (Spady 1977), and much the same applies to competence-based teacher education today. In this chapter we try to identify some of the issues that will have to be addressed if progress is to be made in this field. It can, of course, be argued that all teacher education courses, whatever their approach, aim to produce competent teachers. However, our concern here is with courses which are directed explicitly to the achievement of specified competences.

DEFINITIONS

In any debate about a value-laden activity such as teacher education, difficulties are bound to be encountered in relation to the key concepts employed. Many teacher educators reject the idea of competence-based teacher education on the grounds that it encourages an over-emphasis on skills and techniques; that it ignores vital components of teacher education; that what informs performance is as important as performance itself; and that the whole is more than the sum of the parts. This rejection partly derives from a reading of early American checklists of teacher behaviour, which are ticked by an observer. Yet there are others who argue that a 'reflective practitioner' approach, which often claims to be the very antithesis of a technicist and behaviourist view of teacher education, can itself be expressed in competence terms. Hextall *et al.* (1991:15), for example, argue that 'teaching is not reducible to a set of technical operations'. However, they go on to say that 'they are not running away from the issue of the systematic appraisal of teaching competence' and that even the quality of reflectivity can be formulated as a series of competences that can be monitored. Clearly 'competence' is a term capable of a number of different interpretations.

The courses we have looked at that use the term 'competence' are less than explicit about what it is meant to convey. However, two major approaches to the definition of a competence can be discerned:

- competence characterized as an ability to perform a task satisfactorily, the task being clearly defined and the criteria of success being set out alongside this;
- competence characterized as wider than this, encompassing intellectual, cognitive and attitudinal dimensions, as well as

performance; in this model, neither competences not the criteria of achievement are so readily susceptible to sharp and discrete identification.

Additionally, there is often a lack of clarity about the relationship between different types of competence. Some competences appear to be person-related and others task-related. While some courses restrict themselves to defining a short list of generic professional competences and others embrace literally scores of discrete behaviours, many fail to distinguish between these different types of competence or specify the ways in which they are presumed to relate. Nor are the course documents we have read usually explicit about how performance in terms of the identified competences relates to overall 'competence'. This is reminiscent of some of the early US examples, where it seemed possible to get a tick on a whole list of individual competences and still appear incompetent! Some people therefore argue that competence is more than the sum of a variety of individual competences and that it is more like communicative competence, derived from an underlying grammar that generates individual competences in different unpredictable situations.

In the light of these variations, it would be difficult and probably undesirable to prescribe a particular definition of competence-based teacher education, or to specify particular competences that need to be included in any scheme. Nevertheless, teacher educators attracted by the idea of competence-based approaches will need to clarify their own approach to these issues. As we shall see later, different definitions will have different implications for teaching, learning and assessment.

THE ATTRACTION OF COMPETENCE-BASED APPROACHES

To some extent, even the reasons for choosing competence-based approaches will differ according to the definition of competence employed. Nevertheless, a number of general points can usefully be made. One advantage, which might commend itself to critics of more traditional approaches to teacher education, was put forward by an early advocate of the approach who argued that it would help to 'remove some of the mystique and institutional restrictions that surround teacher education' (Tuxworth 1982). However, that is essentially a plea for clarifying and making public the aims and objectives of a course and the ways in which they are evidenced in assessment, something which arguably should apply to all courses, whether competence-based or not. Beyond that, competence-based approaches can be justified as giving students clear targets of achievement and explicit evidence of their progress, enabling schools to share an understanding of the function of placements, and giving employers a clear idea of what to expect. A subsidiary reason for introducing competence-based approaches, which has been particularly influential in the FE sector, is that it allows teachers to experience the same approach as the students they teach.

Justifications for the particular competences selected also seem to vary. This may relate to the aims of the course in question: whereas an initial B.Ed. is expected to provide a general programme of higher education as well as a professional preparation for teaching, a PGCE is geared to entrants who already have a general education and focuses on their professional preparation. Much of the current debate about the competences that might inform a competence-based approach to teacher education sees them as derived from an analysis of the required competences of the beginning (or continuing) teacher, usually related to performance in the workplace. This is consistent with other forms of training which utilize the approach, as exemplified in the following statement from NCVQ (1989:4):

- the area of competence to be covered must have meaning and relevance in the context of the occupational structure in the sector of employment concerned;
- the statement of competence must be based on an analysis of occupational roles within the area of competence to which it relates;
- the statement of competence must encompass the underpinning knowledge and understanding required for effective performance in employment.

While this last statement extends the notion of competence beyond observable workplace skills, it does not necessarily encompass all the elements of personal education which may be the concern of courses of teacher education. It may well be that an even broader approach to the definition of competences will be necessary in teacher education, especially in B.Ed. courses. All CNAA courses, for example, are required to address the following general educational aims:

the development of students' intellectual and imaginative powers; their understanding and judgment; their problem solving skills; their ability to communicate; their ability to see relationships within what they have learned and to perceive their field of study in a broader perspective. Each student's programme of study must stimulate an enquiring, analytical and creative approach, encouraging independent judgment and critical self-awareness.

(CNAA 1990: Section 4.3.3)

However, such elements of education are notoriously elusive in practice and some argue that, in a competence-based approach to education, they can be addressed more explicitly (Jessup 1991). The notion of transferable skills is now seen as significant in relation to a wide range of degrees that are not, on the face of it, vocational (see UDACE 1991) and it is particularly significant in the context of credit accumulation and transfer and the assessment of prior learning. These concerns are part of a wider concern to relate life and work-based learning to award-bearing higher education courses, and vice versa.

Those considering adopting a competence-based approach will therefore need to address the extent to which it is possible to adapt B.Ed., PGCE, Cert.Ed. (FE) and INSET courses to a method which appears to judge the value of a learning experience largely in terms of the ability to demonstrate competence. Whether broader aims can be accommodated within a competence-based approach may well depend on how broad a definition of competence is employed. A narrow definition based on observable workplace skills is certainly in some tension with the rationale of a liberal education and even with the notion of the reflective professional. On the other hand, a broader definition can make it difficult to define criteria of competence in any meaningful way. The possible limitations of a competence-based approach need not, however, lead to its out of hand dismissal or to the assumption that there is no place for competences in a broader view of teacher education. A parallel from which some lessons might usefully be learnt is the development of the Certificate in Management Education award which incorporates the competences identified as a result of the Management Charter Initiative (CNAA and BTEC 1990).

THE USE OF COMPETENCES IN COURSE DESIGN

A few teams have designed courses on criteria other than competences but then tried to define exit competences for use in student profiles. A distinctively competence-based approach to teacher education implies that competences play a more significant role in the planning and implementation of courses. All course design should be informed by the characteristics of the learners who are to benefit from the course. In a competence-based course, it might be expected that those learner characteristics which provide a basis for entry to the course will be identified in greater detail, thus facilitating a common understanding of the skills, knowledge and attitudes which potential students should bring to the course, and affording a foundation upon which the programme of study will build. Such an approach might be of particular benefit in relation to progammes of study for licensed teachers who bring a wide range of skills, knowledge and understanding which need to be assessed if courses are to be devised to meet their needs. However, its potential application is by no means restricted to such programmes.

The philosophy underlying extreme competence-based approaches implies that if a student can demonstrate a competence s/he can gain credit for it, without necessarily having followed a course at all. Such a strategy places the entire burden of assuring the attainment of the required standards on the assessment process. It has also been suggested that students might be permitted to leave a course of initial teacher education and enter teaching once they have reached a certain threshold of competence (Hargreaves 1989). There are, however, legitimate concerns about the extent to which this approach can undermine the experience of a coherent programme of study, often seen as a necessary part of teacher education. Whether or not the extreme approach is adopted, there is considerable scope for using competences as a basis for the accreditation of prior learning – including experiential learning – and thus giving access to courses with advanced standing. Judgement about prior learning, even expressed in competence terms, may though prove difficult to agree upon. Competences have, however, been seen as providing a particularly useful basis for designing bridging courses into the Cert.Ed. (FE) and shortened B.Ed. courses.

The extent to which a competence-based approach will inform mainstream course design will vary. Some course teams have used the approach only for part of their courses and it is perhaps not surprising that the most extensive use of competences has been in relation to school experience and to the work-based elements in FE courses. Indeed, some tutors believe that, in principle, the approach should be limited to this area, particularly where a narrow definition of competences is being used. Other course teams, usually working with a broader definition, have tried to adopt a competence-based approach to a whole course. School-based courses, such as articled teacher schemes, provide a particularly good opportunity for trying to relate all elements of a course to the achievement of workplace competences.

The specific competences used in course design can be derived from a variety of sources. The various task analyses of teaching or attempts to specify the attributes of the teacher as professional might be one starting point. Some competences may be specified by external agencies. In initial teacher education, for example, they might include those derived from the exit criteria specified in Circular 24/89 (DES 1989b). In other cases, they might be determined by the staff designing the courses, probably in consultation with teachers and LEA advisers. There is also considerable scope for students to negotiate the competences which they wish the course to help them develop and this is likely to be a central feature of INSET provision which adopts this approach.

TEACHING, LEARNING AND ASSESSMENT

It may be argued that a competence-based approach has no epistemological basis: it is concerned with what can be done (and perhaps what has been understood), rather than with *how* skills are developed and knowledge acquired. This creates tensions for higher education courses which are concerned with fostering learning through course curricula and learning processes as well as with the assessment of achievement. Nevertheless, Jessup (1991:138) argues that the whole point of specifying outcomes is to promote learning. If competence-based approaches encourage teacher educators to be more explicit about the characteristics of skilled professionalism that they seek to encourage, this is likely to have implications for teaching and learning. In some cases, it will lead to whole-course policies on teaching and learning. In theory, courses designed with an emphasis on exit competences might be expected to be non-prescriptive about the methods used to encourage their attainment. Indeed, they should provide considerable scope for the negotiation of teaching and learning methods. In practice, teaching methods are likely to be influenced by the particular definition of competences adopted and by the actual competences being encouraged. The competences required of the reflective teacher are likely to require rather different methods of teaching and learning from those of the instructor.

The early association of competence-based approaches with vocational training, especially in some of the narrowly behavioural approaches adopted in the USA, has nevertheless led to a view amongst teacher educators that competence-based education implies an instructional form of pedagogy. A narrowly skills-based definition of competence has, as in earlier courses based upon behavioural objectives, sometimes led to teaching that stresses performance at the expense of understanding. Narrow competence-based approaches to education and training have also relied particularly heavily on the assessment of observable workplace skills. Again they are associated in the minds of many teacher educators with the behaviourist and technicist approaches of their American pioneers, such as one scheme in which 121 separate teacher behaviours had to be checked off by an independent observer and fed into a computer to produce a competence level (see Gitlin and Smyth 1989).

The early work of NCVQ was sometimes criticized for similar excesses, but it is now widely accepted that such an approach is inappropriate in the assessment of higher-level professional skills. NCVQ now acknowledges that for levels four and above, it may be necessary to assess underpinning and understanding separately from performance. One of the last acts of the Training Agency was to mount a research project to look at the assessment of underpinning knowledge and understanding, because it was recognized that, while knowledge was essential to performance, it could not always be inferred from direct observation in the workplace. It is therefore likely that, in a field such as teacher education, a range of assessment methods will be employed, even in a course based entirely around the achievement of workplace competences. In this context, some useful lessons might be learned from the field of management education, where some guidelines for the assessment of management competences have been identified (CNAA and BTEC 1990). Those guidelines suggest that the following principles should govern assessment. It should:

- meet national standards, be based upon criterion-referenced processes and explicit criteria;
- employ a wide and appropriate array of methods;
- include work-based assessment of candidates' performance;
- involve collaboration between candidates, course providers, employers and assessors: there should be a clear delineation of the various participants' roles and of the weighting of their contribution to the assessment;
- be independent of the pathway to assessment, although assessment may contribute to learning;
- be available to individual candidates as well as to a cohort of students.

Knowledge and understanding should be explicitly related to past and current work-based performance and indicative of future performance. If it were possible to arrive at some form of consensus about the levels of competence for beginning teachers, it might be possible to ensure similar standards of entry to teaching despite the diversity of routes into the profession.

Definitions of competence that go beyond skills to include knowledge, values and attitudes raise particular problems for assessment. Some lists of professional competence include personal attributes which demand considerable sensitivity in assessment. On the other hand, many competence-based approaches make extensive use of self-assessment. Indeed, the competences of the reflective practitioner can be expected to include the capacity for self-assessment and the exclusive use of observer checklists on a course designed to develop this mode of professionalism would seem to be a contradiction in terms.

The assessment of competences obviously raises issues of validity and reliability, though arguably these only seem greater than in other types of courses because they sometimes take different forms. Nevertheless, Jessup's view that reliability diminishes in importance in competence-based approaches (Jessup 1991:191–3) is surely contentious, while ensuring validity is itself by no means straightforward in the assessment of sophisticated professional competences. Whatever approaches are adopted, we need to acknowledge that assessment of the attainment of competences requires inferences to be made on the basis of a range of evidence: the less specific the criteria enunciated, the higher the level of inference will be, and the more informed judgement will be called for. One strategy for attempting to ensure that the competences being assessed are not based on too narrow an experiential context is to specify range indicators which describe the context within which a performance should take place; for example, a student-teacher may be required to demonstrate practical ability in more than one type of school.

The competences specified in some courses are the minimum or threshold competences necessary to perform particular teaching activities and, in others, those characteristic of the 'good teacher'. More generally, there are differing views about whether a competence is something that is either a specific achievement or, alternatively, a dimension of performance in terms of which one can perform at different levels. In the former case, one might expect distinct lists of competences for ITT and INSET courses, while the latter approach implies a similar (or overlapping) list of competences with different levels of attainment. Specialist courses may, of course, use a restricted range of competences or introduce additional ones. Courses in education management, for example, draw upon generic management competences. In any case, the criteria and/or indicators to be used in determining whether a particular achievement or level of achievement has been attained need to be specified as clearly as possible. Furthermore, it is necessary to decide how the assessment of individual competences relates to the criteria used in making the overall award. In hybrid courses the relationship of the assessment of competences to any other forms of assessment employed on a course also needs to be clarified. Procedures for the aggregation of components to produce degree classes in the case of the B.Ed. degree need particular attention here, although the issues are in principle no different from those currently involved in relating degree class and performance on teaching practice.

Competence-based approaches lend themselves to clear reporting of assessments for both students and potential employers. They are therefore highly compatible with current trends towards the use of profiles in teacher education courses. Like other approaches to profiling, their use can be formative and/or summative and they raise similar issues about ownership to the profile of achievement. This could become particularly significant in the context of teacher appraisal.

IMPLICATIONS FOR INSTITUTIONS

In so far as the adoption of a competence-based approach to teacher education brings about significant changes to the nature of courses, it will make new demands on staff and on the quality assurance processes of institutions. Institutions that choose to employ a competence-based approach will need to examine the implications of that approach for course design, assessment, course structures, admissions and innovation and the management of change. A further consideration will be the resource and staff demands; these become increasingly acute if a competence-based approach is associated with a student-centred learning approach, negotiated programmes and learning contracts. If the programme is to involve 'work-based trainers', this might call for a fundamental rethinking of roles and could call for the sorts of strategies that are currently being explored in relation to mentor training for articled teacher schemes. If the assessment is to involve a large number of competences, that will have implications for academic and support staff resources. Assessment of prior learning is particularly demanding in terms of staff time.

CONCLUSIONS

Competence-based approaches to education are often considered problematic because of the central focus of competence upon outcomes rather than upon course content and the learning process. However, such approaches may have a number of benefits:

- demystification of teacher education;
- a clearer role for schools/colleges in the training process;
- greater confidence of employers in what beginning teachers can do;
- clearer goals for students.

The difficulties of the approach have also been rehearsed:

- it may lead to reductionism;
- it may shift the emphasis toward outcomes at the expense of learning processes;
- it may be difficult to reach agreement on a definition of competence;
- it may be difficult to specify which competences should be included;
- it may be difficult to arrive at valid and reliable criteria for assessment.

Given the growing official interest in competence-based approaches, teacher educators can expect to come under increasing pressure to explore the extent to which the use of competences can enhance the quality of teacher education. Nevertheless the advantages of using a competence-based approach remain to be proven, and it seems unlikely to be the panacea that its staunchest advocates often imply. On the evidence of the courses we have seen so far, most institutions are at an early stage of development, except perhaps in the field of FE teacher training. There is certainly insufficient experience to date to justify the national imposition of any particular approach, but there is considerable scope for further exploration and evaluation of the range of approaches that is currently developing.

REFERENCES

CNAA and BTEC (1990) *The Assessment of Management Competence: Guidelines*, London, CNAA/BTEC.

DES (1989a) *Attachment to the Education (Teachers) Regulations, Circular 18/89*, London: HMSO.

DES (1989b) *Criteria for the Approval of Courses of Initial Teacher Training, Circular 24/89*, London: HMSO.

Eraut, M. (1989) Initial teacher training and the NVQ model, in: Burke, J.W. (ed.) *Competency-based Education and Training*, Lewes: Falmer Press.

Gitlin, A. and Smyth, J. (1989) *Teacher Evaluation: educative alternatives*, Lewes: Falmer Press.

Hargreaves, D. (1989) PGCE assessment fails the test, *Times Educational Supplement*, 3 November.

Jessup, G. (1991) *Outcomes: NVQs and the emerging model of education and training*, Lewes: Falmer Press.

Hextall, I., Lawn, M., Menter, I., Sidgwick, S. and Walker, S. (1991) *Imaginative Projects: arguments for the new teacher education*, London, Goldsmiths' College.

NCC (1991) *The National Curriculum and the Initial Training of Student, Articled and Licensed Teachers*, York, National Curriculum Council.

NCVQ (1989) *National Vocational Qualifications: criteria and procedures*, London, National Council for Vocational Qualifications.

Spady, W.G. (1977) Competency-based education: a bandwagon in search of a definition, *Educational Researcher*, 6, 9–14.

Tuxworth, E.N. (1982) *Competency in Teaching: a review of competency and performance-based staff development*, London, FEU Research Development Units.

UDACE (1991) *What Can Graduates Do? A Consultative Paper*, Leicester, National Institute of Adult Continuing Education.

Chapter 19

Expertise and competence in further and adult education

Terry Hyland

COMPETENCE AND TEACHING

In a 1989 discussion paper on the potential impact of competence schemes on adult learning, the Unit for the Development of Adult Continuing Education (UDACE) identified a number of concerns and anxieties including the 'erosion of breadth and quality' in learning programmes and the loss of professional autonomy on the part of teachers. Recognizing that there may be some benefits to be derived from utilizing a competence model in certain spheres of adult education, there was speculation about whether, in the face of the powerful influence of the NCVQ and the government-backed training lobby, it would be possible for educators to 'resist or redirect change' (UDACE 1989:33). Given developments over the last few years, it is now even more urgent that teacher educators address these fundamental issues.

The ways in which competence-based strategies have brought about a 'quiet revolution' (Burke 1989:1) in VET in just a few short years have been fairly well documented, though the motives of leading players and the power politics of top-down decisions which have led to this state of affairs invite more careful inspection. In the case of teacher education (particularly the recently announced DES reform of school teacher education) there can be little doubt that recent trends add up to a serious threat to the profession (John 1992). Against the background of rapidly shifting demands and a contracting service, it is understandable how pragmatism might easily come to replace professional commitment. In relation to the move from an objectives-based CGLI 7307, for instance, there is an open admission that the chief motivation for change (which, we are assured, will not dramatically affect the 'integrity and substantial reputation of 7307') was the desire to 'ensure some compatibility with the standards framework being developed by the Training and Development Lead Body' (CGLI 1991:1, 2).

The increasing vulnerability of the profession to these external pressures perhaps serves to explain why McAleavey and McAleer would want to endorse a model of teacher education which has so many obvious weaknesses and shortcomings. Certainly, it is difficult to see how such an approach can do anything at all to enhance the professional status of teachers. In relation to the further education certificate course we are told that a major consideration was that 'the work role of lecturers in further education should be expressed in terms of competences' which would be 'derived from the functions which lecturers are required to fulfil' (McAleer and McAleavey 1990:9). This is fully in line with the functional analysis model used for NVQs, but why on earth should a model of teacher education take the occupational requirements of lecturers to be paramount rather than the knowledge, skills and values required to promote and enhance qualitative practice? Even if we accept (as most teacher educators now seem to) that 'work role competence can only be assessed adequately in the workplace' (McAleavey and McAleer 1991:21), there are still fundamental questions to be asked about what that 'work role' consists in and how it is best assessed.

In the rapidly changing world of post-compulsory education, lecturers will need the wherewithal to cope, not just with curricular and organizational innovation, but also with the internal and external conflicts and tensions which inevitably arise in periods of change. Coping with all this requires, not competence, but the knowledge and understanding to evaluate alternative perspectives and to apply this reflective criticism to the improvement of practice.

Programmes of teacher education which concentrate on specific occupational roles are likely to produce lecturers who are uncritical of change but well able to perform the duties required of them by college management. On this account teachers certainly do come to look like the 'labour force of a nationalised industry' in which (particularly with the setbacks of the last decade or so) they 'may be less powerful in decision-making than miners or railwaymen' (Midwinter 1977:20). Certainly, there seems to be ample evidence for Collins' claim that competence-based models are ones in which 'management interests are well served' but in which 'education and training programmes are trivialised' and 'occupations are increasingly deskilled through the deployment of narrowly defined prescriptions' (Collins 1991:90).

Against this background the claim that the new Advanced Diploma in Education at Ulster is based on a 'view of professionalism as the development of teacher autonomy' (McAleavey and McAleer 1991:22) seems wilfully perverse. How can autonomy be developed if teacher education and training courses are geared towards the assessment of competences derived from a functional analysis of work roles? A person is autonomous, according to Dearden (1972), to the extent that 'what he thinks and does is determined by himself' [sic] and that autonomy is typically displayed and developed through the 'bringing to bear of relevant considerations in such activities of mind as those of choosing, deliberating, reflecting, planning and judging' (p. 461). All this is clearly a long way from preparing people to perform particular work roles!

If there is indeed a genuine commitment to promoting autonomy in teacher education, it is more likely to be achieved through the use of a model which emphasizes what Collins calls a 'transformative pedagogy' in which 'educators can begin to envisage themselves as intellectual practitioners rather than technicians' (1991: 118). In a similar vein, Usher (1989) has argued that adult education is a 'practical activity' which should 'enable practitioners to develop a reflexive awareness of practice and to engage truly in praxis' (p. 90). All this seems to be fully in line with the experiential learning model based on Kolb's theories which, with its insistence upon making links 'between theory and action . . . the doing and the thinking' (Gibbs 1988: 9), has become recommended standard practice for students and tutors in further education in recent years. In order to facilitate such practice, however, we need a framework for teacher education which incorporates, not just the requirements of work roles, but also the sense of vocational commitment captured by the notion of expertise.

TEACHING AND PROFESSIONAL EXPERTISE

McAleavey and McAleer's comprehensive list of task, management and role skills required by teachers in their 'continuously changing role in the contemporary college' (1991: 21), adds up to a formidable repertoire. Similarly, the knowledge and skill components of CGLI 7307 courses and the wide range of CNAA Certificate in Education (FE) courses are quite complex and sophisticated. If we add to this the findings of a recent HMI survey on further education teacher training which reported a generally favourable picture of 'challenging and rigorous' courses, though it did recommend that students 'should be encouraged to read more extensively' (HMI 1991: 2, 7), then the use of competence to describe professional requirements begins to look seriously inadequate.

It has always seemed to me that, certainly beyond the level of basic skills (say, NVQ levels 1 and 2), the term 'competence' is being asked to bear far more weight than it can possibly carry. Of course, it is relatively easy to *describe* something as a competence (or, indeed, as a 'generic competence' or even 'meta-competence', see Fleming

1991), but whether this is actually appropriate or justified is an entirely different matter. In the draft specification for GNVQ Level 3 in Leisure and Tourism, for example, an element of competence in Unit 4 (Providing customer care) is described as 'staff and customer views are sought in establishing needs' (NCVQ 1991: 29). Although the range and evidence requirements in relation to this element are identified, it seems to me to be wildly unrealistic to try to capture all that is involved in such a complex aspect of human activity by means of competence statements. It is in just such contexts that a competence statement, as Ashworth and Saxton clearly explain, becomes merely a 'constrained grammatical form' which is 'empty and uninformative' (1990:19).

Competence (which according to dictionary definitions is synonymous with 'sufficient', 'adequate' and 'suitable') implies the satisfaction of basic minimum standards whereas the sort of organizational, management and interpersonal skills – not to mention the specialist knowledge and experience! – required by further and adult education lecturers and tutors goes well beyond this and incorporates a collection of sophisticated knowledge, skills and qualities which are much better described through the notion of professional expertise. A widely accepted interpretation of this kind of expertise picks out highly proficient and successful activity 'built upon the knowledge and skill gained through sustained practice and experience' (Tennant 1991: 50). There is now a substantial body of empirical work on the nature of occupational expertise which has closely examined the characteristic features of the work of experts in such diverse fields as chess playing, racetrack handicapping, judicial decision-making and medical diagnosis.

The study of clinical diagnosis by Schmidt *et al.* (1990) suggested that expertise develops from a 'conceptually rich and rational knowledge base to one comprised of largely experiential and non-analytical instances' (p. 619). In summarizing a large number of such studies, Chi *et al.* (1988) were able to establish a range of common characteristics and noted that experts tended to excel in their own domains, spend a lot of time analysing problems qualitatively, have systematically organized specialist knowledge and have strong self-monitoring skills. All of these provide a good match with teaching requirements and are fully in line with the knowledge and skills components typically included in professional courses.

The concept of professional expertise seems to provide a far more appropriate model for further and adult education teacher training than the competence-based alternatives on offer. McAleavey and McAleer did, in fact, examine an approach to professional education and training used by the Harvard Business School which involved the observation of 'superior performers' but rejected this in favour of one based on a 'functional analysis of the occupation and its necessary duties and tasks' (1991: 21). In the light of the current demands on post-school lecturers and tutors, the reassertion of the importance of the mentor role in mainstream teacher education, and the general weaknesses and inconsistencies in competence-based approaches, I would suggest that this is a serious mistake which could have far-reaching implications for post-compulsory education and training.

The pace of change in further and adult education in recent years has produced a fluid and uncertain post-school sector (Oxtoby 1991) in which teachers are required to be flexible, critical, reflective and knowledgeable about a vast range of curricular and organizational matters. Added to this are the increased expectations outlined in the DES White Paper on further education and the Further and Higher Education Act that lecturers and tutors in this sphere will take a lead in giving 'more young people opportunities for further education and training' and responding to 'the demand from students and employers for high-quality further education' (DES 1991: 58). In order to meet all these different demands teachers will need rather more than the ability to satisfy occupational work tasks; they will also need, in the words of the recent HMI survey, 'to develop a more independent and critical perspective on educational matters' (HMI 1991: 7). Teachers in further and adult education will, in short, need to be experts. Competence is not enough!

REFERENCES

Ashworth, P.D. and Saxton, J. (1990) On Competence, *Journal of Further and Higher Education*, 14(1), Summer, 3–25.

Burke, J.W. (1989) (ed.) *Competency Based Education and Training*, Lewes: Falmer Press.

Chi, M. *et al.* (1988) *The Nature of Expertise*, Hillsdale, NJ: Lawrence Erlbaum Associates.

Collins, M. (1991) *Adult Education as Vocation*, London: Routledge.

Dearden, R.F. (1972) Autonomy and Education; in Dearden, R.F., Hirst, P.H. and Peters, R.S. (eds.), *Education and the Development of Reason*, London: Routledge & Kegan Paul, 448–65.

DES (1991) *Education and Training for the 21st Century*, London: HMSO.

Fleming, D. (1991) The Concept of Meta-competence: *Competence and Assessment*, 16, 9–12.

Gibbs, G. (1988) *Learning by Doing*, London: FEU.

HMI (1991) *Training for Teaching in Further and Adult Education*, London: HMSO.

John, A. (1992) School-based Teacher Training, *NATFHE Journal*, March, 9.

McAleer, J. and McAleavey, M. (1990) Further Education Teacher Training at the University of Ulster, *Competence and Assessment*, 13, 9–11.

McAleavey, M. and McAleer, J. (1991) Competence-based Teaching, *British Journal of In-Service Education*, 17(1), 19-23.

Midwinter, E. (1977) Teachers: Organised Labour Force of a Nationalised Industry, *Journal of Further and Higher Education*, 1(1), 6-21.

NCVQ (1991) *General National Vocational Qualifications*, London: NCVQ.

Oxtoby, B., (1991) Growth, Uncertainty and Change, *NATFHE Journal*, Autumn, 9.

Schmidt, H. *et al.* (1990) A Cognitive Perspective on Medical Expertise: Theory and Implications, *Academic Medicine*, 65(10), 611-21.

Tennant, M. (1991) Expertise as a Dimension of Adult Development; Implications for Adult Education, *New Education*, 13 (1), 49-55.

UDACE (1989) *Understanding Competence*, Leicester: Unit for the Development of Adult Continuing Education.

Usher, R. (1989) Locating Adult Education in the Practical, in Bright, B. (ed.) *Theory and Practice in the Study of Adult Education; The Epistemological Debate*, London: Routledge.

Chapter 20

The limits of competence
A cautionary note on Circular 9/92

John Furlong

When responding to Kenneth Clarke's consultation document on the future of Initial Teacher Education it seems that many teacher educators indicated a broad support for the proposal that the revised criteria should include a list of competences that all students should follow throughout their training. And it was perhaps because of that support that this aspect of the original proposal survived intact when the new criteria were eventually published in June as Circular 9/92 (35/92 in Wales) (DFE 1992). In this chapter I want to concentrate on what I see as some of the limitations and dangers of over-simplistic interpretations of the competence approach advocated within the Circular.

Writing a critique of competence-based teacher education today presents considerable difficulties because of the enormous variation in interpretations of the approach. When writers as theoretically diverse as Jessup (1991) and Elliott (1990) can both claim to be writing about competences, any critic must approach the area with caution. In this chapter I therefore intend to limit discussion to the view of competence training advocated within Circular 9/92, recognizing that it represents only one amongst many competing interpretations. It is also important to note that the Circular takes a broadly based approach to competences, perhaps deliberately allowing for a wide range of interpretations in the construction of particular teacher education programmes. Once again this makes critique problematic; one can therefore do no more than highlight the *possible* weaknesses that can result from too simplistic an adoption of the approach.

A competence approach to teacher education is powerful in that it can influence a variety of different dimensions of teacher education programmes. A notion of competences can obviously be used to construct the *curriculum*; but the approach can also implicitly and explicitly construct *pedagogy* as well as *assessment*. In this chapter I will examine the adequacy of Circular 9/92 if it is utilized unquestioningly in the construction of each of these different aspects of teacher education programmes.

COMPETENCES AND THE CONSTRUCTION OF THE CURRICULUM

In examining the adequacy of Circular 9/92 in relation to the teacher education curriculum, the first question to ask is, do the items identified within the Circular actually constitute the competences of teaching? What is the origin of the competence items listed in the Circular? Have they, for example, been derived from a systematic analysis of the occupational role of a beginning teacher, as NCVQ would advocate (NCVQ 1989). Clearly the answer is that they have not been so derived; they do not, nor do they purport to cover all dimensions of teaching. Simply stating what is required in an active form ('Newly qualified teachers *should be able to* . . .) does not in itself add up to a competence approach. Rather than deriving from systematic analysis, each item that is included has its own history that can be tracked back through earlier DES and HMI reports, advice and directives on initial teacher education. In evaluating the list as the basis of the teacher education curriculum, it is important to recognize that the items that are included (just as those that are excluded), have been so as the result of political debate both within the profession and outside it. They are, and must continue to be seen as a 'partial' interpretation of teaching competences in both senses of the word.

In fairness to the Circular it is stated that the list of competences 'do not purport to provide a complete syllabus' (DFE 1992: para. 11). However, the fact the Circular also states that 'Higher education institutions, schools and students should focus on the competences of teaching *throughout the whole period of initial training*' (Annex A 2.1, emphasis added) and that the competences 'specify the issues on which the case for approval will be considered' (para. 11) means that individual courses could be forgiven for interpreting the list as a syllabus. Indeed it seems that HMI and CATE will have little grounds for objection if courses mechanistically train students in these dimensions and nothing else.

A repeated criticism of competence training has been that it is both behaviourist and functionalist (Marshall 1991); such a criticism would certainly appear to be valid in relation to some of the more extreme proponents of the approach such as Jessup (1991). Writers such as Elliott (1990) argue that professional education demands more than developing a string of behavioural competences whose performance is measurable. Professional competence is more than 'know-how' or technique; inevitably it includes knowledge, attitudes and under-standings as well as skills, and these too must therefore form part of the curriculum.

And it is clear that those drafting the Circular have to some degree recognized the importance of addressing more than mere behavioural skills. Students are also expected to 'understand' the school as an institution; to 'judge' pupil performance; to have an 'awareness' of individual differences.

While the explicit inclusion of knowledge and understanding in some areas of the curriculum is to be welcomed, the Circular could still lead to the interpretation that certain areas of professional work merely demand behaviour skills. But as Elliott (1990), following Pearson (1984) argues, there is a difference between know-how, or 'habitual skill knowledge', which enables an individual unreflectively to perform certain necessary routines, and 'intelligent skill knowledge' which involves the exercise of capacities for discernment, discrimination and intelligent action. In other words, even in areas where the Circular implicitly defines the curriculum in terms of behavioural skills it is necessary for those responsible for constructing teacher educa-tion curricula to take a broader view.

COMPETENCES AND THE CONSTRUCTION OF PEDAGOGY

There is a considerable history in this country of attempts to intro-duce systematic training into the practical aspects of initial teacher education. In more recent times, systematic training became partic-ularly popular in the 1970s with the development of interaction analysis and micro-teaching. There was also some interest in Ameri-can competence-based teacher education. In their early formula-tions, all of these approaches adopted a behaviourist pedagogy, focusing on narrow skills training, though in America the devel-opment of clinical supervision has demonstrated the possibility of establishing a more broadly based approach to systematic training. It is perhaps because of the narrowness of most British models that the majority of British teacher educators have only utilized systematic training techniques as one amongst many pedagogical strategies (Barrett et al. 1992). To date it seems that very few teacher education programmes have been based exclusively on systematic principles.

Circular 9/92 now formally encourages the placing of systematic training at the heart of all teacher education programmes. Higher education institutions, schools and students are to focus on the competences of teaching throughout the whole period of initial training. As those involved in the development of clinical supervision have demonstrated, the use of competences does not necessarily lead to the adoption of a behaviourist pedagogy, though naive interpretations will inevitably be made; schemes for skills training will abound. My concern, though, is not with behaviouristic pedagogies; even they have their place. Rather it is with the notion that learning to teach can best be promoted by the adoption of any single pedagogical strategy.

Current research being undertaken on mentoring at Swansea (Maynard and Furlong 1992) (see Chapter 1) would suggest that students' learning needs are developmental and effective mentoring demands the adoption of a range of different pedagogical strategies at different stages of development. In the very earliest days in the classroom it seems that students are unlikely to be able to benefit from systematic training (behaviourist or not). The sheer complexity of classroom processes means that at the earliest stages students are unable to 'see' in order to focus on particular competences. At those early stages, forms of collaborative teaching where students can model themselves on experienced teachers are likely to be far more effective than systematic training.

Once students have established some schemas and routines for making sense of and managing the process of teaching, they may then benefit from systematic training of some kind. However, if it is too 'systematic', if it concentrates only on skills it will only take them so far. From our research it would seem that a common problem identified by mentors is that students who have gained basic practical competence in teaching 'hit a plateau'. The challenge is then to move them from a focus on their own teaching to a focus on children's learning. Inevitably this demands a deeper understanding of the processes of teaching and learning than is implied by behaviouristic notions of skills training; it also demands that students find their own professional 'voice' that may well be different from that of their mentor. Supporting students in this sort of learning demands a very different pedagogy from that implied in systematic training. It demands a more open and enquiring relationship between the student and the mentor where teaching strategies can be examined critically and the theoretical, moral and political dimensions of teaching can be discussed.

Circular 9/92 does not demand the adoption a single pedagogical approach. Our research would suggest that it is essential to see systematic training as just one amongst many possible pedagogical strategies each of which may contribute to different dimensions of students' professional development.

COMPETENCES AND THE CONSTRUCTION OF ASSESSMENT

The final dimension of initial teacher education programmes affected by competences is that of assessment. Clearly this is central to the Circular in that it is stated that 'The progressive development of these competences should be monitored regularly during initial training' and 'Their attainment at a level appropriate to newly qualified teachers should be the objective of every student taking a course of initial training' (DFE 1992: Annex A:2.1). As the Circular recognizes, many institutions have already developed their own competence-based approaches to the assessment of students and it seems that CATE may well be utilizing a similar approach in establishing a national monitoring system for all newly qualified teachers.

Once again, the Circular is helpfully open in its approach in this area; it does not specify how competences should be monitored. Inevitably, though, naive interpretations will be made with the competences simply turned into a rating scale for completion by students, teachers and lecturers. If the competences are to be used as a basis for structuring *professional* judgements made by teachers and lecturers, then they would seem to be generally helpful. If, however, they are used as a basis for constructing free-standing assessment instruments then they need closer attention.

There are two weaknesses with such assessment instruments. The first is that they imply that, even if the list of competences on which they are based were complete, teaching performance can be understood and evaluated in terms of a number of discrete elements. Clearly teaching is not like this for, as Walker (1992:3) emphasizes, professional competence demands far more complex preparation than mastering an isolated collection of elements, even if those elements include 'knowledge' and 'understandings' as well as skills. 'Teaching is more than a technology; it is a moral practice whose successful performance depends on a "structure of competence" (Klemp 1977) in which abilities are not isolated discrete elements but are linked together structurally.'

The second weakness, and the one particularly pertinent to the construction of any national system based on lists of competences is that such instruments imply a decontextualized view of performance. But teaching performance is not only multi-faceted, it is also highly dependent on context. Performance, as Walker (1992:7) notes, is culture dependent:

> The individual is never merely an individual and the job is never merely a job, [thus] performance is rarely changed by merely changing any single variable, such as bringing a professional's knowledge up to date. In teaching, the combination of complexity

of the work, individual variation among teachers, and multiple cultural affiliations means that quality in performance usually requires the orchestration of variables. Creative orchestration of the many performance variables can enhance both individual and collective performance.

The recognition that teaching is both multifaceted and culture dependent raises deep concerns about the effectiveness of rating scales simplistically lifted from the Circular's list of competences.

CONCLUSION

In conclusion I would suggest that the greatest strength of the Circular is that it has taken a broadly based approach to the issue of teaching competences. As a result, if handled sensitively and professionally, the list may well prove helpful in each of the areas considered. In relation to *curriculum* it may be valuable in establishing a common minimum entitlement for all students; in relation to *pedagogy* it may prove valuable in the recognition it gives to the role of systematic training as one strategy within teacher education programmes; in relation to *assessment* it may prove valuable in helping to structure the professional judgements of teacher and lecturers. In each area however the Circular is open to narrow as well as broad interpretations. A narrowly mechanistic approach to initial teacher education is not demanded by this Circular. If that is the result it will be because we have imposed it on ourselves.

REFERENCES

Barrett, E. *et al.* (1992) *Initial Teacher Education in England and Wales: A Topography*, Modes of Teacher Education Project.

DFE (1992) *Initial Teacher Training (Secondary Phase) Circular 9/92, 35/92*, DFE.

Elliott, J. (1990) *Competency-Based Training and the Education of the Professions: Is a Happy Marriage Possible?* Unpublished paper. Centre for Applied Research in Education.

Jessup, G. (1991) *Outcomes: NVQs and the Emerging Model of Training*, Falmer Press.

Klemp, G.O. (1977) *Three Factors of Success in the World of Work: Implications for Curriculum in Higher Education*, McBer.

Marshall, K. (1991) 'NVQs: An Assessment of the "Outcomes" Approach to Education and Training', *Journal of Further and Higher Education* 15(3), 50-64.

Maynard, T. and Furlong, J. (1992) 'Learning to Teach and Models of Mentoring', in D. McIntyre *et al.* (eds.), *Issues in Mentoring*, Kogan Page.

NCVQ (1989) *National Vocational Qualifications: Criteria and Procedures*, National Council for Vocational Qualifications.

Pearson, H.T. (1984) 'Competence: An Historical Analysis', in E.C. Short (ed.), *Competence: Inquiries into its Meaning and Acquisition in Educational Settings*, University of America Press.

Walker, J.C. (1992) *A General Rationale and Conceptual Approach to the Application of Competency Based Standards to Teaching*. Unpublished paper. National Project on the Quality of Teaching and Learning, Australian National University.

Chapter 21

Integrating values into the assessment of teachers in initial education and training

Bob Moon and Ann Shelton Mayes

INTRODUCTION

Policies towards assessment in teacher education are undergoing significant change. There are a number of reasons for this. From an *educational* perspective the broadening of the concept of assessment in schools has inevitably created a momentum for change in higher education. Advocates for assessment as a formative and diagnostic process, as well as a summation of students' achievement, have been influential in this process (Brown 1989). From a *social* as well as educational perspective there has also been increasing disillusion, if not distrust, with normative assessment processes. Whilst class lists and 'concours' may be appropriate when asssessment serves rigorous selective purposes, they sit less well in the world of vocational and professional qualifications. The emphasis now is not how one student compares with another, but rather on whether can they do the job, or meet the criteria required within an occupational grouping (Jessup 1990). Finally, from a *political* perspective there has, in a number of countries, been an increased concern about the quality of entrants to the teaching profession and, therefore, the means by which students are deemed to achieve qualified status. In England and Wales, for example, teacher education has been a focus of political controversy for a number of years, and assessment procedures have played an important part in government-led reform.

The Open University, an organization committed to expanding access to education through part-time distance education, was given a government grant in 1991 to establish a Postgraduate Certificate in Education (PGCE) qualification for primary and secondary school teachers from January 1994. Over one thousand students are enrolled for the course, making it Europe's largest programme of pre-service distance education for teachers (Moon 1992). This chapter looks at the context of the debate about assessment reform in England and Wales, and explores the way in which this new national programme of pre-service teacher education has developed a framework for assessment.

THE CONTEXT OF ASSESSMENT IN ENGLAND AND WALES

Over the last decade teacher education at the university level has been required to meet criteria laid down by the Council for the Accreditation of Teacher Education (CATE). All course proposals have had to be submitted for approval to the Council, whose regulations have been changed twice during this period. It is not the intention to discuss here the political and academic issues that have surrounded the work of CATE (see MacIntyre 1991). The work of the Council, which includes lay as well as professional members, has been the focus of controversy. What is important, however, is that CATE moved through a series of regulations to a model of teacher assessment that required certain defined competences to be met in any course proposals submitted (DFE 1992). Every institution of teacher education, therefore, has had to address the philosophical and practical implications of the competence approach, one that has been the subject of debate for many years in other countries (notably the USA) but until recently had hardly touched provision for teacher education.

The response to the elaboration of competences at the national level of regulations has, from many quarters, been critical. The British Educational Research Association Task Group on Teacher Education has produced a strongly argued critique (BERA 1992). Whilst accepting that there should be some consensus about the characteristics of good teaching:

> in order to assure quality in the profession and to identify sufficient, relevant skills and qualities in teachers to promote their pupils' effective learning. Defined competences can guide self-evaluation and continuing professional development and provide a framework to cope with the diversity of routes to qualified teacher status . . .

They see the list of competences as having various shortcomings:

> It confuses different sorts of things by committing the behaviourist fallacy of confusing competence with performance. The list of competencies is presented as abilities that teachers should

have. Most are defined in terms of performance outcomes rather than the characteristics – knowledge, skills, and other qualities – involved in the production of such outcomes, e.g. in 'producing coherent lesson plans'. Competence may be manifested in performance but it cannot always be defined in terms of it. The list also confuses criteria or standards for judging performance outcomes with behavioural descriptions of such outcomes . . . The list is a conceptual mess. In fact it is less a list of competencies but rather of the criteria or standards by which to judge the outcomes of exercising competence. And consistency is even lacking in this respect because the distinction between performance criteria and behavioural description is not recognised.

The list provides no guidance for trainers charged with the task of developing competence because it fails to describe what such competence consists of and therefore lacks any diagnostic potential.

(BERA 1992:17)

These strong words echo earlier and parallel debates about the adequacy of the competence approach. In England and Wales a major national initiative to rationalize vocational qualifications had already stimulated debate about the application of new modes of assessment practice to teacher education. The majority of vocational qualifications are being progressively modified to meet national standards on a scale 1–5, with level 5 representing the equivalent of a postgraduate qualification. The implications for teacher education of the National Vocational Qualification (NVQ) model have been discussed by a number of teacher educators. Eraut (1989), for example, expresses a number of worries about the model of competence underpinning NVQs. He sees it as often being used to set minimum targets which limit expectations and he argues the dangers of a competence model, suggesting that progression lies mainly in increasing the number of competences rather than improving those that they have already got. He cites the approach adopted by Dreyfus and Dreyfus (1984) and Benner (1982) as a more adequate way of conceptualising competence. He also questions the way that prevailing competence models fail to assess knowledge whilst accepting that knowledge is the crucial foundation and underpinning of performance. Knowledge, those advocating NVQ type approaches suggest, can be assessed by observation in use. But this, for Eraut, represents a failure to recognize the role of theory in practical affairs and underplays the significance of *reflective* practice in the education and training process.

Yet people use theory all the time; and it is their personal theories which determine how they interpret the world and their encounters with people and situations within it. . . . Once one becomes more aware of the nature and effect of one's own theories, then it is possible to also consider those of others, whether they be immediate colleagues or authors of books. Similarly, by recognising the contexts in which one has developed one's theories, one is better able to judge when new theories are needed to cope with new kinds of contexts.

My challenge to those concerned with vocational training is to ask them how far this concept of the reflective practitioner is relevant to those personal qualities sometimes described as flexibility, adaptability, situational understanding and ability to learn from experience?

(Eraut 1989:184)

Eraut's concern is with the potential misuse and abuse of competence models and the lack of sufficient conceptual and technical development to support their application. Pring (1992) (see Chapter 16) takes a more philosophical stance to condemn what he implies is a new orthodoxy. He sees the attempt to transpose the functional job-related 'can do's' as competences to the professional and academic as a failure to understand the broad vision of education. And here he refers to the importance of judgement, often unspoken, which cannot wholly be anticipated. The search for absolute competence he sees as a shibboleth distorting in the academic and professional world the inevitable shades of performance, those unique improvements and developments over time that characterize the essence of the task itself.

Whitty (1992) (see Chapter 17), partly as a rejoinder to Pring, accepts that in education as a whole 'quality' is a contested concept. But he sees the distinction Pring makes between vocational and academic criteria as perpetuating a hierarchy that many, including Pring, have done much to challenge. He makes an explicit connection with teacher education. Whitty goes on to suggest that the philosophical argument for an element of mystique in teacher education has been pushed too far and he sees the competence movement as offering positive scope for its demystification.

These are important philosophical and technical debates in which the definition of terms themselves becomes problematic. Does competence necessarily imply an absolute standard in the way that some vocational qualifications presuppose? Does the representation of competences exclude an element of uncertainty? Can the assessment of competence only be seen in wholly instrumental terms? Can the explicit statement of competence be construed as an entitlement for the learner, providing access to the terms within which the assessor is making judgements? Or alternatively, does competence constrain and confine the terms within which learner and assessor can negotiate outcomes? Is there a values dimension to the judgements we make about prospective teachers?

VALUES AND COMPETENCE – A NATIONAL OPEN UNIVERSITY FRAMEWORK FOR ASSESSMENT IN TEACHER EDUCATION

The issues raised, and questions posed above, formed the context in which a new Open University national assessment scheme was developed for first implementation in the United Kingdom in 1994. Within the context of national regulation and against the backdrop of international debate about assessment the scheme seeks:

- to formulate learner outcomes in terms of competences;
- to do so in the context of a developmental model giving the student the responsibility for presenting evidence of achievement;
- to fuse within this the recognition that teaching includes the demonstration of professional qualities and values that go beyond the demonstration of classroom competence;
- to place much greater emphasis on the schools' role in pre-service education *and* assessment.

This assessment plan grew out of a parallel model (Winter 1992) which also sought to integrate a values dimension into the assessment of professional competence.

The national Open University model of assessment is conceptualized in terms of two dimensions of assessment. Five broad areas of *teaching competence* are elaborated and each of these are broken down into a further four or five sub-categories. Students must demonstrate *evidence* of reaching necessary levels of competence for each of these sub-categories and, therefore, at the final stage, of having fulfilled the necessary requirements of each of the major categories. In parallel, however, students will be required to demonstrate *professional qualities* in the way that teaching competence is displayed (Figure 21.1).

There are some important points to make here. First, the defined professional qualities (the values dimension to the assessment scheme) are not assessed independently of the normal day-to-day tasks of the teacher. Professional qualities cannot exist in a vacuum, they must have some context for their realization. The model can, therefore, be conceived of in matrix terms (Table 21.1).

Professional Development Portfolio: evidence supporting MENTOR
assessment (validated by CO-ASSESSOR) of school-based experiences
and TUTOR assessment of course assignments.

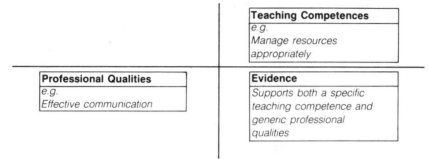

Figure 21.1 Competence-based assessment

In this structure as students demonstrate increasing competence within the defined areas of competence they will *simultaneously* develop a foundation of evidence for their capability in relation to professional qualities. Second, the model is seen primarily as *formative* during the students' progression through the course. Finally, summative judgements are made at the point when all the necessary evidence is accumulated. This stresses the importance of the inter-relation of the various competences and professional qualities and disavows an attempt by assessors to 'tick off' competences in a discrete and isolated way (one of the major criticisms of competence-based vocational assessment). The model therefore allows for *critical reflection*, including some *negotiation* of assessment targets during the course whilst specifying (and to use Whitty's word, demystifying) the judgements made by assessors when the final judgements are made.

Students are primarily responsible for developing a *professional development portfolio* within which they accumulate the variety of evidence to support their progression through the course. Figure 21.2 illustrates how this is organised in a three stage process, each stage involving an increasingly demanding period of school experience.

In this course assessment is primarily school-based. Each student is allocated an experienced teacher, a mentor who works with the student to develop their experience and expertise and to assemble the portfolio of assessment evidence. Mentors receive regular training and professional development materials (text and audio) both in

Table 21.1 Open University PGCE competence model

Teaching competences:	A Curriculum/subject planning and evaluation				B Classroom/subject methods				C Classroom management				D Assessment, recording and reporting				E The wider role of the teacher				
	A1	A2	A3	A4	B1	B2	B3	B4	C1	C2	C3	C4	D1	D2	D3	D4	E1	E2	E3	E4	E5
Professional qualities:																					
Commitment to professional values																					
Effective communication																					
Appropriate relationships																					
Efficient management																					

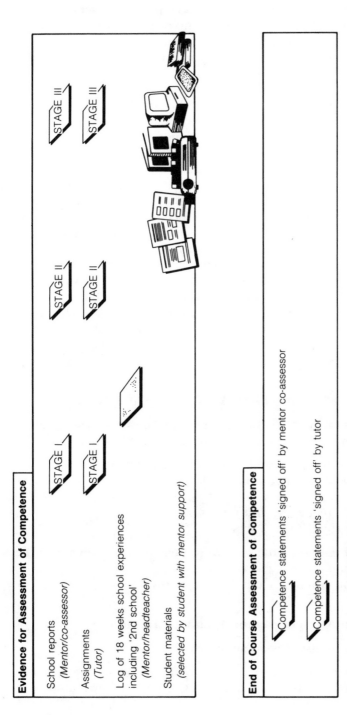

Figure 21.2 Assessment Portfolio, submitted to Assessment Board

the interpersonal and professional skills of supporting student teachers, and in the assessment role. *Indicators* and *examples* of the evidence base for displaying competences and professional qualities are provided (see Appendix) and form the basis for discussion throughout the training process. Mentor judgements, however, are also validated, internally by judgements made by a second *co-assessor*, an experienced teacher and one usually occupying a senior teacher position in the school, and externally through a national system of quality assurance involving regular monitoring of schools, students and mentors.

This assessment model is in the early stages of development. At each stage in its design groups of teachers have worked with the academic team in the Open University to refine its form and structure. It opens up the possibility of a new form of teacher assessment which is school-based and student-led, whilst at the same time specifying clear standards for entry into teaching. The clarity of these standards creates confidence in two ways. In public and societal terms it demonstrates that the teaching profession, like other professions, has explicit and demanding entry standards. At the same time, however, this explicit formulation creates an entitlement to the learner, to the student, which places obligations and responsibilities on the teacher educator and on the schools. The incorporation of a values dimension, focusing on professional qualities, within the model ensures a holistic approach to assessment and one that emphasizes the unique significance of preparing for entry into a profession.

APPENDIX: OPEN UNIVERSITY COMPETENCE MODEL

The Open University PGCE Assessment Model describes the teaching process in terms of five areas of Teaching Competences:

A   Curriculum/subject planning and evaluation
B   Classroom/subject methods
C   Classroom management
D   Assessment, recording and reporting
E   The wider role of the teacher

Evidence is submitted by the student to illustrate competence in the elements of each area.

One teaching competence is set out below:

A Curriculum/subject planning and evaluation

The student demonstrates an ability to:

A1   apply subject and curriculum knowledge (including National Curriculum) appropriate for subject and whole curriculum; e.g.

lesson content coincident with National Curriculum or post-16 syllabuses; content embraces consideration of school documents;

A2   identify diversity of pupil need in the context of appropriate strategies (methods) for ensuring continuity and progression; e.g. planning shows differentiation of activities for different pupils in both strategy and content;

A3   plan and critically evaluate at the level of pupil activity, lesson, sequence of lessons and scheme of work, for whole class, groups and individuals with due regard to how pupils develop and learn; e.g. planning and evaluation sheets for an activity, a lesson, a sequence of lessons (topic); a critical evaluation of pupil learning over a range of lessons.

A4   produce effective resources, and evaluate resources including IT; e.g. examples of classroom resources used (KS1-4 or post 16) with evaluation of their effectiveness.

Teaching, however, is not only concerned with exhibiting certain competences. It is also necessary that the competences exist within a framework of the personal qualities appropriate to the teaching profession. Evidence which is selected by the student to demonstrate one or more of the above elements of teaching competence should also explicitly illustrate one or more of the following four Professional Qualities (and implicitly satisfy all the other qualities):

• commitment to professional values,
• effective communication,
• appropriate relationships,
• efficient management.

A fuller description of one of these qualities is set out below:

Commitment to professional values

Teachers demonstrate this quality, by personal example and through their role in school by, for example:
• respecting and valuing pupils as individuals in order to promote personal growth and autonomy;
• acknowledging the roles and rights of other individuals and groups in the educational process;
• understanding and implementing equal opportunities principles and practices;
• managing and resolving complex ethical responsibilities and value conflicts;
• engaging in self-evaluation, recognizing one's strengths and limitations.

REFERENCES

Benner, P. (1982) 'From novice to expert', *American Journal of Nursing*, 82(3), 402-7.

Bera (1992) 'Reform of initial teacher training. Report of Task Group', *Research Intelligence*, Spring, 16-21.

Brown, S. (1989) *Assessment: a changing practice*, Edinburgh: Scottish Academic Press.

DFE (1992) *Circular 9/92 Initial Teacher Training (Secondary Phase)*.

Dreyfus, H.L. and Dreyfus, E. (1984) 'Putting computers in their proper place: analysis versus intuition in the classroom', in Sloan, D. (ed.), *The Computer in Education: a critical perspective*, Columbia, NY, Teachers College Press.

Eraut, M. (1989) 'Initial teacher training and the NVQ model', in Burke, J.W. (ed.), *Competency Based Education and Training*, Lewes: Falmer.

Jessup, G. (1990) *National Vocational Qualifications*, Lewes: Falmer.

Macintyre, D.G. (1991) *Accreditation of Teacher Education: the story of CATE 1984-1989*, Lewes: Falmer Press.

Moon, B. (1992) 'A new routeway into teaching', *Education Review*, 6(2), 28-31.

Moon, B. (1992) 'The development of initial teacher education in Britain's Open University: implications for Europe', paper given at the 1992 Conference of ATEE, Lahti, Finland.

Pring, R. (1992) 'Standards and quality in education', *British Journal of Educational Studies*, 4-22.

Whitty, G. (1992) 'Quality control in teacher education', *British Journal of Educational Studies*, 38-50.

Winter, R. (1992) *The Asset Programme (Accreditation of Social Services Experience and Training)*, Essex County Council Social Services Department and Anglia Polytechnic University.

Chapter 22

Surrey New Teacher Competency Project

Sue Gifford

The question of 'how' to structure the professional developmental process is answered increasingly these days by the use of competences, target-setting and profiling. The DFE state that they are interested in developing the use of 'profiling and competency-based approaches' (AM 8/92). They also want to promote links between initial teacher training, induction and INSET, and see induction as included in appraisal. The image of a cradle to grave profiling system is hard to dispel. Obviously there are advantages in continuity: however the GTC (1992) point out that where there may be continuity with induction and appraisal, 'much has still to be done to develop the continuum from the initial education and training of teachers'. They argue that training institutions' profiles and records should be used by new teachers in induction record-keeping and that the institutions should continue shared responsibility into the induction year, or arrange for a more local institution to be involved. Presumably they envisage some kind of continued supervision of new teachers, perhaps in conjunction with a continuing profiling system. This would make some sense: it would be interesting to see how popular such a scheme might be with the new teachers themselves, and how the funding for this would be provided.

THE SURREY NEW TEACHER COMPETENCY PROFILE

Surrey Education Authority has been tackling these issues since the late 1980s, when induction coordinators for primary and secondary schools were appointed. There is now a strong tradition of school-appointed mentors, as well as experienced support from the advisory teachers for induction, who provide sessions for new teachers and training for school mentors. Schools are encouraged to provide individualized support, which is tailored to the needs of each new teacher. However, as in many authorities, there is a large number and diversity of schools and experience in mentoring, so it is hard to maintain continuity of approach to school-based induction throughout the authority.

As the result of a successful bid for GEST funding, Surrey LEA Recruitment and Induction Unit has been developing a competence profile. Surrey's initiative is a joint one with the Roehampton Institute. Obviously, for successful induction, the link with experiences in initial teacher education is vital, and the concern of continuing teacher education and development is shared by both parties.

Roehampton Institute is currently developing a competence-based profile with PGCE and BA (QTS) courses and articled teachers, and so is able to contribute this experience to the development of an induction profile.

Surrey decided to adopt the approach of a competence-based profile because it seems to provide mentors with a structured approach to their work as well as linking with practice in initial teacher education. It is also seen as having features in common with Surrey's appraisal scheme, and so forms an initial phase of this.

The competence-based profile approach is seen as providing differentiation related to previous experience. It gives a structure in terms of time and focus and helps to monitor the process of professional development, ensuring the new teacher a certain quality of support, and a say in what happens.

DEVELOPING THE PROFILE

It was decided to write the actual profile with the aid of a working party team of experienced mentors, six primary and four secondary. They were give some 'homework' of issues and examples to consider, including a few relevent newspaper and journal articles. The working party were released from school for meetings altogether and in twos and threes to consider different aspects of the profile. As a result of various kinds of meeting and a residential weekend, the aims, structure, design and actual competences of the profile were created. The group initially suspected that the project team (of induction coordinators, inspector and Roehampton representative) had a Blue Peter version which they had prepared earlier, but eventually they accepted that they were going to be the ones to write it, and the project team would have an editorial role.

We addressed various issues about the nature of the competences and the process that the profile should support. We now have a set of competences which have some validity through being generated by a group of experienced practitioners.

The following are the key features, which reflect the issues identified above. The *competences* reflect a certain model of teaching and learning, where there is a cycle of planning, implementing and reviewing as well as all-pervading aspects of relationships, communicating and self-reflectiveness. It was with some reluctance and considerable difficulty that this complex process was split into twenty-eight competences, arranged in three groups of classroom management, curriculum knowledge and planning, and assessment, recording and reporting. We do not consider these definitive: others may be added, e.g. by agreement, from school policies, or CATE criteria.

We did not arrive at a rigorous definition of a competence: generally the competences describe approaches, personal qualities and attitudes, in broad behavioural terms, as in 'conveys enthusiasm'.

A competence is seen as 'a dimension of performance in terms of which one can perform at different levels' (CNAA 1992): rather than being achieved once and for all, each competence is a continuum, reflecting an aspect of teaching which can always be developed in more challenging contexts or more complex ways.

The *purpose of the profile* is seen as supporting development, not assessing, and this determines the way that it is used. If the process of development is seen as involving self-criticism and the acceptance of critical feedback, then confidentiality is important. The profile is seen as being used jointly by the mentor and new teacher, but at the end of the year as the property of the new teacher, who completes a summary for appraisal purposes, but controls access to the document itself.

Mentors will make classroom observations but, especially in secondary schools, these will also be made by heads of department or heads of year: the evidence from these, in terms of 'logs' and written feedback, is attached to the profile, but these other teachers do not see the profile.

The profile should not be used in the case of a teacher who is giving serious cause for concern, and no evidence from it can be used in case of dismissal: in these circumstances separate procedures are instigated and separate evidence must be collected.

If the competences are to be used developmentally, rather than judgementally, as providing a focus for investigation, observation and discussion, the need for precise definition or pre-specified criteria is not as necessary as if they were to be used for assessment purposes.

The *process* of using the competences is structured, but individualized. It starts with an initial discussion, where questions are suggested that require the mentor to find out about significant aspects of the new teacher's past experiences and training. The new teacher is the one who decides from a 'menu' of competences which they want to focus on: these should include strengths as well as areas for development. At regular intervals throughout the year, the new teacher and mentor review evidence and together select competences and targets. Focusing on a competence requires them both to negotiate 'what it would look like' in the teacher's situation. After various possible aspects of the competence are identified some are recorded as targets. These then become the focus for observation, support, evidence collecting and reviewing. The process of relating a competence to the context in which the new teacher is working, deriving targets and agreeing what successful achievement of these would look like, is seen as an important opportunity to negotiate definitions and exchange viewpoints. Hence the generality and ambiguity of a competence like 'uses assessment to identify individual needs' is used to provoke discussion about methods of assessment and its relationship with planning.

Having identified targets for development, the profile structure requires that the support available is recorded, perhaps in terms of arranging visits, team teaching or observation opportunities.

The *form of the profile* is designed to be manageable: mentors and new teachers are extremely busy people, and so writing should be kept to a minimum, and flexibility of use allowed for.

The finished profile, which is currently being trialled, has some original features, of which we are rather proud. The physical lay-out of the profile is a booklet, including guidance for use. There are pockets inside the covers, one of which may be used for items of evidence (such as notes from observations). The other pocket contains three elements essential to the process of using the competences:

- 'menu cards' to be used when selecting a focus;
- peel-off sticky labels, with the competences written on them, ready to be stuck in the column for the appropriate term (to save time on copying them out); and
- a competence 'tracker' which is used to record coverage of the competences across the three terms. There are also appendices such as criteria from DFE circular 9/92, on the competences required in initial training.

The profile includes a suggested format for an initial interview, with the aim of informing the mentor about the new teacher's previous experiences and current concerns. Following this, and in each subsequent term, new teacher and mentor select a few competences from a menu, stick the appropriate labels on the page and next to these record agreed targets and support to be provided. It is emphasized that the competences chosen should include strengths to be developed. Evidence for the achievement of targets is collected by both parties, and may include written observations by the mentor and other members of staff. Towards the end of the term the evidence is summarized and progress reviewed. Finally, a summary is written of the whole year, including achievements and areas for further development and this forms the basis of a three-way conversation with the new teacher's appraiser.

Throughout the document any writing may be done by the mentor, or by both new teacher and mentor, but it must be agreed and signed by both parties. We expect that there will be different patterns of writing and timing will depend on individual circumstances.

The next stage is to see how useful the profile is, and how it is used in practice. The profile will be trialled in approximately a hundred primary schools and fifty secondary schools. We know that there are a wide variety of situations, according to phase and size of school, experience of the mentor, number of new teachers a mentor has responsibility for and, of course, the job and experience of the new teacher.

During the autumn term there are two days of training for each mentor, during which we hope to develop the next stage of the guidance notes, in collecting examples of targets and support from the mentors trialling the profile.

Initial reactions imply that mentors welcome the structure the profile gives to their role, and that the initial interview schedule gives insights into the previous career and concerns of the new teacher which would otherwise not have been uncovered. There are concerns, however, with practicality of maintaining confidentiality of the document, and in keeping the mentoring process one of support. If heads and ultimately governors are required to assess new teachers and be aware of needs for support and INSET, then pressure may be put on mentors to provide evidence for assessment, and to report on progress, in a way that could damage a relationship of openness and trust.

Whereas we feel that our profile goes a long way in recognizing individual differences of new teachers' experience and in providing a structure for mentors to work with, several questions yet remain unanswered.

Are some of the competences too vague to be useful? Are vital aspects of the complex teaching process missing? How does the idea work in practice of competences being developed in increasingly challenging contexts, rather than being achieved once and for all? Does the target-setting and criteria-identifying process need further structuring? How manageable is it? How variable is the practice in different schools? How is it used differently by different phases or by new or experienced mentors? How do mentors see their role in encouraging reflection? And how do the new teachers feel about their part in the process?

The biggest question of all is, does the profile help mentors help teachers to move from A to B, and how?

These and other questions remain to be answered in the forthcoming year. We now await the reactions of new teachers and their mentors!

REFERENCES

CNAA (1992) *Competence-based approaches to teacher education: viewpoints and issues*, London, CNAA.

DES (1987) The New *Teacher in School: a Survey by HM Inspectors in England and Wales*, HMSO.

DES (1990) *Survey of Initial Teacher Education*, HMSO.

General Teaching Council (1992) *The Induction of Newly Appointed Teachers*, NFER.

Mentoring: professional development and institutional aspects

Introduction

Throughout this book the notion of mentoring to support the development of the 'reflective practitioner' has been put forward. It has also
been noted how in helping others to analyse critically their practice
it is difficult for the mentor not to question their own, and then seek
the means by which to change it. In this final part of the book two
short chapters examine this relationship between mentoring and
professional development; and return again to the theme of the
'mentoring school'. Mentoring, it is suggested here, can be applied
to a range of staff development issues – including induction of new
but experienced teachers, returner teachers and appraisal.

In the first chapter Mike Kelly, Tony Beck and John apThomas, extol
the virtues of applying the mentoring process throughout schools as a
means of achieving professional development. They assert that an organization's greatest asset is the staff and support and development should
therefore be a major priority for school development planning. They go
on to argue that self-development is rarely successful without the support
of other people, and that a system of mentoring can provide this support.
Many schools will be familiar with very similar schemes from a context
of appraisal. And the parallel between the skills required for effective
mentoring and that of appraisal has already been noted (see Earley in
Part C). Note that the practices advocated here fit comfortably with the
ideas of the 'reflective practitioner' and of the 'mentoring school'.

The final words are left to Rowie Shaw. Shaw's chapter revisits the
major themes of this book: from conceptions of mentoring to the impact of mentoring on the whole institution. She concludes that among
the benefits to schools are:

> raising awareness about effective classroom practice; providing a
> climate for discussion about teaching methods and subject content;
> the enhancement of a variety of school processes which lead to
> an improved classroom experience for pupils with an ensuing rise
> in achievement.

Mentoring, from its beginnings in the UK as a mechanism for involving teachers in induction and initial teacher training, would seem to be evolving into an effective strategy for whole-school improvement. It has a pivotal part to play in the improvement not only of the motivation and performance of teachers, but also of quality of learning of pupils.

Chapter 23

Mentoring as a staff development activity

Mike Kelly, Tony Beck and John apThomas

The term 'mentor' is being used to describe an increasing range of activities. It is used in student and staff induction programmes, and in the articled and licensed teacher training schemes. More and more of those involved report the process to be a powerful and cost-effective way of increasing personal and organizational focus and central to the institution's staff development strategies and plans, rather than merely a way of smoothing new staff entry, or offering tips for getting round bureaucratic procedures. Here we consider its use as a significant element in the staff development and target-setting process for all staff including trainees, in the enhancement of their learning and development within their institutions.

THE MENTORING APPROACH

Mentoring as a basis for staff or student development is founded on the notion of learning and learning styles. Staff development, whether of experienced or novice staff, has to be about individuals learning, that is, changing their behaviour. Without going into a major discussion of how people learn, it is pertinent to refer briefly to the ideas of Kolb, who has developed an experiential learning model. it is a model concerned with the systematic and purposeful development of the whole person; it is the kind of learning which leads to people changing. Self-development is rarely successful without the support of other people. A system of mentoring offers that support by providing individuals with someone who can give feedback, question, share, discuss, challenge, confront and guide one through the learning cycle.

The crucial starting point is concrete experience: a happening, or action. Development often starts with a surprise, puzzlement or shock when something has happened that was unexpected or didn't make sense. When this happens a mentor is someone to go to for help.

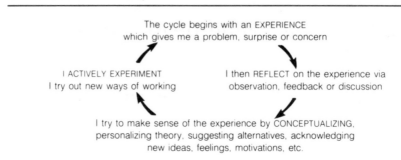

The cycle begins with an EXPERIENCE
which gives me a problem, surprise or concern

I ACTIVELY EXPERIMENT
I try out new ways of working

I then REFLECT on the experience via
observation, feedback or discussion

I try to make sense of the experience by CONCEPTUALIZING,
personalizing theory, suggesting alternatives, acknowledging
new ideas, feelings, motivations, etc.

Figure 23.1 A learning or developmental cycle

Reflection, which can involve observation and discussion and the generation and evaluation of alternative ways of doing things, enables the individual to gain insight into his or her own practice and explore new ways of performing. The mentor can have a vital role to play in this reflection process by observing, discussing, guiding through example, and by coaching.

Stage three involves connecting experiences to conceptual and theoretical frameworks which help make sense of the experiences. Sound development needs new skills underpinned by a rationale, and supported by an understanding of the principles and concepts of good practice. A mentor will probably be able to help in the process of making those connections by dint of greater experience and his or her own prior development as a reflective practitioner.

The last stage involves active experimentation. New ideas need to be internalized and then incorporated into practice; new ways of working and feeling have to be tried out before the learning is complete. The mentor can facilitate and monitor and give feedback on these new actions and help reinforce the development. If the new ideas do not work or are only partially successful, then a further problem arises and the cycle starts again (see Figure 23.1).

HOW IMPORTANT AND USEFUL IS THE MENTORING APPROACH?

There is undoubtedly a tradition of autonomy in the classroom among teachers in British schools, and mentoring does not automatically fit easily into this tradition. However, against this may be seen the growing importance attributed to teamwork.

Working with a mentor system can be effective in meeting such challenges in a developmental and personally rewarding way, while at the same time ensuring that the organization as a whole calls on its stored expertise and experience.

INDUCTION MENTORING: THE NEW HEAD, THE NEW TEACHER, AND THE TRAINEE TEACHER

A significant feature in a successful mentoring scheme is likely to be the quality of the relationship between mentor and protégé – this will inevitably involve issues of hierarchy, confidentiality, trust and openness, and matching or selection. The processes involved appear to identify necessary and distinctive management and staff development needs, and make a real contribution towards meeting them.

An effective induction programme can help protégés to:

- develop an understanding of their organisation
    - its systems and structure;
    - its values and ethos;
    - its politics.
- clarify their new job and role;
- make relationships within their organisation more quickly;
- access the hierarchy of their new organisation.

Mentors have been used effectively in all these ways in induction programmes for new headteachers, lecturers new to higher and further education institutions, teachers in their probationary year and as part of articled and licensed teacher schemes.

Headteachers new in post experience an acute sense of the importance of their new organisation's immediate history. The systems and structures of an organisation may, on the surface, appear easy to understand, but the underlying principles and the values they evidence are far less obvious. Just what messages ae transmitted by following certain procedures, the effect they are having on staff and pupils and what they reveal about the previous headteacher's management style, are all underlying factors which need to be understood by new headteachers. In many cases this growing awareness of their institution is enabled for new headteachers by using an experienced headteacher colleague as a mentor to help interpret the clues they pick up in the early days of their new job. One new head said of his mentor that he appreciated having 'someone to contact when it got really bad,' while another found 'the mentor extended by thinking at different levels' and a third said the mentor helped 'make sense of the clues from staff, children and parents about my school, its history and culture'.

For teachers in their first year, the mentor plays a very different role. People starting out on a career in teaching need to establish themselves in their new school, forming relationships initially with teachers in the same department or section of the school and subsequently with increasing numbers of colleagues across the organisation.

Mentors can provide invaluable assistance in providing access to a whole range of different people who for one reason or another can make the probationer's first year that much easier. Access to resources, support and advice are essential to help first year teachers settle into their new environment.

If mentoring can ease the entry of probationers to the school as an organisation, it can also help initial trainees acquire the knowledge and skills necessary for effective classroom teaching. Graduates can elect to train for teaching through the Articled Teacher Scheme in which mentors are used as role models. Through the scheme trainees work as apprentices, learning alongside their mentors. Understanding of the job is paramount, with learning about children and the curriculum (including development, planning, delivery, monitoring and assessment) seen as central aspects of their training.

Whether as part of a staff development or an induction programme, the use of a mentoring system provides access to an individual, supportive relationship in what can sometimes be a strange and daunting situation. In any organisation, a person can identify a circle of professional contacts/colleagues with whom he or she works. Within that group individuals may consider themselves lucky to have someone other than their line manager with whom they can discuss any problems or difficulty. Indeed in many organisations people who are perceived to have 'problems' are often seen as someone to avoid or are thought of as not being 'up to the job'. How much more effective might a person become working in an organisation which attempts, through an effective mentor system, to provide for more than people's professional needs, and by so doing recognises the worth of each individual?

MENTORING AND THE 'LEARNING SCHOOL'

Mentoring is a high-risk activity. Established in organizations which strive to be 'caring communities' it can and should enhance the development of everyone in that organization. Within the school development plan high priority is given to caring for and developing children, but the support and learning needs of staff colleagues should not be ignored. Mentoring provides a scheme whereby both the mentor and the protégé (and most staff play both roles) can work together to build what Pedler et al. (1989) call 'The Learning Company', i.e. 'an organisation which facilitates the learning of all of its members and continuously transforms itself'. Such organizations:

- have a climate in which individual members are encouraged to learn and to develop their full potential;

- extend this learning culture to include customers (pupils?), suppliers (parents?) and other significant stakeholders (governors and community) wherever possible;
- make human resource development strategy central to business policy;
- have a continuous process of organizational transformation harnessing the fruits of individual learning.

WHAT'S IN THE SYSTEM FOR MENTORS?

So what is in it for the mentors? What do mentors get out of a system which appears time-consuming, difficult to implement successfully without training and as yet largely without credibility?

Much will depend on how seriously schools take the notion of staff development. Current thinking in the management of successful or excellent organizations puts great emphasis on the support and development of the organization's greatest asset, namely the staff. Any worthwhile staff development policy must acknowledge:

- every member of staff's entitlement to development;
- how people learn and develop best;
- that staff development must involve continuous support.

To be a mentor is to contribute to one's own professional development:

- Helping others to reflect on their practice must be beneficial to oneself. It is difficult not to question your own practice when you are discussing the knowledge, skills or attitudes possessed by others. In trying to diagnose the practice of others, you have to relate what you observe to your own experience and behaviour and thereby try to make sense of them before discussing alternatives.
- After questioning your own practice there must follow the challenge of doing something to improve it. Often, in trying to help others, you get insight into your own needs, which acts as a spur to further action - possibly with the aid of your own mentor later.
- Specific skills are required for successful mentoring. Developing those skills (e.g. listening, giving feedback, observing practice, coaching, counselling, motivating, diagnosing performance, etc.) can only help enhance performance in other areas of your work.

Schools probably have the necessary knowledge and expertise among their staff to deliver training programmes for skill enhancement in most of the areas needed. Delivery of such INSET on site is itself valuable staff development for those involved - for both provider and trainee.

- Mentor status can enhance the self-esteem, self-confidence and self-image of those acting in that capacity. Having some responsibility for the development of others can be a satisfying and rewarding experience, providing it is handled sensitively and professionally.

A word of warning: helping others when they may have problems can arouse mixed feelings and emotions. It is surely better, however, for people to share their misgivings, doubts, worries and anxieties about their practice with sympathetic colleagues than to soldier on alone with all the attendant dangers of succumbing to the symptoms and effects of stress.

- Role modelling and helping others develop by example ensures you think carefully about your own practice before demonstrating it in the company of others. Knowing your protégé is to be visiting your classroom tomorrow might make you think a little harder about your own performance.

ISSUES FOR CONSIDERATION

Schools which decide to explore the mentoring approach in their staff development strategies are likely to find the following issues will need addressing in the short to medium term:

- the method of selection or allocation of mentors and protégés;
- training and development needs of mentors, as mentors;
- the agreement of standards for minimum levels of entitlement in a mentoring system;
- the establishment of valid and realistic ways of costing the system;
- the precise ways in which mentoring is related to the introduction and operation of the school's appraisal system;
- ways of handling the likely affective issues, the 'feelings' aspect of such ways of close working, and some of the related issues such as confidentiality, resource levels and staff changes.

The more effective systems using mentoring as and for staff development seem to involve a cyclical pattern, linked with the school and staff development cycles, with a triangle of staff – the protégé, the mentor, and the appraiser – in a complex and delicate balance of development and change. Successful operation of the system can bring the activity of staff development into greater harmony with the activity of pupil and student development which is the heart of the school's purpose.

REFERENCES

Collin, A. (1988). 'Mentoring', *Industrial and Commercial Training*, March/April.

Pedler, M., Boydell, T. and Burgoyne, J. (1989). 'Towards the Learning Company', *Management and Education and Development*, 20(1).

Chapter 24

Mentoring

Rowie Shaw

TRYING TO ARRIVE AT A DEFINITION

What is a mentor?

There are many variants of the function 'mentor' as there are schemes which use them or partners with whom they work. Here are just a few samples:

Trainers and developers.

In teaching:

Supporting a colleague professionally who is less experienced than the mentor.

A supervisor oversees. A mentor guides and teaches.

The mentor has a major role in the support and assessment of the articled teacher in the classroom.

The curriculum tutor and the mentor are together concerned with the professional development of articled teachers in relation to classroom practice. . . . The mentor enters into a voluntary partnership with the curriculum tutor and with the other mentors in that subject. S/he contributes the experience of an established teacher and the perspectives rooted in that experience . . .

. . . a mentor techer with expertise in the specialist subject of the intending secondary teacher . . .

The mentor will be a practising subject specialist within the subject dept. of the GAT's school. The mentor will be an experienced teacher of the subject . . .

In order to provide effective support and a framework of professional development the mentors will need to develop training and supervision skills including: . . . coaching, peer teaching, guidance and counselling, assessment of classroom practice.

Experienced but not very senior . . . someone committed to good teaching and professional development.

Mentors in the USA are also variously known as 'school supervisor', or 'cooperating teacher'. In adult, community and further education mentoring has been routinely used in the training for teachers and other professionals for some time:

Mentors should generally be experienced practitioners who are considered able to offer appropriate advice and support to participants in the scheme. All mentors will be required to attend a specific course of training. . . . A mentor's role is not to direct a participant's activities but rather to enable a participant to work in a self-directed way, by acting as a 'sounding board' for ideas, a source of information about training opportunities and a professional support throughout the process of accreditation. . . . The mentor's role is not as a trainer but a guide and assessor of competence achieved . . .

In health visiting and social work:

Support and assessment of trainees is divided between field-work teachers, health visitor managers and lecturers. In social work there is also a training team consisting of the college tutor, the study supervisor and the line manager.

Subject mentors

This term can be used to describe the head of department, line manager or any experienced colleague who assumes responsibility for some aspect of the school-based training of new teachers. This is not a new nor revolutionary departure as the best team leaders have always been conscious of the need to promote the development of members of their team, especially newcomers. As the central issue should be the performance of the teacher in the classroom, directly affecting pupil achievement, in most cases individuals or pairs of trainees should have a subject mentor from their own department. (This may not be necessary for experienced teachers who come from 'out-county'.)

Phase mentors

Some trainers believe there should be both a subject mentor and a 'phase mentor', that is, someone who could be responsible for guiding and inducting the trainee in general educational matters relating to the school, the LEA and the national framework, leaving issues of classroom practice to the subject mentor. As such induction will often be parallel for students, probationers, licensed teachers and others, this role could be assumed by the professional tutor. Clear forward planning should enable this person to utilize induction programmes both in the LEA and in the school simultaneously for first appointments and other categories.

Mentors for new heads and deputies

Mentoring as a training and induction method is now considered so important that in autumn 1991 the DES announced funding of about £2m to provide mentors for newly appointed heads and deputies. The process of mentoring at this level seems to require the development of an understanding of the school; clarification of the new role and job; providing feedback on performance; highlighting opportunities for greater effectiveness and giving personal support. These functions clearly overlap with the subject mentor role.

Super mentors and generic mentoring

The training of mentors is expensive and time-consuming. For the first cohort of articled teachers mentor training has been undertaken in a variety of different forms, usually by the HE institution in partnership with the school and/or the LEA.

The skills required for mentoring are highly specialized and in some schemes have been on a par with the skills which teacher trainers develop over many years' experience.

Yet there is a core of these skills which, if deployed consistently in our schools, could assist in training and development throughout every stage in a teacher's career, including the support and supervision of staff and pupils as well as appraisal and to which every manager should have access. This is the concept of generic mentoring. It seems clear that a concentration on these skills as a primordial ingredient in the training of teachers as managers would lead to a greater emphasis on the reflective consideration of methodology by individual teachers in our schools. This would in turn lead to higher pupil achievement. It would be more cost-effective for institutions to buy into a super mentor, a person trained in mentoring who could assist, guide and advise subject mentors in schools as well as facilitating meetings and workshops between mentors from different schools. Although the role could be undertaken by the professional tutor there are other ways of achieving this aim.

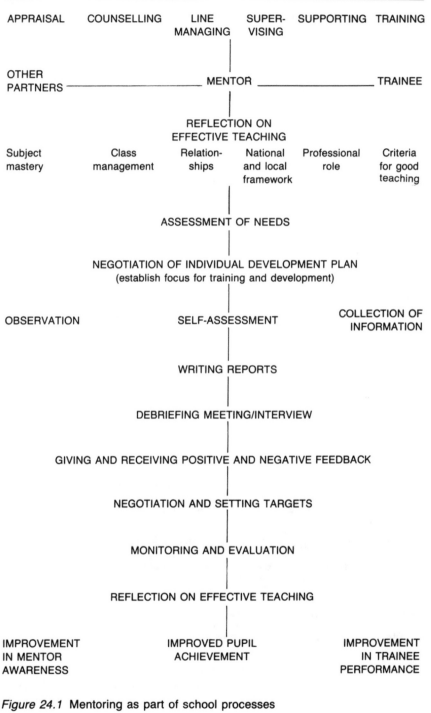

Figure 24.1 Mentoring as part of school processes

Mentoring within other school processes

Schools which adopt teacher training as a whole-school policy will have the benefit of integrating mentoring and supervision within a range of fundamental school processes. This is best demonstrated in tabular form as seen in Table 24.1.

Table 24.1 The role of the mentor and other partners

Mentor works with	HE: universities, polytechnics and colleges	LEA: inspectors, advisers and advisory teachers	School management	Department management where HOD is not the mentor
Student on teaching practice	•		•	•
Articled teacher	•	•	•	•
Licensed teacher	?	?	•	•
Probationer		•	•	•
Supply teacher		?	?	?
Overseas-trained teacher/instructor	?	?	•	•
Out-county teacher			?	?
Returner		?	?	?
Staff development	•	•	•	?
Other trainers and consultants also offer staff development training				

? indicates that partnerships exist in some schemes but not all.
• indicates that partnerships exist.

Mentors and other partners

Table 24.1 shows the different partnerships in which mentors or supervisors may be involved for various categories of trainee. It can be seen that school-based mentors have more support from other agencies in initial training schemes and arrangements for the induction and assessment of probationary teachers, but that for other categories of trainee, in particular the experienced teacher who comes from out-county or who returns after a career break, the mentor or first-line supervisor carries the entire burden of induction and support. The mentor, therefore, has a different role in each case because of the variety of partnerships.

A more standardized approach to these partnerships and clear communication inside and outside school could close some of the gaps seen in Table 24.1. These partnerships can be a catalyst for the generation of new ideas in the school but there can also be problems as we shall see below.

THE RATIONALE FOR MENTORING

This section looks at the benefits of mentoring for individual teachers and schools and at some of the problems that have surfaced.

The benefits for teachers

'In terms of professional development it's the very best thing that has happened to them', said an Oxfordshire head teacher on the teachers who are mentors to interns in his school.

Various incentives are offered to teachers who agree to be mentors. In some schemes (by no means the majority) an incentive allowance is given or a temporary honorarium from GEST funds equivalent to an allowance. More often mentors go unpaid, but most agree that there are rewards associated with mentoring which have nothing to do with money. The professional associations may not agree and there is some debate about the ethics of asking teachers to take on these duties without payment.

In the time-honoured tradition of the teaching profession, where practitioners are not rewarded by higher pay, there can be slightly less tangible but equally important rewards such as being given the extra free time to do the job. Mentors need time for training, meeting with the trainee, observation and debriefing; increased non-contact time is therefore a valuable incentive. Mentors would see it as even more important than payment.

They also value highly the improved career prospects afforded by the role (mentoring looks good on a curriculum vitae or testimonial) and the opportunities for accreditation of their work in school as part of further study. They feel that their status is enhanced and they like being identified as good practitioners and to share good practice. They appreciate having the chance to discuss pedagogy with others and to attend peer group meetings. Those who work in small departments feel that their isolation is lessened.

Mentors attest that there are learning skills which are transferable to their other professional activities such as counselling and negotiation and they enjoy learning fresh ideas from their contact with trainee teachers.

Conversations with mentors from a wide range of schemes revealed that they appreciated the opportunity to reflect on their own practice. Although conscious of the often onerous duties they had taken on, which they clearly articulated, all were enthusiastic about mentoring as an opportunity both for self-development and teacher training.

Benefits for schools

Some of the benefits for schools of mentoring have been described as raising awareness about effective classroom practice; providing a climate for discussion about teaching methods and subject content; the enhancement of a variety of school processes all of which lead to an improved classroom experience for pupils with an ensuing rise in achievement.

Schools can also expect to retain capable people by expanding their rewards and opportunities and by offering better job satisfaction for staff. As well as the opportunities for mentors, trainee teachers have expressed high motivation and improved performance from mentoring. Routes which lead to more effective young teachers will of course benefit schools.

Problems associated with mentoring

There have been real problems experienced by the first formal cohorts of mentors, mainly to do with time management, training and unclear communications.

Some mentor training has not always been systematic and relevant. Sometimes communications between the providers – LEA, HE and the school – are not clear and timely and mentors are confused by conflicting demands on them and not clear about what they or their trainee/s are supposed to do or what deadlines have to be met. They may not receive full and detailed information about course content or dates of meetings to be held outside the school. All these factors put extra pressure on already over-burdened teachers.

In schools where there is not a whole-school approach other colleagues do not always share the same perceptions about the training role, and this can lead to conflicts for mentor or trainee which the mentor has to resolve.

Weak or difficult trainees make heavy demands on the mentors; equally, not all those selected to be mentors have the correct interpersonal skills. Again this can lead to conflict and unhappiness. Finally, mentors report that it is hard to reconcile the role of friend with that of assessor. Not only do mentors have to guide and coach the trainee but in initial training schemes they are also responsible for 'pass' and 'fail'. This burden can be lessened when responsibilities are clearly defined in a supportive way between all partners.

Name index

Subject index